To the Edge and Back

1962 India-China War

To the Edge and Back
1962 India-China War

Lt Col Rohit Agarwal (Retd)

Centre for Land Warfare Studies

PENTAGON PRESS LLP

The Centre for Land Warfare Studies (CLAWS), New Delhi, is an autonomous think tank dealing with contemporary issues of national security and conceptual aspects of land warfare, including conventional and sub-conventional conflicts and terrorism. CLAWS conducts research that is futuristic in outlook and policy-oriented in approach.

CLAWS Vision: To establish as a leading Centre of Excellence, Research and Studies on Military Strategy & Doctrine, Land Warfare, Regional & National Security, Military Technology and Human Resource.

Centre for Land Warfare Studies
RPSO Complex, Parade Road, Delhi Cantt, New Delhi-110010
Phone: 011-25691308 • Fax: 011-25692347
email: landwarfare@gmail.com • website: www.claws.in

First Published in 2020

ISBN 978-93-90095-00-1

Published by

PENTAGON PRESS LLP
206, Peacock Lane, Shahpur Jat, New Delhi-110049
Phones: 011-64706243, 26491568
Telefax: 011-26490600
email: rajan@pentagonpress.in
website: www.pentagon-press.com

Printed at Aegean Offset Printers, Greater Noida, U.P.

Dedicated to
The Bravehearts of the 1962 War

Contents

Conventions Used in the Book

Military designations, ranks, names of units and formations, weapons etc can be confusing for someone not familiar with them. In order to help such readers, I have compiled a ready reckoner of frequently used abbreviations for reference.

In common military usage, the first part of a two-part rank is often dropped, especially when referred to repeatedly in the same sentence or paragraph. For example, Lt Gen Kaul can be referred to as Gen Kaul and Lt Col Singh can be referred to as Col Singh. Also, the formation names are also further abbreviated in subsequent references. For instance, 4th Infantry Division is subsequently referred to as 4 Inf Div or simply as 4 Div.

Troops belonging to a unit are also often referred to by a derivative of the unit name. This may not actually be a reference to their ethnicity, but a reference to the battalion they belong to and not which state they originate from.

Here's a brief outline of the organisation of the army to help lay readers understand the references made in the narrative. The Army Headquarters, which is the apex headquarters of the army, is located in Delhi. It is headed by the Chief of Army Staff (COAS), who is a 4-star General and reports to the Defence Minister. He is assisted by several Lieutenant Generals (Lt Gens) within the headquarters, who are called his Principal Staff Officers (PSOs). In 1962, the PSOs were headed by the Chief of General Staff (CGS) – an appointment that has been abolished, and the appointment of Vice Chief of Army Staff was introduced instead. The Defence Minister is also advised and supported by the civilian bureaucracy of the Defence Ministry, which is headed by the Defence Secretary.

The army is divided into several operational Commands, each commanded by a senior Lt Gen, referred to as the GOC-in-C or Army Commander. In 1962, the Army consisted of only 3 such commands: Western, Eastern and Southern. Each command has several Corps under it. The Corps is also commanded by a Lt Gen, but ones in a junior grade as compared to Army Commanders. Each Corps has a number of Divisions under them, each commanded by a Major General. Each Division usually has three Brigades, each commanded by a Brigadier. Sometimes a Brigade may also operate directly under the Corps headquarters in a specific area or for a specific task. Each Brigade, in turn, has three battalions – the basic infantry fighting unit. Battalions were commanded by Lieutenant Colonels in 1962 (now they are commanded by Colonels). Sometimes brigades may be allotted additional battalions for a specific task/area. Conversely, battalions could be detached from a brigade. Each battalion comprises four companies commanded by a Major, and each company consists of three platoons of approximately 30 men each led by Junior Commissioned Officers (JCOs).

Each infantry division also has supporting arms units and logistics units. These include Artillery, Engineers, Signals, Army Supply Corps and Army Ordnance Corps units. Usually, a division has one Artillery Brigade consisting of three or more artillery regiments. The type of equipment (guns) held by the regiments is correlated with the role of the division. For mountainous terrains, artillery regiments are supposed to be equipped with lighter guns that are easier to transport across the underdeveloped roads and tracks in such terrain, vis-à-vis the heavier guns that are authorized to the artillery regiments in the plains where mobility is not such a big problem.

You would come across the reference of "main" and "tactical" headquarters throughout the text. The main headquarters of a formation like a Brigade or Division consists of all the major commands and control, supporting and logistics elements. This includes the brigade/divisional staff and components like artillery, engineers, signals, supplies and transport. A tactical headquarters is merely the brigade/divisional commander with one or two staff officers and the means to communicate with his command – radio sets and if possible a telephone line.

Sometimes the names of places and posts can be confusing to those not familiar with these areas. The reader is therefore advised to refer to the maps and corroborate these with the text wherever a doubt arises. The place names are also spelled differently in different sources, and for the ease of readability, I have used the easiest versions like Bumla and Bomdila instead of Bum La and Bomdi La. However, wherever I have quoted directly from a source, I have retained the original spelling. Also, there are references to Kameng division or Lohit division at places. These are references to the administrative divisions, and not military formations like 4 Infantry Division.

Since this book is meant for general reading and not an academic work per se, I have omitted footnotes and instead quoted directly from texts to highlight or illustrate the points I make as I go along. A comprehensive Bibliography is compiled at the end to include all the works I have referred to in writing this book. About my usage of rank of Maj Gen DK Palit, he was a Brigadier at the time of the war, and subsequently retired as a Major General. This was the rank he held when he wrote the book referred to extensively in this account. However, I have used his rank during the war throughout the narrative, including at places where I quote from his book. This is not an oversight but deliberate, to avoid confusion in switching between ranks during the narration.

Foreword

The war with China in 1962 came as a timely wake-up call to the country. Undoubtedly, we were unprepared – or at least underprepared – to face the 'well-oiled' fighting machinery of China's People's Liberation Army. Our diplomatic and intelligence setup also failed to read the signs of an inimical neighbour who intented on enforcing its territorial claims through force. The war, besides the destruction, left a nation determined never to allow a repetition of such a situation. It served to bring the nation out of its complacent belief that diplomacy alone was sufficient to deal with external challenges and resulted in the Indian Armed Forces finally beginning to become operationally more effective.

The re-arming, re-organising and modernising of the forces that were set into motion after this defeat have ensured that, we perform well in all wars since then. India went on to fight the 1965, 1971 and 1999 War with Pakistan, where the Indian Armed Forces proved their fighting capabilities, with more advanced weapon systems and operational-oriented training; thereby, setting new limits of warfighting, especially in the sphere of mountain warfare. This book is a reminder of the valour of the Indian soldiers, who over and over again, whether at Rezang La or Nuranang, in isolated outposts, etc. faced an overwhelmingly superior force unflinchingly. They fought back to the last man till they ran out of ammunition, and even refused to abandon their posts. Tales of valour of these heroes continue to inspire generations of soldiers to date.

While writing the book, care has been taken to cater for the lay reader – one who may not be very familiar with military matters; yet keen to read about what actually happened. The book gives an understanding of the background to the dispute, significant events in the years preceding the war that contributed towards the final flare up, and the course of the war itself. It also analyses as to where mistakes were made at different levels and draws some lessons from them.

A book of this nature is important because its not just those directly concerned with the military who need to have an understanding of how a nation goes to war, but also analyses what happens when it does, and what mistakes could be made. Such understanding is important for knowledgeable and enlightened citizens in a democracy who can participate in the national security discourse. This book is also a reminder as to how India faced the failure, only to come out more stronger in the wars that were fought later. The book would be of great interest to both military and civil persons, students of military history, geography and human psychology. It would also bring home a point regarding development of strategic culture among the youth of the country. 'National outlook for national security' should be central to all our actions.

April 2020 **Lt Gen (Dr.) VK Ahluwalia, PVSM, AVSM**, YSM, VSM (Retd)**

Director, CLAWS

(Former Army Commander, Central Command)

(Former Member, Armed Forces Tribunal)

Commonly Used Abbreviations

2/Lt	Second Lieutenant
AR	Assam Rifles
BGS	Brigadier General Staff
BM	Brigade Major
Brig Adm	Brigadier in charge Administration
Brig	Brigadier
Capt	Captain
Cdr	Commander
CGS	Chief of General Staff
COAS	Chief of Army Staff
Col	Colonel
Div	Division
DMI	Director of Military Intelligence
DMO	Director of Military Operations
Gen	General
GOC	General Officer Commanding
GOC-in-C	General Officer Commanding in Chief
GR	Gurkha Rifles
Hav	Havildar
HQ	Headquarters
IB	Intelligence Bureau; International Boundary
JAK Militia	Jammu and Kashmir Militia

JAK Rif	Jammu and Kashmir Rifles
JCO	Junior Commissioned Officer
L/Nk	Lance Naik
Lt Col	Lieutenant Colonel
Lt Gen	Lieutenant General
Lt	Lieutenant
Maj Gen	Major General
Maj	Major
MC	Military Cross (this was a pre-partition decoration)
MEA	Ministry of External Affairs
MoD	Ministry of Defence
MVC	Maha Vir Chakra
Nb/Sub	Naib Subedar
NEFA	North Eastern Frontier Agency
Nk	Naik
OG	Olive Green
PLA	People's Liberation Army
PSO	Principal Staff Officer
PVC	Param Vir Chakra
QMG	Quarter Master General
RM	Raksha Mantri
SM	Subedar Major/Sena Medal
Sub	Subedar
VrC	Vir Chakra

Introduction

The rugged, windswept Himalayan slopes and peaks, where the tiniest blade of grass struggles to sprout, formed the arena for a bloody conflict between Indian Army and Chinese People's Liberation Army (PLA) in the autumn of 1962. Ill-clad, ill-equipped and ill-prepared, short of everything but raw courage, the brave jawans and officers fought against a far better prepared enemy, against overwhelming odds and for as long as it was physically possible. But rout was inevitable.

Fighting to the last breath to uphold the honour of the flag and protect the soil it's planted on is a soldier's *dharma*. His unquestioning obedience of orders comes from an implicit trust in those sending him off to fight. He believes that they will risk putting him in harm's way only if the odds of victory are reasonable enough, and not merely use him as cannon fodder. He also believes that while doing so, they will provide him with the requisite wherewithal to carry out the assigned task – weapons, ammunition, clothing, fire support, logistics and information being some inescapable ones. It was this trust that was betrayed by political and military leadership of the time, who passed orders without due diligence, sending off troops on missions without ensuring they had the means to carry them out. This is a sad fact, and no amount of analysis can prove otherwise.

Volumes have been written already about the events leading up to the war and those fateful days of fighting. Many of those who were closely involved presented firsthand accounts of the events and thought processes behind their own decisions in books authored by them. Each had a slightly different version of the events, which is but natural and can be attributed to differing perspectives from which they observed or participated in the events. Each one of them, also understandably, justified his own role and actions, absolving himself of any blame in the disastrous turn of events. Unfortunately, some of the key players in the imbroglio – Prime Minister Nehru, Defence Minister VK Krishna Menon, COAS Gen Thapar and GOC-in-C Eastern Command Lt Gen LP Sen – did not write their memoirs of the war. Official records, such as minutes of meetings at which critical decisions were taken, were either not kept at all, or are not available in public domain. The official correspondence and war diaries of the units and formations who participated in the war are still classified and thus not available for reference.

For a neutral observer to put together an unbiased picture six decades down the line, it is essential to correlate the mosaic of firsthand and third-party accounts and make allowances for personal biases. In order to do that in this book, I have tried first to focus on narrating the events as they unfolded before attempting to analyse where the faultiness lay. The first few chapters of the book are therefore more or less non-judgemental, while the last few chapters deal with trying to ascertain what went wrong. I have also been assiduous in keeping the primary mandate given to me – to make this a readable account, one that lay readers can easily digest. To that end, I have avoided dwelling too deep in the nitty-gritty of the engagements and battles from a tactical point of view. Wherever possible, I have tried to simplify the actions for those without any military exposure to also be able to follow the course of the battles, which are well documented in previous works by other authors. Detailed accounts of the battles are available in the books mentioned in the Bibliography for those interested in reading about them in greater depth. My efforts have been to condense and synthesise the available literature into a readable narrative that would give a lay reader an overview about the roots of the conflict, events leading up to the war, the skirmishes and battles, the aftermath and causes.

1

Origin of the Boundary Dispute

Historical Backdrop

The boundary dispute between India and China has its origins in the deep past. It is the result of complex interplay between Empires and nations – interactions between emperors, viceroys and prime ministers, generals and diplomats over centuries. Principal players in this drama up to the mid-20th century were three Empires: British, Chinese and Russian; a semi-independent theocracy, Tibet; and subsequently two independent countries, India and China, with a peripheral but not an insignificant role by a third, Pakistan.

The disputed border is 4056 km long and divided into three Geographical sectors: Ladakh (2176 km), the "Middle" sector (554 km) and the North East sector (1326 km). The entire stretch consists of very high mountains with few road tracks or habitation. This was even more so six decades ago, when the war took place. In such terrain, the passes between the high peaks (locally identified by the suffix "La" after the name, such as Nathu La, Shipki La) assume significance. It was through these passes that traditional trade routes in the region passed. Being defiles or bottlenecks, these passes assumed great importance during operations as controlling these passes blocked the route that passed through it. Although small bodies of men could make their way cross country through the rugged mountains (as small infiltrating columns of the Chinese did during the war several times), larger troop movements and logistic columns needed to support them had to confine themselves to the established routes through these passes.

For the purpose of this account, the Middle sector, or the border that falls in the Indian states of Himachal Pradesh and Uttarakhand today, is irrelevant as it did not see any action during the 1962 war. The boundary in the other two evolved separately over centuries, as briefly described below.

Ladakh Border

One of the key points of dispute from which the boundary issue arises is the status of Tibet at various points in history, particularly at those times when it signed border agreements. While the Indian side views these treaties as valid in view of Tibet's status of a signatory as an independent state, the Chinese claim that Tibet was always a part of China and hence ineligible to sign independent treaties. At the Jokhang Temple in Lhasa, visitors can see an ancient stone pillar inscribed with Tibetan and Chinese script. The writing it bears is the text of a treaty between two empires – Tibetan and the Tang Empire of China – dating back to 821-823 AD. The significance of this is that here, etched in stone, is indisputable evidence that back then Tibet was an independent state empowered to sign treaties as an equal of the Chinese Empire rather than being its vassal chiefdom. Its state of independence continued when it formalised its borders with Ladakh under the Treaty of Tingmosgang after a war between them in 1684. However, Tibet lost its independence and became a part of the Chinese Empire in 1792 when an army dispatched by Chien Lung from Peking to Lhasa sent the Nepali invaders scuttling back to the lush valley of Kathmandu and to submit to the terms that the Chinese had no difficulty in interpreting as tributary status. By protecting the Dalai Lama, the Chinese were able to claim that their imperial umbrella overshadowed Tibet's theocracy. Ladakh too lost its independence when the Dogra General Gulab Singh invaded and made it a tributary to the Sikh empire of Maharaja Ranjit Singh in 1834, but this annexation has no significance to the boundary dispute per se.

Gulab Singh continued his advance beyond Ladakh deep into the Tibetan territory, and by 1841 his conquests had extended to include the holy lake Mansarovar. But eventually, his conquests were brought to a grinding halt, not by an enemy with a stronger army, but by the indomitable forces of nature. The severe winters of Tibet ensured he suffered the fate similar to the more famous ones of Napoleon and Hitler against Russia. Marooned at a height of 12,000 feet along with his army, he could neither advance nor retreat. The Tibetan counterstrike to push back his army came shortly afterwards, and it resulted in a stalemate. As a consequence of this, both sides signed a non-aggression pact in October 1842. In this pact, they agreed to respect each other's territories, but the boundary between them remained undefined, with vague reference to "the old, established frontiers."

Shortly thereafter, in 1846, there was a major shift in power in the region when, after the first Anglo-Sikh War, Kashmir became a part of the British Empire. Realising the challenges involved in administering the far-flung and largely inaccessible territories of the kingdom, the British chose the easier option of allowing Gulab Singh to continue administering Kashmir as its Maharaja while owing "suzerainty" to the British. They could thus have effective control over this "guardian of the northern frontier" without the expense and responsibility of actually administering it and manning its frontiers.

As part of the housekeeping by British administrators, two significant decisions were taken. Firstly, they chose to cancel some sections of the treaty signed between Ladakh and Tibet in October 1842 that they considered detrimental to their own imperial interests. In effect, this could be considered as the abrogation of the whole agreement, a fact that had severe repercussions for the legal positions subsequently. Secondly, the British also forbade Gulab Singh from undertaking any conquests to add to his territories without British consent, effectively fixing the boundary between Ladakh and Tibet as it existed at that time.

In order to prevent any future disputes on the boundary, they informed the Chinese government of this decision, and sought its assent on the boundaries thus fixed. The Chinese reply was characteristically vague and evasive – the Chinese viceroy at Canton, who dealt with the issue on behalf of the Emperor, replied that "the borders of these territories (Tibet and Ladakh) have been sufficiently and distinctly fixed, so that it will be best to adhere to this ancient arrangement." However, there was no formal demarcation of borders on ground, despite British attempts at doing so by sending boundary commissioners to the frontiers. The Chinese delegation that was supposed to join them in marking the frontiers never arrived. The British, nonetheless, drew a line on their maps indicating what they accepted as the boundary, and also the line beyond which Gulab Singh was not to extend his territories.

The boundary commissioners spent 1846 and 1847 surveying the terrain and drawing a boundary line using their own judgement over where a practical boundary should be. The resulting boundary extended from a little north of the Pangong Lake to the Spiti River. However, the area between Pangong Lake and Karakoram Pass and the Kuen Lun mountains beyond "could not be correctly defined' and 'must be viewed as *terra incognita*' (unknown land), they concluded. Being uninhabited, and of little economic value, they felt that in any case the area was not of much consequence to either side. This so-called valueless, unknown land was to become to be known as Aksai Chin, and form the heart of the Sino-Indian boundary dispute that led to the bloody war of 1962.

Had this state of affairs of deliberate, delightful ambiguity been allowed to perpetuate, the problem would not have assumed the complicated proportions that subsequent muddling resulted in. If this area had remained un-demarcated till the next century, it might have allowed both India and China some flexibility in mutually arriving at an agreed settlement without either side having to lose face. But in 1865, WH Johnson from the office of Survey of India carried out another survey of the area and drew up a boundary alignment to fill up the gap between Pangong Lake and Karakoram Pass. This alignment, subsequently called the "Johnson Line," was published in an atlas in 1868 as the boundary between Kashmir and Tibet, and was replicated in many maps that were drawn subsequently.

Soon another imponderable was added to British concerns while considering the Kashmir-Tibet boundary. This was their increasing discomfort about Russian intentions in the region. The British were willing to compromise on territory in this distant frontier wasteland if it meant preventing Russian ingress into more vital areas in its Indian territories that, at this time, included the North West Frontier Province. Thus, in 1889, Viceroy Lansdowne noted that the territory between Karakoram Pass and KuenLun ranges was "of no value, inaccessible, and not likely to be coveted by Russia." He felt that it would be better for British interests to allow China to take it rather than leaving it as a no man's land open for Russia to grab. China was thus seen as a "useful obstacle to Russian advance along this line."

As a consequence, in 1892, Chinese were allowed to erect a boundary marker at the Karakoram Pass with an inscription proclaiming the Chinese territory began there. This was welcomed by the British who expressed themselves in favour of the Chinese filling up the no man's land beyond the Karakoram. The Karakoram Pass thus became a fixed and mutually accepted point on the Sino-Indian boundary, but on either sides of the pass, the alignment continued indefinite. The Chinese dispatched an official, Li Yuan-ping, to explore the whole stretch of their southern border. He travelled up the Karakash River to Haji Langar and thence turned south across Aksai Chin, crossing what seems to have been the Lingzi Tang salt pan and reaching the Changchenmo River.

In the years that followed, Chinese began expressing claim over the Aksai Chin region, which was not accepted by the British. The closest the two sides came to an agreement was in 1899, when the division of Aksai Chin between Britain and China was suggested along a boundary following the Lak Tsang range. This was proposed to China on 14 March 1899 by Sir Claude MacDonald, the British Minister in Peking. Of the various conceptions held at different times in London and India about north-western boundary with China, this was the only one that was actually proposed to the Chinese Government, and it has therefore a particular significance. But although the British learned unofficially that the local Chinese authorities in Sinkiang had intimated that they had no objection to the proposed alignment, China never officially replied to the proposal.

In 1902, the fear of Russian intervention in Tibet was resurrected with rumours of a secret treaty between Russia and Tibet with tacit connivance of the Chinese. Despite denials by Russians as well as Chinese, the Viceroy and the British ambassador in China were both convinced of the veracity of this information. The British feared that Tibet would come under the influence of Russia, which they believed would be against British interests. They feared a hostile Tibet, armed and supported by Russia, could cause disturbance on India's frontiers. Although the British government "back home" in England was reluctant to take any actions to secure the far-flung Tibetan frontier that might cause Russian reactions in some other more significant area, they did agree with Lord Curzon's proposal to send a mission to Tibet to explore establishing trade links. Led by Col Francis Younghusband, this mission in 1903 met with a cold reception by the Tibetans. The initial strength of the mission comprising 200 men was bolstered up by a brigade worth of troops under Brigadier-General J MacDonald, and it had a minor confrontation with the Tibetans before pushing its way up to Gyantse in Tibet by April 1904. This led to the signing of the Anglo-Tibetan Convention of 1904, granting a foothold for British presence in Tibet for the purpose of trade. The absence of any Chinese signatory on this agreement is yet another indicator of the sovereignty of Tibet at this point in time.

In 1910, the Chinese re-established their control by invading Tibet, sending their troops ostensibly to secure important trade routes. The Dalai Lama fled from Lhasa in the face of this invasion and sought asylum in India. While Britain always recognised China's suzerainty over Tibet, this was the first time that Chinese troops had actually occupied Lhasa, much against the will of the Tibetan people. However, Chinese overland threat to India itself was never considered serious by the British. Their view was that any such threat could be countered by a far superior British Navy attacking or threatening to attack mainland China by sea. The British were therefore not overly perturbed by Chinese aggressions in the Himalayas. They accepted the opinion of the Secretary of State for India, Lord Morley, that the Chinese were justifiably exercising their suzerainty.

The October revolution of 1911 in China led to the fall of the Quing empire and establishment of the Republic of China, ending the imperial rule forever. As a result, the Chinese focus shifted inwards instead of its disputed frontiers. This put an end to the Chinese invasion of Tibet, and Dalai Lama returned to Lhasa. He re-established his government and declared its independence from China. But it also implied that China was no longer a strong buffer for any Russian designs on British territories in India. Aksai Chin therefore became vital to British interests again, and the unanswered British proposal of 1899 to China, seeking bifurcation of Aksai Chin, was unilaterally abrogated by Britain. Britain was also keen to end any ambiguity regarding the status of Tibet vis-à-vis China, as the newly formed government in China continued to assert its claim over it.

Border in the East

A large portion of North East India was under the rule of the Ahom kings since the 13th century. They exercised control over the Assam plains right up to the foothills. The area beyond the foothills towards Tibet was inhabited by semi-nomadic tribes, with little or no outside influence or control. There was no government structure, or even a unified tribal federation in the whole region. Each forest village was headed by an autonomous headman, and the kings used to keep them from any incursions into the valley by a system of petty bribery.

In 1819, the Ahom kingdom was attacked by Burma. The king sought help of the British East India Company, which had started exerting considerable influence in large parts of India by then. This resulted in the First Anglo-Burmese war, at the end of which Assam came under British rule in 1826. The British administration continued the practice of allowing near independence to the tribal regions beyond the Assam plains as hitherto. They found any attempts to extend military or civil control over the difficult terrain difficult and unnecessary. Instead, they decided to create a buffer zone to reduce contact – and therefore avoid friction – between the hill tribes and the populace in the plains.

Consequently, the Bengal Eastern Frontier Regulation of 1873 was passed, which laid down a buffer zone between an "inner line" running east from the Bhutan border, along the foothills, and an "outer line" running further north and almost parallel to it, but south of the tribal areas. Any outsiders, including the inhabitants of the valley, required a special permit to travel north of the inner line. The area beyond the outer line was considered as part of the British sphere of influence, although it was not formally administered by them. This arrangement worked suitably to protect the British interests in Assam, which was mainly the tea plantations and lumber, from any interference by the tribals. It also saved British the extra effort of extending their control over the difficult terrain inhabited by the tribals. It also suited the tribals, who were left undisturbed as before.

In early 1900s the British government decided to bring the tribal regions under more formal control, but faced some resistance from the tribes. In 1911, a party tasked to collect taxes from the hill tribes led by Noel Williamson, Assistant Political Officer at Sadiya, Assam, was massacred. As a result, a military campaign was launched into the Assam hill tribe areas, led by Major General Hamilton Bower. Besides disciplining the hill tribes, the expedition was also aimed at warding off any Tibetan incursions into the area.

Tibet itself was in an ambiguous status at this time, as the effect of the upheaval in China, which began in 1911 and ultimately led to the overthrowing of the Chinese Empire, was also felt in Tibet. The Tibetans rose in revolt against the Chinese garrison, which was suppressed and in April 1912, the new Chinese Republic declared Tibet to be a province of China. However, in 1913, the Dalai Lama declared Tibet's independence and refused to acknowledge Chinese authority over himself. Between 1912 and 1949, China claimed its authority over Tibet, but this was not accepted by the Tibetans. Neither did the Chinese actively exert their claim or exercise any kind of administrative control over Tibet. The ambiguous status on the border, coupled with the disturbances in the tribal regions, compelled the British to seek a negotiated settlement of the boundaries with Tibet. It was in this backdrop that the Shimla Conference of 1913-14 was held.

Shimla Conference 1913-14

On 23 May 1913, the British India's Foreign Office issued an invitation to the Chinese government for a tripartite conference, including a representative of the Tibetan government. The objective was to arrive at an agreement on the boundary between China, Tibet and India. Inclusion of China in the conference was probably meant to avoid subsequent dissent. It was also in keeping with a convention signed by Britain with Russia in 1907, which prohibited any direct negotiations with Tibet. China, in turn, was keen to attend as it feared British undertaking direct negotiations with Tibet would undermine its own claim of suzerainty over it. The Chinese expressed their preference for the location as either London or Peking, rather than a neutral location like Shimla in India that would put both China and Tibet at an equal footing. But this was not agreed to by the British.

The Conference began in October 1913. The British delegation was led by Sir Henry McMahon, Secretary to Government of India, whose name the disputed boundary line in the North East still bears. He was assigned the role of host and also mediator between the other two participants. He was assisted by Sir Charles Bell. The Tibetan delegation was led by Lon-chen Shatra, a Chief Minister in Lhasa, and Ivan Chen led the Chinese delegation. The latter was a well-travelled diplomat fluent in English, having spent nine years in London.

Tibetans were keen to have the boundary clearly defined, and their larger aim was to get an acknowledgement of their independence now that Chinese troops and officials had been evicted from Tibet. The Chinese counter to this was a firm claim of sovereignty over Tibet citing the conquest of its territories by Genghis Khan, and subsequent protection to Tibet from foreign invasions by Chinese armies over the centuries. The Tibetans produced extensive documentary evidence to support their claim of independence – revenue records, house lists, charters, agreements and other documents. The Chinese, on the other hand, had nothing but oral recounting of ancient history to offer. In order to find a compromise, McMahon proposed an agreement on suzerainty of Tibet – a middle ground between complete independence and being under the Chinese regime.

On the issue of the boundary between China and Tibet, there was once again a great divergence of views between the two sides. McMahon proposed the delineation between "Inner Tibet" and "Outer Tibet" – the former being directly under China and the latter being administered by Dalai Lama as an autonomous region. The British wanted this arrangement as the "Outer Tibet" to serve as a buffer between China and British India, thus preventing any direct confrontation along the borders – "a tract of neutral territory separating two potentially antagonistic neighbours." This roughly followed the model of Outer and Inner Mongolia that had been devised between Russia and China. While the idea was accepted in principle by all the parties, disagreements arose between the representatives of Tibet and China while deciding the exact boundary between Inner and Outer Tibet.

Interestingly the McMahon Line – the boundary between British India and Outer Tibet – was never a subject of dispute during the entire proceedings. This line runs along the crest of the Himalayan watershed, firmly establishing the tribal areas on the mountain's southern slopes as part of India. It was only subsequently that this line became the main point of dispute, remaining so even to this day despite over a hundred years having passed, a border war and decades of subsequent negotiations between India and China.

The negotiations were conducted for about six months, with an adjournment between December 1913 and January 1914 due to heavy snowfall. After prolonged discussions, the convention was signed, on 3rd July 1914, by the British and Tibetan representatives. The Chinese delegate initialled the document instead of signing it, pending the ratification by Chinese government, which never came.

While the deliberations in Shimla were on, dark war clouds were looming over all of Europe. With the outbreak of the First World War, the problems of a mountainous frontier in the far east was driven out of the minds of the British. Probably as a result of this, official diplomatic outcome of the Shimla Conference was not published by Britain immediately. The first mention of it was recorded in the 1929 edition of Aitchison's Treaties, but that too did not include the exact alignment of the boundaries, including the McMahon Line. It also mentioned that the Chinese government had refused to permit their representative to proceed to full signature. Meanwhile, after the Younghusband expedition, the British Government of India had established direct relations with the Tibetan government at Lhasa, and received trade concessions. Trade mission was set at Gyantse and trade marts at Rudok and Taklakot, with telegraph and wireless communication facilities being provided by the Indian government. A small detachment of Indian Army troops was also permitted to remain in Tibet for the protection of the trading posts. Later an unofficial mission was also established in Lhasa (which was converted into Indian Consulate General after the Chinese occupation of Tibet in 1950).

The actual alignment of the boundary was published in the 1937 edition of Aitchison's Treaties. The same year, the Chiang Kai-shek regime disputed the legality of the McMahon Line, and in the early 40s, it published maps in which North East Frontier Agency (NEFA) was shown as an integral part of China.

This did not attract substantial reactions from the British Government of India. They, and subsequently the Government of Independent India, were convinced on the validity of the boundaries as settled by the Shimla Convention. As a result, China continues to reject the settlement reached at the convention to this day, and hence claims that the border was open to a negotiated settlement. The fact that the disagreement during the discussions was regarding the boundary between Inner and Outer Tibet, and not about the McMahon Line, was conveniently overlooked by China. Therein lay the roots to the war that broke out in 1962.

2

Independence at Bandung

When India gained its independence in 1947, it inherited the borders that the British government had acquired "by treaty, agreement and occupation." It also inherited the existing British concessions in Tibet – the trading posts, the army detachments and communication facilities for these trading posts including telegraph lines and wireless equipment. The British government "...hoped the Tibetan Government would continue with that government (of Independent India) the same relations as had formerly existed with the British Government." The British Union Jack at the mission in Lhasa was replaced by the Indian Tricolour, but there was no other change on ground.

At different times in its history, Tibet had come under foreign influence: that of the Mongols, the Gorkhas of Nepal, the Manchu Emperors of China and the British rulers of India. During this chequered history of alternating between independence and under foreign domination over the past many centuries, Tibet was, at this time, by all considerations a sovereign state – a theocracy ruled by the Dalai Lama. The British acknowledged Chinese "suzerainty" over it, but China was too preoccupied with its own civil war to practically exercise this suzerainty in any way. In its independent capacity, Tibetan government sent a telegram to the Indian government on 16 October 1947, asking it to return territories occupied by it on the boundary between the two countries. But this was not taken seriously by the newly independent Indian government at all. These claims were, in any case, not related to specific areas but, if taken literally, the boundary between India and Tibet would have come down to the river Ganges. The Indian reply, as documented in the White Paper released by the Government of India, was delightfully diplomatic: "*The*

Government of India would be glad to have an assurance that it is the intention of the Tibetan Government to continue relations on the existing basis until new agreements are reached on matters that either party may wish to take up." In hindsight, this was a tacit acknowledgement of the boundary being open to negotiation, instead of an outright rejection of Tibet's claims.

Boundary disputes with Tibet, or for that matter China, and the possibility of a conflict over it was not high amongst the issues occupying the minds of the Nehru government at that time. Their entire attention was focussed on the newly demarcated Western borders instead. Immediately on independence, they were occupied in managing the large-scale migration across it, which was accompanied by bloodshed in communal riots on an unprecedented scale. Within a few months, as the violence was gradually brought under control and rehabilitation of migrants began, Pakistan launched an invasion of Kashmir using tribal militia and regular Pakistani army personnel in civil dress.

Nehru was convinced that having won its independence through a non-violent movement, India would continue to be a beacon of peace in the continent and the world. He also had tremendous faith in his own prowess as a statesman at the world stage, the power of diplomacy, and the strength of the United Nations and other international bodies like the Non-Aligned Movement he helped set up later. A testimony to this was India's appeal to the UN in January 1948, asking for a ceasefire in Kashmir just when Pakistani forces were on the run – this, even though India was militarily stronger than Pakistan, and there was no assurance that the UN would accept India's views on the conflict. Nehru also became a proponent of nuclear disarmament and did not pursue the development of a nuclear arsenal despite having the capability to do so.

It was with these utopian ideals that India forged its foreign policy towards China. Even before independence, in his very first broadcast to the nation as the Vice President and Minister in Charge of External Affairs in the interim government, on 7 September 1946, Nehru talked about friendly relations with China: "*China, that mighty country with a mighty past, our neighbour, has been our friend during the ages, and that friendship will endure and grow. We earnestly hope that her present troubles will end soon and a united and democratic China will emerge, playing a great part in the furtherance of the world peace and progress*". India established diplomatic relations with China under Chiang Kai-Shek in 1948, appointing the erstwhile Prime Minister of Bikaner State PM Panikkar as its first ambassador to that country. Panikkar reached China to take up his post amidst a raging civil war between Chiang Kai-Shek's Koumintang government and the Communists under Mao Tse Tung. When the Communists finally won and took control of the government in China, India became the second country outside the Soviet block to recognise the new government – that too at the request of Burma (now Myanmar) to wait as it wanted to be the first. India formally recognised the People's Republic of China on 30 December 1949. Pannikar, who had been recalled to India in the interim, returned as India's ambassador in May 1950.

Meanwhile, after the establishment of the Communist government in China, Tibetan government under Dalai Lama evicted the Chinese mission in Lhasa, with the assertion that since the Chinese National Government, which had sent the mission, had fallen, the mission was no longer representing the official government in China. Fear of spread of communism to Tibet was possibly the reason behind this action. Tibetan government also sent out feelers to India about receiving weapons and ammunition to arm the Tibetan army against a possible invasion by Communist China. While the request was accepted, India continued to publicly recognise Chinese suzerainty over Tibet, as it wanted to avoid offending the Chinese. When questioned in parliament about the status of Tibet on 8 February 1950, Nehru said,

> *In the early years of this century, a convention was held … and at this certain decisions were arrived at ... about the boundary of Tibet and India called the McMahon Line, that Tibet should be treated as an autonomous country, and subject to China agreeing to this, some kind of Chinese sovereignty should be acknowledged. … But later the then government of China did not accept this agreement and, therefore, did not sign it. In fact, although this agreement has been acted upon in India and Tibet, there has been no formal signature to it by the Chinese government. So the matter stands there. Tibet is treated as an autonomous country and its exact relationship to China was not accepted by China.*

This indicates that even at this early stage, Nehru was cognisant of Chinese not accepting the McMahon Line as an adjunct to their refusal to sign the Shimla Convention. However, he did not consider the ambiguity as a possible future threat to relations between India and China, and he took no measures to address it.

He was, however, personally invested in fostering friendly relations with China, given the millennia-old historical and cultural ties between the two civilisations. He thought that as two new Asian nations, India and China also shared common problems and challenges for the future. In promoting friendship with China, he was willing to brush the boundary issue under the carpet rather than insisting on Chinese recognition of the McMahon Line. Instead, he took up the cause of integrating China in the comity of nations with the greatest zeal. He was a strong proponent of entry of the new Chinese regime into the United Nations (which still recognised the nationalist government now limited to the island of Taiwan as the official government of China).

During his visits to Britain and United States, Nehru actively pleaded China's case for entry into the UN. Whether it was apparent to Nehru or not, several members of his cabinet recognised that this spirit of bonhomie was not completely reciprocated by China. His proximity to western leaders and popularity with their people was viewed with suspicion in China, which had to date remained almost completely isolated from the western world. The western leaders, in turn, were wary of communism and their openly anti-communist stance served to further fuel distrust. There were several extremely unflattering references to Nehru in China's state-controlled media, wherein he was referred to as "*a hireling of Anglo-American imperialism.*" One Chinese magazine accused him of aiding imperialist designs for the annexation of Tibet and charged him with the "*beastly ambition of aggression*". Another publication, the *Shanghai Observer*, wrote on 11 April 1950, "*It is a matter of Nehru weighing his desire for US assistance against his need to assume hypocritical role of a progressive leader to deceive the Indian people.*"

The expansionist designs of the new Chinese regime soon became apparent, when on 7 October 1950, approximately 40,000 troops of Chinese PLA marched into Tibet to "liberate" it. An official announcement from Peking on 25 October stated, "*Units of the Chinese People's Army have been ordered to cross over into Tibet in order to free three million Tibetans from Western Imperialist oppression and to consolidate national defences on Chinese Western Border.*"

The October invasion changed the status of Tibet from an autonomous country to a province of China, and effectively removed the "buffer" between India and China carefully maintained by the erstwhile British Indian government. India's protest of this action was viewed by China as vindication of their suspicions about Indian intentions in Tibet. A telegram sent by the Chinese Ministry of Foreign Affairs to its embassies around the world on 24 November 1950 spoke about "*Indian government's intention to interfere with our internal affairs, prevent our liberation of Tibet, and maintain Indian and capitalist privileges in Tibet.*" The Chinese stance on the issue was summarised in the same telegram thus: "*Tibet is an inalienable part of China and the People's Liberation Army must enter and liberate Tibet and safeguard the frontier of China. The Tibet issue is a domestic issue of China and no foreign interference is allowed.*"

Sardar Vallabbhai Patel, the Home Minister in Nehru's cabinet, wrote a strongly worded letter to Nehru on 7 November 1950, warning the Prime Minister on the implications of the Chinese invasion of Tibet, which he termed as "*little short of perfidy*". He reminded Nehru,

> *We have done everything we could to assuage Chinese feelings, to allay its apprehensions and to defend its legitimate claims, in our discussions and correspondence with America and Britain in UNO. In spite of this, China is not convinced about our disinterestedness; it continues to regard us with suspicion and the whole psychology is one, at least outwardly, of scepticism, perhaps mixed with a little hostility.*

With almost prophetic vision, Patel went on to warn Nehru,

> *Chinese ambitions in this respect not only cover the Himalayan slopes on our side but also include important parts of Assam. ... While our western and north western threats to security are still as prominent as before, a new threat has developed from the north and north east. Thus, for the first time, after centuries, India's defence has to concentrate itself on two fronts simultaneously. Our defence measures so far have been based on the calculations of a superiority over Pakistan. In our calculations we shall now have to reckon with Communist China in the north and north east – Communist China which has definite ambitions and aims and which does not, in any way, seem friendly disposed towards us.*

He concluded the letter with some issues he felt that needed immediate attention to take preventive actions against the Chinese designs, as under:

- *A military and intelligence appreciation of Chinese threat to Indian both on the frontier and internal security.*
- *An examination on of our military position and such re-disposition of our forces as might be necessary, particularly with the idea of guarding important routes or areas which are likely to be the subject of dispute.*
- *An appraisement of the strength of our forces and, if necessary, reconsideration of our retrenchment plans for the Army in the light of these new threats.*
- *A long term consideration of our defence needs. My own feeling is that, unless we assure our supplies of arms, ammunition and armour, we would be making our defence position perpetually weak and we would not be able to stand up to the double threat of difficulties both from the west and north west and north and north east.*

- *The question of Chinese entry into UNO. In view of the rebuff which China has given us and the method which it has followed in dealing with Tibet, I am doubtful whether we can advocate its claim any longer. There would probably be a threat in the UNO virtually to outlaw China, in view of its active participation in the Korean War. We must determine our attitude on this question also.*
- *The political and administrative steps which we should take to strengthen our northern and north eastern frontiers. This would include the whole of the border, Nepal, Bhutan, Sikkim, Darjeeling and the Tribal territory in Assam. Measures of internal security in the border areas as well as the states flanking those areas such as UP, Bihar, Bengal and Assam.*
- *Improvement of our communications, road, rail, air and wireless in these areas with frontier outposts.*
- *Policing and intelligence of frontier posts.*
- *The future of our mission at Lhasa and the trade posts at Gyantse and Yatung and the forces which we have in operation in Tibet to guard the trade routes.*
- *The policy in regard to the McMahon line.*

On 15 December 1950, just over a month after writing this prophetic letter, Sardar Patel passed away. Unfortunately for India, the steps suggested by him were not pursued vigorously enough. It is easy to imagine a different outcome if the timely warning, 12 years before the Chinese invasion, had been heeded to and acted upon in right earnest. But Nehru continued to ignore the seriousness of the challenge that China posed, preferring to rely on diplomatic parleys. While reliance on diplomacy was not wrong in itself, a simultaneous buildup of military capability and communications infrastructure along the borders would have been a prudent safeguard against such diplomacy not succeeding. But this did not happen. Nehru was questioned about the last point mentioned by Sardar Patel in his letter above, i.e., McMahon Line, in the parliament a few days later. When Dr SP Mukherjee, who had recently resigned from Nehru's Cabinet, pointed out that maps of China in circulation include portions of Assam (in Tibet), Nehru said, "*Our maps show that the McMahon line is our boundary and that is our boundary – map or no map. That fact remains and we stand by that boundary and we will not allow anybody to come across that boundary.*" With Nehru making his rigidity on the border issue public, the Chinese were bound to plan their further strategy accordingly.

India's stance on Tibet, however, was a study in ambiguity. In an attempt to retain the sympathetic attitude and friendship for the people of Tibet, without offending China in any way, it was at best an awkward balancing act. Nehru stated that he was "interested in Tibet's autonomy, but without challenging China's suzerainty over it." He told the parliament that "*we were aggrieved at a certain turn of events in Tibet, but we did not allow that to affect our policy or our desire to maintain friendly relations with China. I am glad to say that our relations with the new China are friendly at present.*"

For the record, India did lodge a protest to China for its suppression of independence and human rights in China. In return, it got an assurance from China that it would not use force in coming to a settlement with the Tibetan people. India not only took this assurance at face value, but also offered it on behalf of China when the Chinese occupation of Tibet came up for discussion in the United Nations Security Council. India's assurance on the subject led to dropping of the discussion in the Security Council. India's ambassador to China during this period, KM Panikkar, played a significant role in building an optimistic view of China's benevolent intentions vis-à-vis India, not only with the Prime Minister, but within the government and Foreign Ministry as well. In his periodic meetings with the Chinese leadership, they constantly assured him of China's best intentions about Tibet and friendly relations with India, and convinced, he dutifully conveyed the same back to India.

BN Mullik, who was the Director of the Intelligence Bureau and one of the key advisors and confidants of Nehru, and also amongst the key decision makers on our China policy, writes in his book *The Chinese Betrayal*,

> *I was present at a meeting held in 1950 by the Foreign Secretary, at which KM Panikkar, our Ambassador in China, and the Chief of Army Staff, General Cariappa, were present. At this meeting Panikkar gave a long dissertation on Chinese suzerainty over Tibet and tried to make out that it really meant no more than acknowledging the titular overlordship of China but did not in any way interfere with the practical independence and internal autonomy of Tibet. No one else at the meeting was convinced by the argument.*

At the same meeting, as per Mullik, the feasibility of a military intervention to assist Tibet was discussed:

> *On the question of India sending troops to stop the Chinese, Panikkar explained that legally India's action would be indefensible. However, when the question was put to General Cariappa, he quite categorically said the he could not spare any troops or could spare no more than a battalion for Tibet, so hard pressed was he with his commitments on the Pakistan front and with the*

internal troubles raised both by communal and Communist forces. He was also clear that his battalion could not go much farther than Eating or at the most might be able to place a company at Gyantse. Moreover, he explained that the Indian Army was not equipped or trained to operate at such heights and would be at a serious disadvantage against the Chinese army which had much training and experience in fighting in these extremely cold plateau and were even better armed, having acquired all the arms which the USA had poured into China to bolster the KMT army.

Mullik goes on to say that while he personally favoured a military intervention, and was disappointed by Gen Cariappa's refusal, he also acknowledges the merit in his reasoning. India was definitely not in a position to intervene militarily. Nor did it take any substantial steps to build up such a capability in the years that followed.

Having acknowledged that there was no military solution possible, the only recourse was to manage the situation diplomatically. And diplomacy in India in 1950s was largely the exclusive persevere of the Prime Minister, who had also retained the portfolio of Foreign Minister with himself. In his book *India's China War*, Neville Maxwell writes,

Nehru's highly personal style was, if anything, more marked in his handling of foreign policy than of domestic affairs. There was a cabinet committee for foreign affairs but that, too, he ignored more often than not, and time and again crucial foreign policy decisions were taken and announced – even acted upon – without either the committee or the cabinet being aware of them. This was true of the handling of the boundary question with China, which was kept not only from the cabinet and its foreign affairs and defence committees, but also from Parliament until armed clashes made it impossible to suppress.

India's foreign policy in the 1950s was thus the conception of Nehru himself, and its implementation the concern of Nehru and the senior officials of the External Affairs Ministry. Even there, in the early years Nehru tried to run the ministry as if that were his only charge, often drafting even simple telegrams himself and not consulting his officials. Of the Indian Foreign Service in Nehru's days one perceptive observer wrote that 'it was not a good service – nothing like good enough for a country of India's importance. There was not enough training or professional competence, not enough espirit de corps, and too much eagerness to please the boss. Nehru was too busy and too preoccupied to get to know the necessary detail, or to get to know the officers except for a handful of very senior ones or a few favourites. This encouraged sycophancy, personal ad hoc approaches, and a mixture of amateurishness and subjectivity.

Simultaneously with the Chinese invasion of Tibet, trouble was brewing in the Korean peninsula. The war between North and South Korea, the two states carved out of Korea by the Cold War adversaries in 1948, had the backing of the respective blocks. On 25 June 1950, troops of North Korea, backed by Soviet Union and China, invaded South Korea after a series of border skirmishes. This rapidly escalated into a full-blown war that lasted three years and ended on 27 July 1953 on signing of the Korean Armistice Agreement. China's active involvement in the war resulted in the Tibet and border dispute with India being put on the back burner by her for the time being. Yet it wasn't ignored altogether, as China continued to consolidate its grip on Tibet through force during this period.

Nehru, meanwhile, continued to back China, or at least shield it from international criticism at various world bodies during this period. In his own words, he thought "*it become [sic] necessary for India to avoid bickering with China on the issue of Tibet, so that she might play the role of an honest peace broker between the warring parties.*" In accepting the Chinese claims over Tibet, Nehru seemed to overlook the fact that he was also giving fillip to the Chinese claim that the Shimla Agreement of 1914 was not binding as Tibet did not have the authority to sign it. On 1 February 1951, India voted against a resolution in the United Nations General Assembly that fixed the blame on China as an aggressor in Korea. He was rewarded with several complimentary articles in the Chinese state-controlled media, which was a refreshing change from the scathing, almost abusive criticism they had reserved for him earlier. Perhaps this led him to feel buoyant and optimistic about the future of Sino-Indian ties.

Notwithstanding the optimism, a high-powered committee was constituted under Maj Gen Himmat Singhji, the Deputy Defence Minister, to recommend the improvements required in border defence, communications and administration consequent to the Chinese occupation of Tibet. It included representatives from Ministries of Defence, Communication, Home and External Affairs, besides those from Intelligence Bureau. It was formally named the North and North East Border Defence Committee. While the committee's report has not been declassified to date, the subsequent re-deployments, administrative changes and construction of roads initiated are supposed to have been an outcome of this.

One major development, possibly following the recommendations of this committee, was the establishment of formal Indian administrative control over Towang in NEFA, and now in Arunachal Pradesh. Major Bob Khathing, an officer of 2nd Assam Rifle belonging to the Thangkul Naga tribe, who was serving as an Assistant Political Officer in the Indian Frontier Administrative Service, led a force of 200 troops of 5th Assam Rifles to undertake this task. Under direct orders from Jairamdas Daulatram, the Governor of Assam, Major Khathing set out on 17 January 1951 for this assigned task. Making their way through Sisri, Dirang, Sela Pass, Nuranang and Jang, the party reached Towang on 7 February.

Major Khathing interacted with the Tibetan revenue officials who he found present at Towang, and forcefully conveyed to them that Towang was part of India as per the Shimla Convention of 1914. He then met with the representatives of the Towang monastery and the village elders and reiterated to them the control of Indian government over the area. As per local accounts, he was advised by the village elders that the people of the village would not comprehend an authority that did not collect taxes from them. It was based on this advice, the story goes, that a system was instituted where every house was to pay Rs 5 as an annual tax to the Government of India – a tax that's apparently still collected to date.

Amongst other decisions taken this time, again possibly on recommendations of the Himmat Singhji Committee, was to make the Intelligence Bureau responsible for foreign and strategic intelligence. The bureau had been set up as a special police organisation during the British rule, with the basic task of collecting internal and political intelligence. This amounted to gathering intelligence about criminal activity, and more importantly, on the freedom fighters and revolutionary organisations. It was a small organisation with no experience in gathering external intelligence and was manned by officers on deputation from police with no specialised training in gathering or interpreting intelligence. They had to undertake a drive to induct large number of new people to gear up for the enhanced task. A major problem was lack of people who could speak, let alone read or write, Tibetan or Chinese. As a result, while we had the technical capability to monitor radio transmissions, deciphering or translating the intercepted messages was very difficult. This was an area that received immediate attention, and slowly a language and cryptography section was built up.

On 23 May 1951, while the Korean war had still been raging, Tibet had been coerced into signing the "Sino-Tibetan Agreement on Measures for the Peaceful Liberation of Tibet" – a 17-point agreement that sealed the fate of Tibet's autonomy. This was the first agreement between Tibet and China since the one signed in 821 AD mentioned earlier. It declared that "*the Tibetan people shall unite and drive out imperialist aggressive forces from Tibet; the Tibetan people shall return to the big family of Motherland – the People's Republic of China.*" It laid down the integration of Tibetan Army into PLA and gave Peking total control over external affairs of Tibet. Logically, this should have sent alarm bells ringing in New Delhi even if the invasion of 1950 hadn't. India's limited presence – military, communications and trade – in Tibet, and India's control of territories considered disputed along the borders could be the only possible things being referred to when talking of driving out "imperialist aggressive forces" in Tibet, since there was no other foreign presence in that country whatsoever. Yet no such concerns were evident in Delhi.

On 27 September 1951, Chinese Premier Chou En-Lai, in an informal conversation with KM Panikkar, the Indian ambassador to China, said that "*there was no territorial dispute or controversy between India and China.*" It was perhaps similar assurances in the past also that formed a strong belief in Panikkar that there was no threat of a dispute with China over the boundary, and he continued to convey the same impression to his ministry and to Nehru, lulling them into a false sense of security despite the timely warning by Sardar Patel and the ominous wording of the 17-point agreement.

India, secure in China's purported friendliness and dismissal of talk of any territorial dispute, reciprocated by making concessions in Tibet. In September 1952, the Indian Political Agency in Lhasa was re-designated as Indian Consulate General. Panikkar observed, "*the main issue of our representation at Lhasa was thus satisfactorily settled and there was no outstanding issue between us and China.*" This indicates that India had no issues with Chinese subjugation of Tibet, since that continued unabated.

After the ceasefire in Korea in 1953, the Chinese immediately started moving more troops into Tibet. Their benign stance towards Indian presence in Tibet also changed drastically. They objected to the despatch of fresh Indian troops to replace the guards at Gyantse and Yatung, and seized the wireless set of the Indian Trade Agent at Gartok and prevented him from proceeding to the trade marts at Rudok and Takalakot. The Chinese military buildup into Tiebet was simultaneous and swift, using motor and air transport. Since movement and sustenance of a large army in Tibet required a much better road infrastructure than what existed, the Chinese initiated extensive road building programs. India remained blissfully unconcerned about these developments.

In December 1953, talks between China and India to settle the niggling issues began in Peking. The Foreign office at New Delhi had deliberated raising the frontier between Indian and Tibet during negotiations with Chinese Government. Girija Shankar Bajpai, former diplomat and then the Governor of Bombay, advised that India should get the Chinese to recognise the MacMahon Line to finally settle outstanding questions between India and Tibet. But the Indian ambassador to China, Panikkar, advised Nehru that India should not touch upon this and Nehru was in agreement. So far as India was concerned, the border was well established and well understood. If the Chinese wanted to raise any question, it was for them to do so.

Position of the Indian government continued to be short sighted and confused. The Prime Minister, during a debate on foreign policy in the parliament on 24 December 1953, said, "*Tibet is a part of China and our relations with the Chiense government are friendly. I do not believe there is the least chance of even an attempt of invasion of India. I'm not aware of any massing of troops across the Tibetan frontier. In fact, such troops as were there had been lessened because of difficulty in feeding them.*" It seems that extreme care was being taken not to antagonize the Chinese, lest it affect the outcome of the talks.

During the talks, the Chinese premier said that discussions would settle the questions "which were ripe for settlement." He said two large countries like India and China with a common frontier were bound to have some questions but all these could be settled smoothly. They seemed to be waiting for an 'appropriate' time to 'settle' the boundary issue, possibly once they had sufficiently recovered from the Korean war, consolidated their hold on Tibet and were in a position to enforce their stance militarily. Outwardly, the Chinese leaders continued to convey a false sense of security to India in all their interactions. In a prophetic comment, the Indian newspaper *Pioneer* wrote of the talks: "*Nothing has been secured to rule out further penetration of Chinese communists into regions bordering on China. India has yet to waken to the reality on her north-eastern frontiers and to events that are likely to follow.*"

The deliberations finally led to signing of the (in)famous Panchsheel Accord in April 1954. As per this, India agreed to completely withdraw the military escorts present in Tibet, and hand over the postal, telegraph and public telephone services it maintained. Trade agencies in Yatung and Gyantse were also relinquished. In exchange, there was no concession whatsoever from China. The boundary issue was not referred to at all beyond generic references to "mutual respect for each other's territorial integrity and sovereignty" and "mutual non aggression." Hailed as a huge milestone in India's foreign policy in general and its relations with China in particular, it was soon to become a millstone around India's neck instead.

The couple of years following the Panchsheel Accord were the high point of Sino-Indian relations – at least outwardly so. Premier Chou En-lai visited India in June 1954, in an unplanned stopover on his return to Beijing from Geneva. Nehru, who was slated to go on a 10-day holiday to Shimla, had previously cancelled the trip in anticipation of the visit. A specially chartered Air India Constellation aircraft "Maratha Princess" was sent from Bombay to fetch him from Geneva. At his charming best, the Chinese premier wrote in a note of appreciation to the crew, "*Skilful piloting and wonderful service. All is worthy of being learnt by the Chinese airline. I am grateful to the Indian government for sending a special plane to take me to India.*" There had been a minor confusion when a telegram from the Ministry of External Affairs (MEA) was misread by the crew as the premier being a vegetarian, but this was clarified, and he apparently relished the butterchicken served on board.

This was his first visit to Delhi, and also the first time Nehru and he met face to face. He was given a warm, rousing welcome by Indians lining the streets shouting "*Hindi Chini Bhai Bhai*" (Chinese and Indians are brothers). A hundred buses were run from different parts of Delhi to bring people to the airport for this public reception. He started his visit with a visit to Rajghat to pay tributes to Mahatma Gandhi and was also given a civic reception at the *Diwan-e-Khas* in the Red Fort. He also visited Qutub Minar in Delhi and Taj Mahal in Agra. Besides formal receptions, banquets and call-ons, he held several rounds of talks with Nehru and also extended a formal invitation for him to visit China, which Nehru accepted. In a broadcast before leaving Delhi, the Chinese premier spoke of the ancient ties between China and India and their "*common desire to construct our respective great motherlands in peaceful environments.*"

Nehru returned the visit with a 10-day trip to China in October 1954 and was greeted with what the *Times of India* called a "Himalayan welcome." "*Nearly a million people lined the 12-mile route from the airport, singing and cheering in a tidal wave of exuberant enthusiasm and affection,*" reported the newspaper. There were multiple receptions, meetings, discussions and banquets during the visit, where Nehru also met the Dalai Lama for the first time. At every forum, paeans were sung about the everlasting friendship between India and China by speakers from both sides. The visit also received a great deal of attention from western media, much to Nehru's delight. The News Chronicle, a London newspaper wrote, "*The meeting of Mr Nehru and Mr Mao Tse-tung may change history ... No one could do more than Mr Nehru to help pave the way for a better understanding in the future.*" Chinese newspapers were equally complimentary in their coverage of the visit in general and of Nehru personally in particular. Breaking protocol, Mao Tse Tung for the first time attended a banquet given by a foreign ambassador in someone's honour.

When, during this visit, Nehru brought up the issue of Chinese maps showing NEFA in China at a separate interaction, the Chinese premier Chou En-lai assured him that these were reproductions of old maps that they hadn't had the opportunity to correct. The matter was not pressed, and Nehru remarked at the end of his visit, "*I am convinced that the people of China, like the people of India, are devoted to the cause of peace.*"

The spirit of goodwill in Sino-Indian relations continued, and India was instrumental in getting China on board the Afro-Asian Conference (referred to as Bandung Conference after its venue in Indonesia) in 1955. Nehru took visible pride in bringing Communist China slowly out of its self-imposed isolation and into the fold of world diplomacy.

Chou En-lai visited India once again in November 1956, and this time he did bring up the border issue, but rather dismissively. He said that while there was no dispute regarding the border, there were certain petty problems that could be settled amicably. He did not go into the details of what these problems were. Nor did India insist on knowing more about them. India's view continued to be that our borders were well settled, while China, on the other hand, was waiting for an opportune time to bring it up. In 1957, there was another high-level visit when the Indian Vice President S Radhakrishnan went to Peking. This visit too was conducted amidst cordiality and expressions of goodwill from both sides. This period saw growth of the bilateral trade between India and China. But soon all this was about to change.

3

The Downward Spiral

Aksai Chin Highway

Amidst all this bonhomie, unknown to India, China was building up infrastructure in Tibet to support large-scale induction of troops from the mainland. The most significant amongst these was the highway connecting Tibet with Sinkiang (Xinjiang), another "autonomous" province of China. This road passed through Aksai Chin, the north-east tip of Jammu and Kashmir as per the Indian maps. In effect, China had unilaterally occupied, and built a large highway over territory that it knew was claimed by India. China began the construction of the road in 1955. Aksai Chin was an area that, though claimed by India, was not even covered by it through regular patrolling, let alone any permanent deployment of troops. It was an area that was uninhabited, with no communications, and so barren that, as Nehru famously remarked in the parliament, "not a blade of grass grew there." For all these reasons, the Chinese encroachment, including construction of a massive highway, through this Indian territory remained undetected for several years.

Journalist DR Mankekar in his book *Guilty men of '62* writes that Brig SS Mallick, the Indian Military Attaché at Peking, had heard word of construction being undertaken in Aksai Chin to provide a strategic link between Sinkiang and Tibet. Brig Mallick included this matter in his routine report to the MEA in New Delhi in November 1955, but this did not ring any alarm bells back home. Five months later, he sent a special report to highlight the construction, despite heavy opposition by the Ambassador RK Nehru, and marked a copy of this report to the Army Headquarters as well. Yet there was no official reaction from India, and no protest was lodged with the Chinese about this large-scale encroachment into India territory.

BN Mullik also claims in his book *The Chinese Betrayal* that the IB had inputs about the construction of this road, and had kept the government informed about it, even before the Military Attaché reported it. As per him, they had reported the construction of a jeep track as early as in November 1952. In 1953, he claims, they reported the jeep track had been completed and regular jeep traffic had been commenced over it. Reports from the Indian trade agent at Gartok indicated that Chinese were then upgrading this road to take heavier traffic. To quote Mullik, "*Enough information was available about the construction of the road from 1951 to 1957, when the road was formally declared open. All through these years no questions were raised by Army Headquarters or MEA (Ministry of External Affairs) about this road. It was only after the road had been completed and heavy traffic started plying that some attention was turned on it though even then, it was only considered to be of nuisance value and not one that affected our security.*" Recently declassified CIA notes, including one dated 15 July 1953 dealing with "Road construction, Sinkiang to Tibet and Ladakh", confirm that the US intelligence agency was aware of the construction of this road. It is quite likely that they would have shared this piece of information with their Indian counterparts. There is no doubt that the Indian government, including the Prime Minister, MEA as well as Ministry of Defence, was aware of the Chinese transgression. Yet they chose to ignore it for as long as they could, not wanting to confront the reality as it was rudely in contravention of the spirit of conviviality that marked the relations with China till then.

The news of the 1,179-kilometre-long Sinkiang-Tibet Highway, claimed to be the highest highway in the world, with a stretch of 95 km being 4,000 meters above sea level, having been completed, was published in a Chinese newspaper on 6 October 1957. The Indian ambassador and Military Attaché were invited to be present at the inauguration of the road, but both declined to attend. With the information becoming public, it was no longer possible for India to ignore the blatant encroachment on its territory. Shortly afterwards, India's Foreign Secretary Subimal Dutt wrote to Prime Minister Nehru suggesting sending a patrol to ascertain if the road passed through Indian territory. Nehru agreed, albeit reluctantly, being of the view that it will "*not perhaps be very helpful.*"

Two patrols were sent out as recommended by the Foreign Secretary. The first was of the Army, led by a young officer called Lt Iyengar. This patrol was accosted by the PLA and the soldiers were detained. They were returned only after protracted negotiations for two months with the Chinese. The second patrol was from the border police, led by Karan Singh, and it managed to reach the Aksai Chin road undetected. Karan Singh photographed Chinese convoys plying on it. They could thus confirm that the road had indeed come up on the Indian territory and was being used by Chinese military and civil traffic.

Nehru now instructed the External Affairs Ministry to send an "informal note" to China, along with the map showing our claimed boundary. Incredibly, the note included protestations as to why "*no applications for visa from Chinese personnel working on the road or from Chinese travellers traversing this road have been received by the Government of India.*" But lest this offend them, it went on to assure the Chinese government that "*the Government of India is anxious to settle these petty frontier disputes so that the friendly relations between the countries may not suffer.*"

Mullik pins the blame for not taking the blatant occupation of Indian territory by China seriously enough squarely on the Army Headquarters and MEA. As per his book *The Chinese Betrayal*, the Army Headquarters "*knew that they were in no position to prevent the Chinese from constructing this road across Aksai Chin*" due to lack of communications, and thus difficulty in maintaining any troops in the far-flung area. "*So he* (Gen Thimayya, the Army Chief) *tried to play down the importance of the road.*" The External Affairs Ministry, says Mullik, thought "*this part of the territory was useless to India. Even if Chinese did not intrude into it, India could not make any use of it. ... It would be pointless to pick up quarrels over issues in which India had no means of enforcing her claims.*" Gen Thimayya was only being realistic. Since the government had accorded low priority to arming and modernising the armed forces ever since independence, it was not strong enough to enforce its rights against a militarily more powerful China. As for the MEA, being headed by the Prime Minister himself, it is expected that it was his views that it was expressing.

The outcome of this helplessness was an ostrich-like stance by the government, which took recourse to just burying its head in the sand and ignoring the issue completely. The government did not take the parliament or the people into confidence about the Chinese occupation of Aksai Chin and construction of a road through it at this stage. Two years later, in a debate in the parliament in November 1959, Dr HN Kunzru – an experienced parliamentarian and freedom fighter – charged the government with deliberately hiding the construction from the parliament. He said, "*We have been told that the*

Government of India did not know that the Tibet-Sinkiang road was being built through Ladakh. Perhaps the government received information about it first in 1957. Whether it believed that this information was correct or not, I do not know but it did, I believe, receive information at least two years ago about the fact that the Sinkiang-Tibet road was being built through Ladakh. It came to know with complete certainty that the road had been built at least a year ago."

Revolt in Tibet

Resentment against China had been brewing up in Tibet ever since the occupation by PLA troops and subsequent thrusting upon them of the 17-Point Agreement in 1951. The opposition was particularly strong in the Kham and Admo provinces, and the revolt that ultimately broke out is referred to as the Khampa revolt after the residents of the former. Being part of 'Inner Tibet', and hence closest to China, the Khampa had borne the maximum brunt of the Chinese occupation. During the initial years of occupation, while they were busy consolidating their hold and, more importantly, building roads and infrastructure, the Chinese were more benevolent towards the local population. This attitude changed around 1956. Having firmed up its presence, the Chinese now started attempting to introduce land reforms and reduce the power of monasteries, bringing Tibet more in line with the communist system. A large number of Tibetan youths were dispatched to China for "training" and "special education" classes. Youth and women organisations were set up in Tibet to spread the communist ideology. Village elders were pressurised to extort consent for these measures, and attempts were made to indoctrinate them politically. The locals resented these measures, and the building resentment ultimately led to the Khampa revolt.

The Khampas took to guerrilla warfare, attacking Chinese installations and disrupting communications. An escalatory cycle of attacks, reprisals and further attacks led to large-scale atrocities on innocent Tibetan men, women and children. With their complete control over the region, which was virtually isolated from the rest of the world, the Chinese perpetuated the most heinous atrocities without any check or international reactions. Even the Dalai Lama wasn't fully aware of the gravity of the situation in the outlying areas, till people migrating from Kham towards Lhasa recounted stories of the horrors they had faced at the hands of the Chinese. To pacify people's sentiments, China announced a postponement of the proposed land reforms and reduced troop presence in Lhasa. The people weren't mollified, and the agitations continued. In this backdrop, the Chinese insisted that Nehru, who was to visit Tibet in 1958 on their previous invitation, cancel his visit. Instead, he visited Bhutan, completing the four-day journey by plane, car, pony and on foot. He did traverse through the Tibetan territory, where he was even given a guard of honour by the Chinese army.

The Khampas now formed a militia that took control of the territory south of Tsangpo up to the Indian frontier in NEFA. The Chinese, meanwhile, resumed their attempts to impose communist ideology and suppress Buddhism. The revolt further intensified in 1959, and the Chinese accused the Dalai Lama of actively encouraging the rebels. The Chinese started building up their forces in Tibet, bringing in almost 2,00,000 troops. Tibetan people started fearing for Dalai Lama's life when he was "invited" to the Chinese military headquarters on 10 March 1959, for a theatrical show, with instructions for his guards not to accompany him. Large crowds started gathering in Lhasa to dissuade him from going. They maintained a round-the-clock vigil outside his residence, and vowed to protect him against Chinese designs. Demonstrations were also held in front of the Indian Consulate General in Lhasa, protesting India's inability to do anything on their behalf. The crowd was further agitated when they received news that the Chinese had brought in artillery guns into Lhasa. Dalai Lama's followers feared that they may bombard the palace, and his close advisors mounted pressure on him to get away from the palace and go as far away from Lhasa as possible.

Asylum to Dalai Lama

On 17 March 1959, Dalai Lama escaped from Lhasa into rebel held territory in the south. He was accompanied by some family and cabinet members and a few bodyguards. With a complete lack of information flowing from Tibet, there was widespread concern about Dalai Lama's safety in India. Nehru informed the parliament that he had "*no correct information as to where he* (Dalai Lama) *is, but I certainly hope he is safe.*" He emphasized that India had no desire to interfere in "China's internal affairs" yet spoke of India's concern in view of the ancient cultural ties with Tibet. The initial plan was to set up a government in exile there, but his advisors thought the Chinese threat to him while he remained in Tibet was too grave. Being the figurehead, sovereign, religious leader and the biggest rallying point for any Tibetan movement, elimination of the Dalai Lama would have been high on the Chinese wishlist. The advisors came to a conclusion that it would be safer for him to seek asylum in India, out of reach of any nefarious designs of Chinese forces. Accordingly, on 31 March, Dalai Lama's party crossed over into India, where he sought and was granted political asylum. India initially denied any information about the whereabouts of Dalai Lama in response to a Peking radio broadcast declaring his escape to India. Finally, on 4 April, Nehru confirmed his arrival in an announcement in Parliament.

The Tibetan revolt and grant of asylum to Dalai Lama was possibly one of the key turning points in this saga. Relations between India and China kept sliding downwards from this point onwards. The Chinese were now openly hostile towards any Indian overtures, the Panchsheel Agreement notwithstanding. As per a National Intelligence Estimate prepared by CIA in 1960, "*outbreak of the Tibetan revolt in early 1959 caused China to take rapid and ruthless action to put it down. Peiping* (Peking) *was suspicious that the revolt was supported by India, and gave little thought to Indian sensibilities.*" No amount of balancing acts by Nehru, who continued trying to convince China that India's moral obligations to Tibetans did not translate into any predatory territorial designs there, served to assuage Chinese doubts. The asylum, combined with India's now open protestations against Chinese occupation of Aksai Chin, changed the language of interlocution between the two countries from the friendly terms of Bandung days to acrimonious accusations against each other. Shortly after Dalai Lama's arrival in India, Nehru held meetings with him at the hill station of Mussoorie, which were widely reported in the media, causing further instigation to the Chinese.

Using Dalai Lama's escape as an excuse, the Chinese unleashed a fresh reign of terror in Tibet and brought the entire region tightly under its control. If there remained any doubts about the threat China posed to India after it initially occupied Tibet in 1950, these should have been completely removed by now. Yet, even at this stage, there were no thoughts given to military preparations to counter a possible Chinese threat.

Border Clashes

Up until now, there had been some sporadic incidents of border violations and clashes. Such incidents are not unusual when two armies are deployed across disputed, un-demarcated borders through long stretches of an uninhabited territory with inaccurate maps. Patrols from one side wander into the other side, and are spotted, possibly engaged. Incidents are reported up the chain of command and formal protests are lodged diplomatically.

One such incident had taken place within a few weeks of signing the Panchsheel Accord, when Indian troops accosted Chinese soldiers at a place called Bara Hoti, on the Indian side of the Tibet border in Uttar Pradesh (the area now falls under Uttarakhand). The intruders were asked to leave Indian territory, and there was no physical engagement. This intrusion was repeated once again at several places in 1955, and Indian Foreign Ministry lodged formal protests on both occasions. Nehru, in his capacity as the foreign minister, continuously urged the ministry not to lose a sense of perspective and not to "*indulge in strong language in notes to the Chinese*", as former diplomat Subimal Dutt recounts in his book *With Nehru in Foreign Office*. He writes, "*Nehru was still unconvinced that the Chinese had large territorial claims against India or that they would use force in settling their claims. He rather felt that the violations of Indian territory by the Chinese personnel were due to the expressive enthusiasm of the Chinese border force.*"

While on one hand, it was becoming increasingly obvious that national security was under unprecedented threat, on the other hand, the defence budget was being inexplicably cut. As per an article in the *USI Journal* (January-March 1959),

> *The Parliament of India expressed during the budget debate its concern for Indians defence and security in the face of growing threats. The debate on the demand for the Ministry of Defence which took place in the Lok Sabha on April 10 1959 was marked by the assurances given by the Defence Minister in the course of his reply that the cut in defence budget was entirely done on the initiative of the Ministry and that in effecting this reduction the Ministry had taken into consideration all relevant facts like defence needs the context of the existing situation and the capacity of the country to bear the cost. In effecting this reduction there was a calculated risk taken, but* ***"if anybody should be so unwise or unkind and ungenerous as to seriously violate our frontiers, the defence forces of the country would meet the attack to the best of their ability and capacity."***

The basis of this assertion, or whether the ability and capacity was a match for the Chinese, was not questioned by anyone including the opposition. There were few parliamentarians, if any at all, who had even a cursory understanding of military matters to enable them to assess the government's claims vis-à-vis the capabilities on ground, and to raise such questions.

The Chinese threat was not very real in the minds of the military as well as political leadership. The latter had developmental priorities that they were loath to override for spending more on defence. Besides, they were still confident of resolving the issue diplomatically through talks between the two countries. The military leadership, confident in the diplomatic ability that the leadership put so much of reliance on to avoid an open conflict, never considered the Chinese as a clear and present danger.

The frequency and intensity of the border clashes increased after the arrival of Dalai Lama in India. In July 1959, six men of an Indian reconnaissance patrol were arrested by the Chinese. While the earlier incidents were limited only to the Western (Ladakh) or Central (HP/UP) sectors of the border, they were now extended to the North East. This was also possibly because now Chinese had full control over Tibet and were therefore now in a position to launch such incursions from the areas bordering NEFA. On 7 August, 200 Chinese troops pushed back the Indian picket at Khinzemane in the Kameng subdivision of NEFA. A serious clash took place at a place called Longju on the McMahon Line on 26 August 1959 when another strong Chinese party crossed the McMahon Line and opened fire on Indian troops. This resulted in a long standoff between the two parties. As a report in the *Time* magazine dated 7 September 1959 quoted Nehru, "*38 Indian soldiers had fought with 300 Chinese invaders and barely escaped encirclement. An Indian plane had tried to drop munitions to surrounded men but had failed.*"

A similar incident took place on 21 October 1959 at Kongka Pass in Ladakh, leading to a number of casualties to an Indo-Tibetan border force party. Nine policemen lost their lives and some members of this party were taken prisoner. The full scale of atrocities committed by the Chinese on the Indian patrol became known only when these were released. The leader of the patrol was tortured and abused, forced to give statements in accordance with the Chinese version, and to make a propaganda film. Chinese also intruded in several areas along the border in Ladakh, including Sapnggur in the Pagong Tso area and at Khurnak Fort to its east. These sporadic border incidents while not major in themselves were clear indicators of the increasing friction in Sino-Indian relations. Vice President Dr Radhakrishnan declined a Chinese invitation of a goodwill visit in view of the increasing tensions.

The article quoted above speculated,

> *Red China, beset by internal troubles, made plain its determination to cause friction and perhaps war all along its southern borders. ... The long unrealistic era in which the two largest nations on earth coexisted peaceably because one of them saw no evil or heard no evil seemed at last to be ending. ... In India's*

lower house of Parliament, Jawaharlal Nehru described, in blunt language he had never used before, the 'continuing aggression' of Red China's troops against India's northern borders. The frontier incidents were clearly a Chinese testing of India's willingness to defend itself. "We must not become alarmist and panicky and take wrong actions," cautioned the ever cautious and neutralist Nehru, but he added ringingly that 'there is no alternative to us but to defend our borders and our integrity.

Nehru's statement above, and his instructions to the Foreign Office as recounted by Subimal Dutta above are a perfect expression of the confused state of mind that he and the entire government was in on how to deal with China at this stage.

It was on 28 August 1959, after the encounter at Longju, that Nehru formally took the country into confidence about the ongoing issues with China along our borders, when he spoke about it in the parliament for the first time. Significantly, he made a clear distinction between our stance (at that time) regarding the borders along Ladakh and the McMahon Line. He admitted that "*The actual boundary of Ladakh with Tibet was not carefully defined. It was defined to some extent by British officers who went there. But I rather doubt if they did any careful survey. ... As people do not live there, by and large, it does not make any difference. It did not make any difference. At that time nobody cared about it.*" But he emphasised that "*McMahon Line has to be accepted, and so far as we are concerned, it is there and we accept it. ... But having broadly accepted the McMahon Line, I am prepared to discuss any interpretation of the McMahon Line; minor interpretations here and there ... That I am prepared to discuss with the Chinese Government. I am prepared to have any kind of conciliatory, mediatory process to consider this.*"

In this speech, Nehru grandly announced placing the border in NEFA directly under the Army. If anything, this increased the ambiguity of the situation. In Nehru's own words, "*We have in fact placed this border area of NEFA directly under the military authorities. That is to say it was being dealt with by the Assam Rifles, which was functioning under the Governor of Assam, and the governor is an agent of the Government of India, in the External Affairs Ministry. ... The Assam Rifles will of course, remain there and such other forces as will be necessary will be sent, but they will function now under the army authorities and their headquarters.*" This announcement appeared to satisfy the parliament, with the limited military understanding of most of its members, that adequate action was at hand to deal with the situation. However, he seemed to have overlooked two implications of his statement. Firstly, the army had virtually no presence in NEFA at that time, and hence would require time and resources to gear up for this new task. The poor road network in the border areas (virtually non-existent in most of them, in fact) would hamper building up and maintenance of any large-size force capable of realistically meeting a Chinese threat. Moreover, to the Chinese, this statement indicated an escalatory step on India's part. It served to further aggravate their suspicions about India's intentions and harden its own stance, as it soon became apparent.

While Nehru came under criticism from the opposition for keeping the country in dark about these developments so far, they were broadly supportive of his proposed measures to deal with the Chinese. However, the Communist Party of India (CPI) came out strongly in support of the Chinese stance on the border issue. In a 12-page article titled "India China Relations," BT Ranadive of CPI questioned the validity of India's boundary claims and the validity of the McMahon Line. His reasoning for this was in line with the argument forwarded by China herself. He argued that it "*arose out of an attempt of British imperialism to separate Tibet from China and make it safe for further penetration.*" He also parroted Chinese line about it not having ratified the Shimla Accord, making it null and void.

Thimayya's Resignation

One unforseen outcome of Nehru's announcement of "handing over the situation to the army" was a showdown between Gen Thimayya and VK Krishna Menon, the Defence Minister. Since the army had not been consulted or even informed about the Prime Minister's decision, the announcement came like a bolt out of the blue. It appeared that the Army was being given a *fait accompli* in order to bail out the Prime Minister, who was facing criticism for his handling of the whole affair so far. An impression was being built up that now that the army had been called in, everything would soon be in order. However, there had been no taking stock of whether the army was equipped with the wherewithal to deal with the situation immediately. There was also a major disagreement between Thimayya and Menon regarding promotion of some officers whom Menon wanted promoted and Thimayya felt weren't deserving. Thimayya handed over his resignation to Nehru in protest. When the news about the resignation came out, there was a huge furore in the media, and Menon was blamed for precipitating this crisis. An article in the *Time* described this sordid event thus:

> *The worst furore of all broke when the New Delhi Statesman headlined the*

shocking news that India's popular and able army chief of staff, General K.S. Thimayya, had handed in his resignation. The reason: months of incessant bickering, especially about promotions in the armed forces, between Thimayya and the civilian Minister of Defense, crotchety, Mephistophelean Krishna Menon.

Press and public opinion erupted. Krishna Menon, 62, is so oblivious of his own mistakes and so coldly cruel about the mistakes of others that even his well-wishers frequently find him intolerable. The fact that he had apparently precipitated strife in the high command at a time when India might be facing battle with Red China set off loud demands that he be sacked. The Hindustan Times proclaimed: "Krishna Menon must go!" The Indian Express called Menon "preeminently the guilty man."

This put Nehru in an embarrassing situation, leaving him open to attack by the media and the opposition. Nehru summoned Gen Thimayya and persuaded to withdraw his resignation. While the records of Thimayya's discussions with Menon or Nehru are not available, accounts by contemporary writers suggest that Nehru appealed to Thimayya's sense of duty as a soldier. He implored the General to reconsider his resignation in view of the ongoing situation with China, which could turn into a crisis any time. As an honourable man and a good soldier, Thimayya did what was asked, and withdrew his resignation. However, the very next day in a statement in the Parliament, Nehru virtually insulted Thimayya. He insinuated that the resignation was prompted due to a personality clash between Menon and Thimayya, making no mention of the grave reasons that prompted the differences between the two, or Thimayya's views on the preparedness of the army to face a Chinese threat. He dismissed these aspects as being "*trivial and of no consequence.*" On the contrary, he expressed his satisfaction on the progress made in making the army ready for war. He said,

About midday on August 31, I received a letter from General Thimayya offering his resignation. … It seemed to me peculiarly unwise that this action should have been taken in the conditions prevailing in India today. On the evening of August 31, I sent for General Thimayya and pointed out to him that his sending me his resignation in that way did seem to me not a right thing at all. I advised him to withdraw it and he accepted my advice… . Though General Thimayya assured me that the Army was in fine mettle, the morale of the offices and men was excellent and that good progress had been made in production of ordnance factories, he told me he was not feeling happy about various matters connected with the Defence Ministry. He gave

> *me some instances but they were, to my thinking, rather trivial and of no consequence. I realised that the difficulties that had arisen might be called temperamental. …*

Brig Dalvi writes that the cause of the falling out between Gen Thimayya and Menon was probably the government's China policy. "*General Thimayya was a seasoned, disciplined soldier. … He would hardly have made an issue over trifles. Only over-riding national interests would have provoked him to the extreme step of resignation: and later withdraw the resignation in dutiful obedience to his Prime Minister.*"

Chinese Bombshell and Diplomatic Parleys

On 8 September 1959, Chou En-lai dropped a bombshell on India when he spelt out that China claimed over 90,000 square kilometres of Indian territory, including all of Aksai Chin and NEFA. In a letter addressed to Nehru, he wrote, "*…there is a fundamental difference between the positions of our two governments on the Sino-Indian boundary question.*" Tracing back the boundary question to the aggressive attitude of the British empire, he alleged a British design to "*separate Tibet from China*" by constant instigation of Tibet and application of pressure on China. He went on to emphasize the Chinese stance that the boundary had never been delimited, questioning the legal grounds of the territories as depicted on British and subsequently Indian maps. Dismissing the Ladakh Treaty of 1842 and the Shimla Conference of 1914 as part of the British design mentioned earlier, the letter claimed that the McMahon Line had never been recognized by any Chinese Central Government and "*is, therefore, decidedly illegal.*" In a veiled threat, he said that though the Chinese government did not recognize the McMahon Line, its troops never crossed it "*for the sake of maintaining amity along the border to facilitate negotiations and settlement of the boundary question.*"

Time, it seems, was finally ripe in Chinese reckoning, to confront India on the boundary dispute, after years of dismissing it as minor misunderstandings. Chou completely disowned any validity of the Shimla Accord of 1914, and therefore refused to recognise the legality of the McMahon Line as having been arbitrarily defined by an Imperial power. He insisted that the borders between India and Tibet needed to be redefined afresh based on negotiations between China and India as independent nations. This was the outcome of a series of correspondence in 1958 and 1959 wherein Nehru had questioned the continued issue of Chinese maps with parts of India shown as Chinese territory. He had reminded Chou En-lai of his assurance to Nehru in 1954 that there were no major territorial disputes between India and China. The Chinese premier's response was that though the boundaries had never been formally delimited, Peking had not raised the issue earlier as "conditions were not ripe for settlement." Although it is evident from his earlier statements that Nehru all along knew that China did not recognise the Indian alignment of the boundary, with China now officially disowning it, the problem could no longer be ignored.

Nehru persisted with his rigid stand, and in a note dated 4 November 1959 to the Chinese embassy, the Indian MEA replied that the boundary issue had been long settled and could not be reopened. On 7 November, Chou replied, proposing a withdrawal of armed forces of both sides by 20 kilometres from existing positions, creating a de-militarised zone of 40 kilometres all along the border. He suggested this as a means to avoid any further clashes while the two countries settled the border dispute through negotiations. This proposition was distinctively disadvantageous to India. The Chinese "existing positions" advanced into territory claimed by India as its own in Ladakh way beyond Aksai Chin, through which the Chinese had constructed the vital highway linking Sinkiang with Tibet. India had no holding beyond the McMahon Line in Arunachal Pradesh. Accepting the Chinese proposal would effectively mean that Indian forces would have to withdraw 20 kilometres from the McMahon Line, while the Chinese would still retain a hold over Aksai Chin and even Indian-claimed area beyond it towards Ladakh. As an American editorial of that time observed, "*acceptance of this proposal would have seriously jeopardised Indian defence positions in the east and would have at the same time made a gift to the Chinese of the vital Aksai Chin area.*" This was also not acceptable to India, as it feared that China could renege on the agreement and surreptitiously occupying area south of McMahon Line, as it had done earlier in Aksai Chin.

On 23 November 1959, Nehru placed a White Paper on the table of the Lok Sabha, giving out Indian government's stance and their correspondence with China on the border issue. In the ensuing debate, Nehru agreed that there had been "*a worsening of the situation … both actually and in the public mind*". He asked the house for opinion and advice on the broad policies that the government should follow, and steps that should be taken to implement these policies. He referred to his government's policies of non-alignment and peaceful co-existence. He admitted to the latter not having succeeded vis-à-vis China but defended both the policies being principally valid. On the implementation of these policies, he spoke about military power, or the lack of it, arising from the presence or absence of a strong industrial base. He claimed that while his government had not ignored the importance of military strength, he admitted to giving priority to industrial development, from which he hoped military power would ultimately flow. "*Of course, we can go and buy – to meet a temporary emergency – warlike material and equipment, but thereby cut short all our planning and the other schemes we have in view. I hope it will never come to that.*" (Unfortunately for him and the country, this was exactly what the government had to resort to under dire circumstances as events unfolded). He went on a philosophical monologue about our commitment peace in the long term before seeking the views of the house. He came under criticism from the opposition about ignoring signs of Chinese expansionism right from 1954, being obsessed instead with the Panchsheel agreement. His assertion about the defence forces being adequately prepared was also questioned. B Shiva Rao, a Congress MP, sought assurance that "*should the necessity arise ... there will be no hesitation on our part to obtain aid from friendly countries for the safeguarding of our frontiers. ...*"

It was still three years before the Chinese attack. If the government had seriously considered the possibility of an all-out attack by China even at this stage, they could have ensured the nation and the armed forces were better prepared to meet the challenge. However, this did not happen, and efforts for a diplomatic resolution continued without a simultaneous military preparation.

On 5 February 1960, Nehru wrote to Chou En-lai, refuting the Chinese stance on the border issue and suggesting a meeting between the two of them to discuss the problems at an early date. He invited Chou En-lai to be an "*Honoured guest*" to discuss the issues face to face: "*I confess I do not particularly like this long-distance correspondence which consists of a reaffirmation of our respective views*". But even before the planned visit, China sent another note on 3 April 1960, rejecting the "Watershed principle" that India had considered as the basis of demarcation of the boundary between the two countries. It said, "*...even though some sections of the Sino-Indian traditional customary line may have comparatively distinct natural features, it is still necessary for the two sides to define jointly their starting and terminal points and their specific alignments.*" Although the letter reassured India that no preconditions were being set for the upcoming talks, the content and tone of the letter seemed to suggest that the Chinese were not inclined towards accepting the Indian point of view *in toto*.

Amidst the ongoing diplomatic exchange aimed at resolving the border dispute, the Indian government simultaneously kept up its effort of convincing the parliament and people that our defence preparedness was adequate to meet any threats. As per a report in the *Times of India*, during a debate on the budgetary demands of the Ministry of Defence in the Lok Sabha on 9 April 1960, Defence Minister Menon "*firmly assured the House that the strength of the Army had been increased and that India's defensive power and productive capacity were now greater than before. Army units had, moreover, been moved to forward positions.*"

Chou En-lai arrived in New Delhi from Rangoon on 19 April 1960 aboard an Indian Air Force Viscount aircraft "Raj Hamsa," ceremonially escorted by eight Vampire jets. In Rangoon, he had assured of peaceful settlement of the border between Burma and China. The crowd at the airport and lining the route to Rashtrapati Bhawan, unlike his previous two visits, was sparse and outnumbered by the policemen deployed. There were no waves and cheers, but there were also no demonstrations as feared by the government. A few persons carrying black flags were arrested before they could wave these.

Chou En-lai met and held talks with the President, Vice President and several cabinet ministers including Menon besides holding multiple rounds of talks with Nehru. There was no movement towards a resolution during the talks with both sides adhering firmly to their previously stated positions. The only outcome at the end was a confirmation by both sides that there were serious differences about their respective understanding of the basic facts about the border. Chou En-lai insisted, "*the only possible approach to a settlement would involve India's tacitly or formally recognising Chinese rights in the Aksai Chin area in Ladakh in exchange for reciprocal forbearance by Peking from any assertion of her claims for territory below the McMahon Line in the east.*" Nehru categorically rejected what he saw was linking of China's illegal claim over Aksai Chin with India's legal jurisdiction up to the McMahon Line. He was against any such "barter".

The prime ministers decided that the officials of the two governments would meet and examine all the relevant documents to verify claims of either side. Meanwhile, they agreed, every effort should be made to avoid friction and clashes in the border areas. The talks between officials of the two sides dragged on endlessly over multiple sessions alternating in either country. Journalist Prem Bhatia wrote in an editorial in the *Times of India*, "*It is now understood that the talks among officials in Peking on the frotnier disputes between India and China are going according to plan – the Chinese plan. Apparently, in the two weeks that our representatives have been in Peking, the talks have recorded no progress. When the Nehru – Chou En-lai joint communique was issued in New Delhi at the end of*

April, no one thought that much good would result from the discussions in Peking. Few, however, foresaw the kind of difficulties which the Chinese are now reported to be creating."

While there was an honest attempt from the Indian side to provide accurate answers to queries raised by the Chinese, there was no reciprocation of sincerity from the Chinese side. They evaded questions, and whatever replies they gave were framed in ambiguity. They did not even clearly spell out the coordinates of their claim line. Mullik writes in his book *The Chinese Betrayal*, "*This vagueness was deliberate because in the western sector* (Ladakh), *unlike in the east, the Chinese were in occupation nearly up to their claimed line and so had no difficulty in giving the coordinates. This was a clever manoeuvre so that they could go on pushing forward their boundary as they had been doing since 1954 onwards.*" Simultaneously, in a possible bid to showcase their reasonableness vis-à-vis India's obduracy, the Chinese came to a settlement of their boundaries with Burma and Nepal.

By February 1961, it had become obvious that the border negations between the two countries had reached a deadlock, as was apparent from the report on the discussions published by the MEA. The Indian embassy in China received a message that RK Nehru, the Secretary General of the MEA and former Indian ambassador to China, was being dispatched by Prime Minister Nehru to China to find a way to break the impasse. Being a relative of the Prime Minister, RK Nehru was supposedly amongst the "inner circle" of the few who were trusted by Nehru in diplomacy. He arrived in Peking and seemed to be in a foul mood on the low-key reception accorded to him by the Chinese government. Instead of the one-on-one meetings with Mao and Chou En-lai he expected, he got to meet only the titular head of the government, Liu Shao Chi. He did manage to meet Chou En-lai during a stopover at Hong Kong during his return flight, but as per the then ambassador to China G Parthasarathi, the discussion did not extend to the border issues. It remained more of an exchange of pleasantries.

The news of this unofficial mission caused outrage in Delhi with the opposition in Parliament up in arms, demanding to be taken into confidence about the outcomes of this unannounced and unexpected initiative of the government. The Prime Minister played down the visit as an informal stopover by RK Nehru while returning from an official visit to Mongolia, and assured the opposition that he had not carried out any negotiations with the Chinese.

However, RK Nehru held a press conference in Hong Kong and gave a statement contradicting this. He said that in his conversation with Chou En-lai, he had taken "*a strong and clear stand against Chinese violation of Indian territories and gave them suitable warning.*" This, in turn, caused a storm in Peking. The Foreign Ministry summoned the Indian ambassador and lodged a strong protest against the "*incorrect and untrue statements made by Mr RK Nehru.*" As per them, RK Nehru had informed the Chinese ambassador in Delhi that the Indian government wanted him (Nehru) to visit China to discuss matters of "mutual interest." An invitation was extended and normal diplomatic courtesies extended including formal meetings with leaders. However, there were no discussions about the border issue during any of these meetings as was falsely claimed by RK Nehru in his press conference at Hong Kong. The Chinese accused him of abusing Chinese hospitality. The incident typifies the cavalier attitude of the Prime Minister and the External Affairs Ministry under his favoured protégés towards such a serious, contentious issue. They looked at playing to the gallery as being much more important than substantive progress in sorting out the issues. This grandstanding, which was not hidden from the Chinese leadership, who also had access to Indian newspapers, probably served to enhance their distrust of India.

In his book *My Peking Memoirs*, PK Bannerjee, who took over as the Indian ambassador to China shortly after RK Nehru's disastrous visit, describes an interaction with Chou En-lai that gives an insight into the Chinese thought process at that time. Recalling his interactions with Nehru during the heady days of Bandung friendship, the Chinese Premier said, "*The great need was for India and China to work together again. He was concerned that certain powers were trying to influence Mr Nehru for their own national goals and widen the gap between India and China.*"

It is quite possible that the repeated mentions of India or Indian leaders being "misled by foreign powers" was to do with Chinese suspicions that India and US were working closely together to support rebels in Tibet, and India was helping CIA with its operations there. It's ironic that it was in fact Pakistan, not India, who was helping CIA in Tibet. As per Bruce Riedel, American security expert and author of *JFK's Forgotten Crisis: Tibet, the CIA and Sino-Indian War*, CIA was running an extensive operation in Tibet in this period. This operation was being run with East Pakistan (now Bangladesh) as the base, and the Pakistani government was actively complicit in it. He writes, "*The CIA was supporting a rebellion in Communist China's Tibet province from another Pakistani Air Force base near Dacca. ... Tibetan rebels trained by CIA in Colorado were parachuted into Tibet from CIA transport planes that flew from Pakistani air base, as were supplies and weapons. U-2 aircraft also landed in East Pakistan after flying over China to conduct photo reconnaissance missions.*" As per Riedel, Mullik and Nehru had an inkling of some covert action by the US in Tibet, but chose to turn a blind eye to them. There is no indication of any Indian collaboration with the US in running these operations.

As per a monograph by Sunil Khatri published by IDSA, the CIA covert operations in Tibet had three major components: ST CIRCUS, assistance for armed resistance in Tibet; ST BARNUM, airlift operations for CIRCUS; and ST BAILEY, political action in India and other countries, UN and other human rights organisations worldwide. India was never officially informed about these. Chou En-lai, however, seemed to have an inkling of some CIA operations underfoot, and was suspicious about Indian involvement. He mentioned "*subversive activities encouraged by US agents taking place in Kalimpong.*" Nehru assured him that Indian government would not allow anti-Chinese propaganda from its soil. He did find it difficult to explain to Chou, however, the articles appearing in the Indian press in support of Tibetans – the concept of free press possibly being completely alien to the Chinese premier.

China, however, was apparently working towards a pre-planned design all along. Keeping India diplomatically entangled in talks on one hand, it continued building up its military strength and logistics capability in Tibet simultaneously on the other. Reports of Chinese reinforcements were published regularly in Indian newspapers. A report in the *Times of India* dated 4 June 1960 quoted Tibetan sources about the move of "*rockets and armoured cars into Western Tibet.*" Another, dated 12 June, spoke of a string of airfields having come up, including at Rudok, Gartok and Tashigong. It also reported presence of "*heavy artillery pieces, including mountain batteries, in Rudok and other military bases in western Tibet*" besides setting up of military outposts where Chinese troops were "*equipped with mortars and provided with wireless sets, tents, horses and mules.*" Nehru acknowledged information of "*large buildup of Chinese forces in Tibet*" when questioned about it during a press conference on 24 June 1960. However, he underplayed the importance of this saying some of these stories had no foundation in fact: "*Most of the stories, I take it, come from refugees or odd people coming over. There may be some little truth occasionally but they tend to get exaggerated.*" Consequently, as we will see later, the Indian counter-preparations were far from commensurate to meet the serious situation that seemed to be developing.

4

Military Preparedness

Despite Nehru and Menon's frequent assertions to the contrary in parliament and to the media, the state of readiness of the Army to meet a full-fledged war with the Chinese at this point left a lot to be desired. The reasons behind this were many, primary amongst them being that such a war was not considered a realistic eventuality by almost everyone in the decision-making apparatus of the government and the army.

The coming of independence along with the partition of the country had posed numerous challenges for the Indian Army. The complicated task was of dividing one army between two nations – allocating everything between the two countries, from tanks and artillery guns down to mundane equipment like typewriters, and of course, the men. Division of the latter was on the basis of religion, with a few notable exceptions of Muslim officers who chose to stay back in the Indian Army. The other ranks did not have an option. Most of the fighting units – Armoured and Artillery Regiments and Infantry Battalions – were composed of subunits of men belonging to one specific class. For example, a unit could have two companies of Jats and two of Punjabi Muslims. The distribution at partition caused major upheaval as many units were carved up with one or two companies going over to Pakistan, being replaced by others coming from units that had been allocated to that country. The shortage of senior officers was another problem, as most of the senior appointments had been occupied by British officers. 'Indianisation' of the officer cadre had started only after the end of First World War, and the senior most Indian officers at the time of independence were a handful of Brigadiers. A number of senior British officers were retained on loan to temporarily tide over the shortage, while Indian officers received accelerated promotions to fill in the rest of the slots. Field Marshal Cariappa, who was promoted from Brigadier to Major General at the time of independence, went on to take over as the first Indian Commander-in-Chief of the Army within 18 months. In this duration, the Army was also baptised by fire when Pakistani irregulars, backed by Pakistani Army, invaded Kashmir in October 1947. This first Kashmir war lasted over a year, within which the intruders were beaten back from almost two thirds of the state before a UN-brokered ceasefire came into force at India's request.

Once the war was over, the outfitting and modernisation of the army did not receive the attention it warranted. The Army was considered by the policy makers and political leadership of the time as, at best, a necessary evil for a peace-loving country like India that harboured no expansionist designs. Scarce resources were, it was thought, best utilised for other means in a poor and underdeveloped country like ours. Unfortunately, there was no strategic thought or crystal gazing to evaluate future threats the country might face that went into deciding on allocation of resources to the armed forces.

The thought process of the policy makers of the nascent nation is apparent from the correspondence between Baldev Singh and Nehru while both were part of the pre-independence transition government formed in the run up to complete transfer of power. Baldev Singh, who was heading the Defence Committee in the interim government, wrote to Nehru, the Vice President of the interim government, on 7 April 1947, "*The question of peace-time strength of our Armed Forces will come up before the Defence Committee of India tomorrow. You will have seen my official note. I am writing this to you personally as I feel that consideration is not being given to all the implications involved in this matter. I fully realise the difficulties before us particularly of finance. As I have said before, I am not in favour of a big armed force. I do however emphasise that it must at least be the minimum India needs....*" Who was to determine what was "the minimum India needs," and on what basis, was something the inexperienced government didn't give due thought to. In the same letter, Baldev Singh mentions the cabinet directive to his committee "*to produce a scheme of the possible strength of the armed forces with the limit of Rs 100 crores.*" He goes on to say that the Commander-in-Chief has "*made it clear that within this limit the armed forces will not measure up to the needs of the country; it will not be able to withstand a sudden attack; it would barely suffice for the internal security; it would certainly not be a 'balanced force', that is, one that is capable of rapid expansion in case of an emergency. In fact such a force would be but a magnified police force and not worth calling an armed force at all.*"

Despite a timely wake-up call in the form of the Pakistani invasion of Kashmir, due priority was never accorded by the political leadership to arming the nation against a military threat. Brig Palit writes, "*The years between 1947 and 1955 must go down in our history as wasted years, in our defence thinking and military preparedness. The political assumptions for our defence policies were invalid and dangerous.*" These political assumptions were that we would continue to have friendly relations with China and that American pressure would prevent any hostilities with Pakistan.

SS Khera, former Cabinet Secretary, writes in his book *India's Defence Problem*,

> *Throughout the nineteen fifties, and until 1962 no one, neither the Government of India, nor the top military commanders appear ever to have made up their mind as to what should be the strength of the Indian Army, Indian Navy and the Indian Air Force, nor even what kind of army, navy or air force the country should have. From the point of view of sheer man-power, the army during the nineteen fifties was sufficiently large. But it lacked the essential core in the way of equipment and training. Things like the reserves and buildings, and general logistical support were almost out of the picture altogether.*
>
> *This state of affairs persisted until 1962. While the army acquired more and more in personnel (for recruiting men in a country like India is the easiest part of it), the whole military apparatus was getting more and more attenuated as equipment got worn out without being adequately replaced, leave alone requisitioning the additional equipment of the kind and in quantities essential to match the recruitment. This in turn affected the training....*

What he fails to mention is that there were no political directions to the armed forces on the basis of which any estimation of force levels required could be worked out. Secondly, instead of assessing the threats to our security and then planning for a force level to meet those, the planning was based on what we could afford within the limited budgetary allocations for defence over the years.

A large part of this neglect can be attributed to the absence of a Defence Minister with any real understanding of – or even genuine interest in – defence or security matters. As per Brig Palit, "... *we did not have the required ministerial talent, and if one is honest, the professional ability, to keep a watching brief on the activities of our neighbours and take far-sighted and timely decisions. Lacking firm higher directions, the armed forces merely coasted along, and began to lose the professional efficiency gained during World War II and in the Kashmir Operations."*

The tragedy of the defence setup of Independent India was that the country had a series of Defence Ministers who were neither qualified for, nor interested in the crucial task of providing political direction to the armed forces of the country. As SS Khera further puts it in his book, "*The sequence of Defence Ministers in independent India is interesting, and could well be the subject of a separate study by itself.*" Baldev Singh, the first Defence Minister was, as per Khera, "*a man of considerable personal charm, happy to leave those responsible to get on with their jobs ... as Defence Minister he was more or less run by his Personal Secretary and staff.*" Lt Gen Thorat confirms this in his book *Reveille to Retreat*. He writes, "*Sardar Baldev Singh was a perfect gentleman but did not have the courage to control officers of his ministry even when he was satisfied that they were being unreasonable with the sole object of establishing the superiority of the Civil over the Army.*"

About Gopalaswami Ayyangar, the next incumbent, Khera writes, "*... he was a tired old man. He never wanted the job of Defence Minister, but he took it on ... and he could not last, and died some months after he had taken over as Defence Minister.*" Dr KN Katju, another stalwart of the freedom struggle, was next. Khera describes him as "*a dear old boy, endearing himself to all who came in contact with him. But he had the reputation that he could never take a decision upon anything. He was charming to everyone, but simply did not appear to know the difference between the army, the navy and the air force.*" After Katju, for a while the Defence portfolio was handled by Nehru himself, but "*obviously it was impossible for him to give this ministry the detailed attention it needed.*"

Finally Nehru appointed one of his prodigies, Krishna Menon, who had been India's High Commissioner in London and then its representative at the United Nations. A strong personality with keen intellect, he had the added advantage of being close to Nehru and having his ear. However, he had his own idiosyncrasies, strong likes and dislikes. He treated most military officers with disdain and was at loggerheads with them. His biggest disadvantage in this appointment, as it turned out, was his open and strong bias for the leftist ideology and implicit trust in Communist China. Being the Defence Minister in the run up to the war with China, this misplaced trust was one of the major contributors to the subsequent setbacks. To top this, he was strongly suspicious of the people around him, specially the senior military officers. Khera writes, "*... his distrust and suspicion of the men in the defence apparatus for whose performance in security* *and safety of the country he was responsible as the country's Minister of Defence affected their morale, and their will to work together."*

Till 1959, responsibility for manning the borders in peacetime rested with the police and not the army. The borders with Tibet were manned by the state police of Jammu & Kashmir, Punjab (and later, after the new state was carved out of Punjab, Himachal Pradesh), Uttar Pradesh, and in the NEFA it was manned by Assam Rifles. The Himmat Singhji Committee report had recommended the handing over of this task from state police to the IB, but IB lacked the requisite manpower to take on this task. Besides, the rationale of an intelligence agency being asked to take over border policing duties was not clear. This also led to the unusual situation where the location and deployment of posts on ground was being dictated by the Intelligence Bureau (IB) rather than the army. However, assistance was provided by the army to overcome the shortfall. Yet Indian presence in the far-flung areas along the border remained almost insignificant, in the form of "checkposts" rather than tactically sited military posts. A joint Army-IB checkpost was set up in 1950 at Panamik near Shyok on the Leh-Sinkiang route. By 1952, there were a total of 30 checkposts in Ladakh, Punjab (later Himachal Pradesh), Uttar Pradesh by the respective state police and NEFA by Assam Rifles. A recruitment drive was started for IB, and it was only by 1958 that IB personnel became available for all these posts. By 1960, the total number of posts had gone up to 67, but these were still grossly inadequate to cover the vast expanse of land along the long boundary. There were huge gaps between the posts, and large stretches of land in the furthest corners remained uncovered except by patrols sent out during summers. Of course, we also lacked the technological aids available today, like satellite monitoring and drones, and thus had no means of preventing or even detecting Chinese incursions till it was too late.

Another peculiar arrangement at that time was that the control of border management in Jammu & Kashmir, Punjab and Uttar Pradesh fell under the jurisdiction of the Home Ministry, while in NEFA it was the responsibility of the MEA, under which Assam Rifles also functioned. This was in continuation of British legacy where such arrangements suited the British Indian Government. No thought had been given post independence, and even after clear signs of trouble brewing on the Tibetan front ever since 1950, to bring the border management under a single umbrella. There was therefore a lack of coordination between the agencies manning different stretches of the border. Since the Prime Minister kept MEA under himself, it obviously had a greater say.

The Army and even the Ministry of Defence were therefore merely peripheral players in the boundary issue right up to the time Nehru announced 'handing over' NEFA to the Army during his speech in Parliament in August 1959. Up until then, the entire focus of the Army was on India's western border with Pakistan. Neither the government, nor the Army hierarchy itself, were seriously worried about the threat of a full-fledged war with China. In his book *1962: The Unfought War*, Shiv Kunal Verma quotes Gen Thimayya, who had taken over the Army Chief in 1957, as having said, "*Whereas in the case of Pakistan I have considered the possibility of a total war, I am afraid I cannot do it in regard to China ... we could never hope to match China in the foreseeable future. It must be left to politicians and diplomats to ensure our security.*" And from every statement emanating from the Prime Minister, who was also the External Affairs Minister, or from the Defence Minister, it appeared that they did not foresee any possibility of an actual confrontation with China. Therefore, there were no army formations that had been previously earmarked for employment along the Tibetan border if the need arose. The climate, terrain and consequently the tactics and equipment employed in mountains are completely different from those in the plains. With army's sole focus on the western border with Pakistan, the training, equipment and even clothing were solely suited for fighting in the plains or deserts.

Besides being underprepared, there was also a general underestimation of the capabilities of PLA within our own army. An article by Major Edgar O'Ballance that appeared in the *USI Journal* in 1959 evaluated the capabilities and intentions of the PLA as under:

> *China now has a large, modern army and we must accept that it is more efficient and capable than ever before. At present it is limited basically to home defence and can only find small expeditionary forces of limited strength and mobility. As a whole the Red Army is not a mobile army, and unless the production of oil is boosted up to a fantastic degree it does not look like become so, although there is much scope and need to increase the armoured and mobile element.*
>
> *It would seem that for the next 5 years perhaps, China will have to be content with "creeping" progress into adjacent countries to the south and east, with the accent on political doctrine and propaganda, rather than on military force. But after that length of time, the situation may change as the Red Army will have improved and then the countries on her fringe may be in danger. The unconcealed aim of Communism is world domination.*
>
> *Once Red China acquires nuclear weapons she will be able to bargain with any country in the world on equal terms.*

Even after the Chinese incursions in NEFA and Ladakh in August 1959, an appreciation by the Military Intelligence Directorate deduced that with the existing state of development, China was unlikely to "*launch a major incursion on any part of the country or create a situation where there is a likelihood of major operation taking place.*" It was felt that China would, instead, continue to create border incidents "*unless threatened by major retaliatory action by India.*" It recommended the protection of vulnerable points on our frontier against possible Chinese incursions.

Given the growing tensions between the countries, it would be expected for the Indian intelligence and military apparatus to extensively study their Chinese counterparts, irrespective of the degree of probability of the tensions resulting into a full-fledged conflict. One would expect Chinese tactics and strategy during its most recent war in Korea to be closely followed and appropriate lessons be drawn vis-à-vis our own situation. Surprisingly, there is no evidence of this kind of analysis. Bruce Riedel writes about US engagement with Chinese in the Korean war,

> *In late October the Eight Army fought a bitter and costly battle with CCF forces at Unsan in the North. The Americans were routed, but then the Chinese pulled back. They wanted to entice the Eighth Army northward to trap it far from their supply lines and to isolate it near the Chinese frontier. Willoughby dismissed the Unsan battle as unimportant and continued to claim that the Chinese would not intervene in force. So did MacArthur. The Chinese decision to trap an American unit in Unsan, then stop and regroup, would be unerringly similar to the Chinese invasion of India twelve years later in which they used the same tactic – attack, halt, and then attack again – to defeat the Indian army.*

The invaluable lessons that could have been learnt if only someone had thought of studying the opponent – or even actually realised that China was an opponent in the first place – remained unlearnt.

As late as January 1961, as per a Chief of Staff Paper, from which the Defence Policy emanated, the charter given by the Government of India to the armed forces was "to be prepared for and to resist external aggression, mainly by Pakistan." Brig DK Palit writes, "*The emphasis implied in the last phrase was curious, to say the least, because it was obvious that the very necessity for a new government directive had arisen from China's hostile activities in 1959. It was almost as a postscript that the Chiefs of Staff Paper recorded: 'We are required by the Government to resist to the full and evict any further incursions or aggressions by China on our territory.'*" He comments that the complete lack of addressing the logistical requirements of meeting a possible Chinese onslaught given the altitude and existing state of communications was incredible. Having commanded a brigade in NEFA in the years leading up to the war, he had firsthand experience of the challenges.

Morale of the troops and officers, a critical factor in war, was another facet that the government was oblivious to during the critical years leading up to the war. Nehru supporting his prodigy Menon, even at the cost of a public humiliation of Thimayya (during the episode where the latter had submitted his resignation as described in the previous chapter), would have certainly brought the morale of the army to a rock bottom at this critical juncture. Thimayya was personally liked and was almost a legendary figure amongst the troops, and the shabby treatment meted out to him would have saddened them. It is difficult to imagine Menon and Thimayya working together effectively for the next almost two years that Thimayya was in office. Friction between the two also grew on the issue of promotion of some senior officers who were considered to be hand-picked favourites of Menon. Prominent amongst these were Lt Gen BM Kaul and Gen PN Thapar. Both, in fact, were also favoured by Nehru for various reasons, which immediately brought them into the "inner circle" of Menon as well.

About Gen Kaul, Brig Dalvi writes in his book *Himalayan Blunder*,

> *It was Nehru who, many years previously, first established this irregularity (practice of general officers establishing direct access to politicians). He had come across Kaul in the years just before independence and found him a refreshing change from the stereotyped, British aping and politically uncommitted senior officer of the Indian Army. A strong rapport had sprung up between the two distant kinsmen. It was Nehru who allowed that relationship to growing an official link after he became Prime Minister. He frequently summoned Kaul for various purposes, some outside the call of army duty, when Kaul was only a colonel. On one occasion he even entrusted to him the task of political troubleshooter in Kashmir. … Prominent among his characteristics was hypersensitivity about his lack of regimental and combat service; and he was ever on the lookout for an intended slight in this respect.*
>
> …
>
> *His instability was another outstanding characteristic, one exacerbated by his proclivity to be tossed about in a whirlwind of random events.*

Gen Kaul had been commissioned into the infantry, but due to "personal reasons" had sought transfer to the Army Service Corps, which provides logistic support to the combat soldiers. He writes in his book *The Untold Story* that he did this due to financial compulsions, as his mother was suffering from a prolonged illness and he needed extra money for her treatment, and the assignment came with better allowances. As a result, through the long years of Second World War, he did not gain any combat experience. Instead, he was in charge of the troupé for entertainment of troops, and later worked as a Public Relations Officer (PRO). It was during this appointment that he developed contacts in the western media, which he leveraged to his advantage in later years. Unlike his peers – other senior Indian officers of that time – he never commanded an Infantry Battalion. But later, due to his closeness to Nehru, he was brought into the mainstream by giving him the command of an Infantry Brigade and Division as a Brigadier and Major General, respectively. Coincidentally, this was the same division that was subsequently moved to NEFA and played a main role in the war. During his command of the Division, he came up with the idea of "Project Amar." This involved using troop labour to construct living accommodation for themselves. The idea sounded extremely noble and creative, and received great accolades from politicians. However, it came at the cost of time for training of troops.

When Gen Kaul's name came up for promotion from Maj Gen to Lt Gen, Gen Thimayya was strongly against it. An upright soldier himself, Gen Thimayya had served with Kaul in several assignments and knew him well. He was also blunt enough to state his mind, and thus he did not recommend Kaul's name. He was overruled by Menon and Nehru. Not only was Kaul promoted to Lt Gen, but was also appointed as the Quarter Master General (QMG) to Thimayya. The QMG is one of the Principal Staff Officers (PSOs) of the Army Chief, and is responsible for planning and providing logistics support to the entire army. He took over this appointment at a time when its role was critical in view of the war in the horizon, and the obvious handicap Indian troops at the border faced in logistics vis-à-vis China. His promotion was one of the reasons that had prompted Gen Thimayya to submit his resignation in the incident described before.

Gen PN Thapar replaced Gen Thimayya as the Army Chief on his retirement shortly thereafter. He was also a distant relative of Nehru by marriage, and was not Thimayya's recommendation as his replacement. He had recommended Lt Gen SPP Thorat, who had considerable combat experience and a formidable reputation as a thinking General. But Gen Thimayya was overruled, and Gen Thorat resigned soon after that. Brig Palit writes in his book *War in the High Himalayas*, "*As for Thapar, his* (Menon's) *choice as 'Timmy's'* (Gen Thimayya's) *successor was a disappointment to many senior officers. Upright and conscientious by reputation, professionally well groomed, Thapar's was nevertheless a lacklustre personality and he did not possess the réclame and professional reputation of Thorat who, though a name lower in the army list, was a more charismatic figure and one of a handful of Indian officers who had operational experience at battalion command level during the Second World War. Most people had expected that Thorat would be nominated as the next Army Chief. Thus, Thapar's appointment was regarded as another example of the Menon-Kaul conspiracy.*"

On taking over, Gen Thapar placed Gen Kaul as his Chief of General Staff (CGS), which is de facto the number two to the Chief. This appointment is now called the Vice Chief of Army Staff (VCOAS). With this, Gen Kaul became in charge for planning and conduct of all operations, intelligence and logistics of the army, responsible only to the Army Chief.

There are several indications that Gen Thapar and Gen Kaul were preferred as they were viewed as more compliant to following orders without raising issues about their feasibility, adequacy of resources and military soundness as Gens Thimayya and Thorat had been. In his book *The Battle of NEFA*, GS Bhargava writes, "*... a new class of Army Officer who could collude with politicians to land the country in the straits in which it found itself in September–October 1962.*"

It was no wonder that the Director IB, BN Mullik, who was virtually calling the shots about army deployment with the blessings of Nehru and Menon, was full of praises for them. This was as opposed to his harsh criticism for Gen Thimayya, who questioned every order which wasn't militarily sound. Mullik writes in his book *The Chinese Betrayal*, "*In March 1961, a wind of change had come over the Army Headquarters. Thapar had taken over as the COAS and Kaul as the CGS. Both showed much alertness regarding the frontier situation and were also responsive to the strong feelings in the country against making any more concessions to the Chinese... This change from the negative attitude we had encountered so far was naturally most welcome to us.*" It is rather unfortunate that officers providing sound military advice to the government were considered negative and obstructive, while those more compliant and willing to ignore military viability of political instructions were considered "responsive." It was this responsiveness, or hesitation to say no to instructions that were virtually impossible to execute, which was ultimately responsible for the loss of lives and face for the army and humiliation for the nation.

5

On the Edge

Induction of 4th Infantry Division

Consequent to the government decision of handing over the border in NEFA along the McMahon Line to the Army, the 4th Infantry Division (4 Div) had been moved from its peace location in Punjab to NEFA, and took over responsibility for the entire border from Bhutan to Burma, in November 1959. The division had a glorious history. It had participated in the Second World War and distinguished itself in many battles. Lord Wavell, the Viceroy and Governor General of India, had praised it thus: "*The fame of this Division will surely go down as one of the greatest fighting formations in military history; to be spoken of with such as the Tenth Legion, The Light Division of the Peninsular War, Napoleon's Old Guard.*" But even the best of formations have their limitations if given unrealistic tasks for which they haven't trained, and then their hands are tied behind their back because of outdated equipment, non-existent logistics support and shortage of everything but courage.

As per the role assigned to it before its sudden move to NEFA, the division was tasked to fight against Pakistan in the open plains of Punjab. The equipment it held, and all its training to date, had been geared up towards this. Fighting in the rugged mountainous terrain of NEFA was a different ball game altogether, for which the division would require extensive training. Such training requires time, and needs units and subunits to be withdrawn for operational deployment to suitable areas where it can carry out training. Since the division was hurriedly rushed in and immediately deployed in penny packets strung out along the wide frontier, this opportunity was never given to it. To make matters worse, even in the years before its sudden deployment, routine training activities had been disrupted because of the troops had been engaged in constructing houses under "Project Amar" mentioned in the previous chapter. In June 1958, almost 18 months ago, Maj Gen BM Kaul, who had been commanding the Division, had come up with the idea of using troop labour to construct living accommodation. The troops worked round the clock to construct 1,450 houses for themselves. As if this wasn't enough, Gen Kaul volunteered the services of his troops to build a huge pavilion in New Delhi for hosting an exhibition. And if the reader thinks this cannot get any more ridiculous – it does. The same division was asked, in February 1958, to give a firepower demonstration, involving all the combat power and showcasing all the weaponry and equipment of the Division, to a visiting Chinese military delegation – the very army they were being inducted to fight now.

The troops were armed with .303 Lee-Enfield bolt action rifles of First World War vintage, while the world over armies (including Chinese) had upgraded to semi-automatic rifles. For the uninitiated, in the bolt action rifles, the soldier had to manually pull back the bolt of the rifle after firing every round to load the next one, whereas in a semi-automatic rifle, the next round is loaded automatically on firing. This not only ensures firing a greater number of rounds in the same timeframe, but also helps in accuracy as the movement of the rifle isn't as much after every round. (The difference between this and an automatic weapon is that in a semi-automatic, the trigger has to be pressed again and again to fire successive rounds, while in an automatic weapon keeping the trigger pressed results in automatic firing.) Every other piece of equipment was in short supply, including winter clothing desperately required for the cold climate in NEFA. Even the transport and artillery that they did have was not suitable for mountain warfare. Lighter load carriers (one-ton vehicles) were required to move along the rugged roads and tracks of NEFA, while bulk of the transport held were three-ton vehicles that were of no use. Similarly, lighter artillery guns and mortars are employed in mountains, while the division had heavier field and medium guns that could not be moved over the rugged terrain and deployed. Much of this heavy equipment had to be left behind, and this necessitated leaving behind manpower to maintain it as well, thereby denuding the frontline of valuable hands.

On arrival at NEFA, the division came under the command of 33 Corps headquartered at Shillong, which in turn was under the Eastern Command with its headquarters at Lucknow. 33 Corps was being commanded by

Lt Gen Umrao Singh, while Lt Gen SPP Thorat was the Eastern Army Commander. Gen Thorat resigned shortly afterwards when Gen Thapar became the Chief, and Lt Gen LP Sen took over as the Army Commander. The division had three brigades: 5, 7 and 11 Infantry Brigades. The area allotted to it for safeguarding the border stretched from Bhutan on one end to Burma on the other, a total of about 1300 kilometres. To give the reader an idea of the enormity of this task, a division has nine battalions, and each battalion has 12 platoons, the smallest subunit normally deployed independently. The principle on which platoons or companies are deployed is that they should be in mutual support, i.e. if one is attacked, the other should be in a position to support it. The support can be in the form of the automatic weapons of one platoon being able to fire in support of the other. Alternatively, it should be able to send timely reinforcements to a neighbouring platoon under attack.

If the platoons were strung along the border to cover the entire area of responsibility, the distance between neighbouring platoons would be 12 kilometres. While supporting any neighbouring platoon by fire in this situation would be out of question, even sending reinforcements over this distance in the rugged mountainous terrain could take up to two days. Thus, the deployment of troops within these parameters meant that only selective areas, considered to be more vulnerable to Chinese incursions, could be occupied. And even in these, the deployment of the posts was akin to border checkposts or flag posts occupied by border guards rather than tactically sited military defences. However, *"there was complete satisfaction in Delhi where maps of NEFA sprouted in the offices of the big Brass, with little pins showing our defence preparations. A little blue pin-head can be very satisfying and re-assuring in Delhi. Politicians can get up in the Lok Sabha and assert that Government had initiated military counter measures to prevent any further incursions by the Chinese,"* writes Brig Dalvi in his book *The Himalayan Blunder.*

Two of the infantry brigades – 11 and 7 – were allotted sectors astride the two ancient trade routes between Tibet and India, Sikkim and Kameng. The third, 5 Infantry Brigade was given the responsibility of the vast area of Subansiri, Siang and Lohit frontier divisions. This was estimated to be a lower threat area because of the rugged terrain and lack of any traditional routes. The Div headquarters was located at Misamari, and thus was able to exercise command and control effectively only over 7 Brigade. The deployment and force level was dictated, not by tactical considerations, but by the administrative capacity – the quantum of troops that could be maintained in a particular area over the almost non-existent network of roads and tracks.

NEFA, a horseshoe-shaped region lay between two tri-junctions: in the west the borders of Tibet, India and Bhutan, and in the east the borders of Tibet, India and Burma (now Myanmar). The Brahmaputra river (known as Siang within the region) flows through it from Tibet and into Assam. Four of its five administrative divisions, Kameng, Subansiri, Lohit and Siang, lie along the McMahon Line (see Map 1). Since the ridges of the Himalayan range run north to south in the region, movement from north to south (Tibet into India) is possible along the valleys, while lateral movement is difficult having to go over successive ridges.

Map 1: NEFA Overview

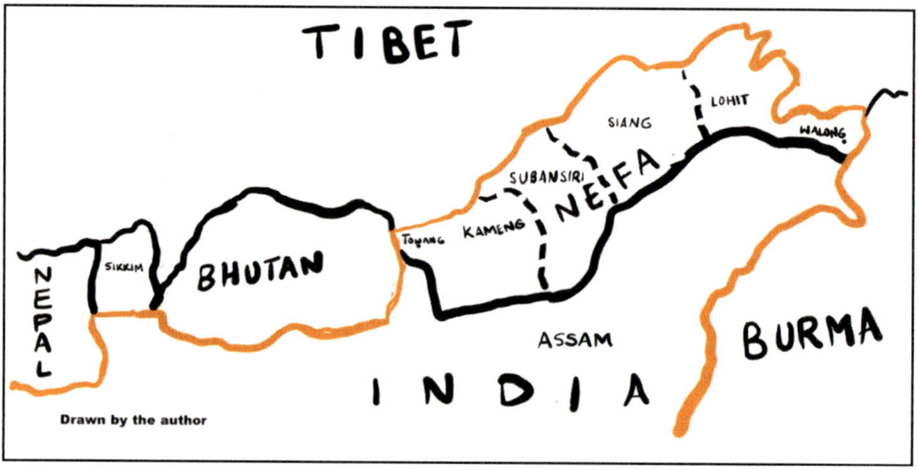

From a military perspective, when a commander evaluates an area for deploying his troops to defend it, he starts out by first deciding the vital area or vital ground. This is the part or features within the area of responsibility which, if falling into the enemy hands, would make holding the entire area no longer possible. It could be a vital communication hub, or some feature like a mountain pass which the enemy cannot bypass while advancing deeper into our territory. After this, the approaches an enemy can adopt to attack the vital ground are evaluated. Then suitable defensive positions along each approach are identified, where the troops can deploy to prevent any enemy reaching the vital area. While the extent of area and characteristics of the vital ground vary with the size of the unit or formation tasked to defend it, the basic principle remains the same whether deploying a division or a platoon. Based on such an appreciation, the entire NEFA was subdivided into three sectors: western, central and eastern. To the extreme west, Khinzemane to Tuting La, in the centre between Tuting La and Gelling, and in the East from Gelling to the tri-junction with Burma.

The Kameng frontier division, for which 7 Brigade had been given responsibility, coincided with the western sector. The western sector had a number of passes from Khinzemane to Tuting La, all converging at Towang. This had been the traditional trade route between Tibet and India for centuries. From the enemy's perspective, this was the easiest approach into NEFA, and was therefore considered the most threatened sector.

The eastern sector extended from Gelling to the tri-junction of India-Tibet-Burma border. Here the approach for the enemy was possible but much more difficult as compared to the western sector. The central sector between the two was where the ground made it almost unviable for the enemy to approach. The eastern and central sectors combined were the responsibility of 5 Brigade. It was too large an area for a single brigade (not that even just the western sector alone wasn't), but it was considered to be relatively less threatened. The fact that the areas allotted to the brigades were far beyond their capability for effective tactical deployment was not considered relevant, since the assumption was that the brigades would be deployed for more of a policing – flag showing role to assert claim on the boundary. China was not expected to attack, and hence the defence capability wasn't a consideration for the senior leadership.

In the western sector, a number of mountain ranges emanate from the tri-junction of Bhutan, Tibet and India. One called the Thag La ridge runs eastwards from the tri-junction. There are three depressions on this ridge: Dum Dum La, Yumtso La and the Thag La. In the valley below the Thag La ridge, a small river called Namka Chu flows from west to east, and after a few kilometres it turns northwards, cutting the Thag La ridge. On the Namka Chu, there were seven bridges that receive frequent mention in all the narratives of the action that subsequently took place there. These were nothing but a few logs thrown across the river at places where it was the narrowest, by the local herders who grazed their cattle on either side of the river. On the southern side of the valley formed by Namak Chu is another formidable feature called Tsangdhar ridge. This extends to the east of the river towards Bum La. Main features or peaks on the Tsangdhar ridge are Tsangdhar (approx 4,880 meters) and Karpo La I. Hathung La (approx 4750 meters) is a prominent pass on the Tsandghar ridge.

Map 2: Namka Chu – Thag La Area

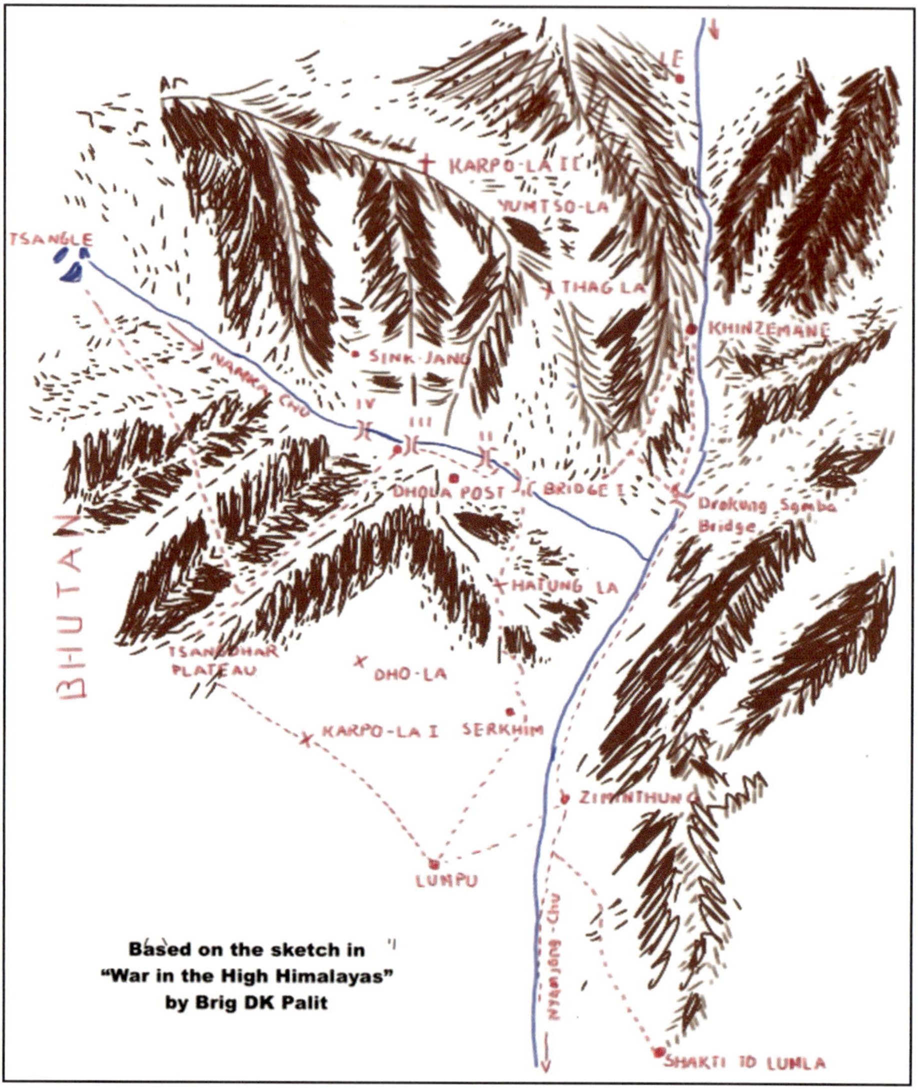

Based on the sketch in
"War in the High Himalayas"
by Brig DK Palit

Because of the high features with no tracks leading up, movement in the area was only possible through the passes, most of which lie at very high altitudes. Thus, to move from the hinterland to the border, you had to cross several ridges, climbing up to a pass on each ridge and then descend into the valley separating it from the next. The best routes were along the mountain valleys, running north to south, which ideally suited movement from Tibet into NEFA. But even these were nothing more than foot tracks, at best usable by sturdy pack animals like yaks or mules, and had traditionally been used by traders and herders over centuries.

The road communications leading up to the border were extremely underdeveloped in NEFA and in the other sectors as well. The Indian government had woken up to the necessity of improving these very late. The Border Roads Organisation (BRO), or General Reserve Engineering Force (GREF), its official name, was set for this task after its raising. It was given the task to construct strategically important roads leading up to the Tibet border in various sectors. The roads included in this was Misamari – Bomdila, Shimla – Rampur – Karchama – Chini – Shipki La, Siliguri – Gangtok – Nathu La and Manali – Leh.

Road construction was a slow, laborious process in the mountainous terrain on our side of the border, while it was much easier on the flat Tibetan plateau on the other side. We also had reservations about building roads too close to the border itself. This was probably out of fear of alarming the Chinese about our intentions. There was also the apprehension that if the Chinese attack, they could use these roads to speed up their movement into our hinterland. As Gen Kaul later wrote in his book *The Untold Story*, "*As a matter of policy, we had orders at the highest military level, not to build roads within close vicinity of our borders. … Moreover, we had started building our roads even up to Towang quite recently which we should have done at least five years earlier, like the Chinese had done. And every so often, financial sanctions for our road construction were held up for months in prolonged meetings and ceaseless administrative wrangles instead of Government giving us emergency sanctions in a situation like this.*" Considering that as QMG and then as the CGS, Gen Kaul himself was part of the decision making at the highest level at that time, this realization is of little comfort as a hindsight.

The only road in Kameng division or the 7 Brigade sector was the one running from Misamari near Tezpur in the foothills up to Towang. When 7 Brigade was initially inducted, this road was usable only by light transport like jeeps. By 1962, the BRO had upgraded this to allow plying of one-ton vehicles. From the foothills, the road climbed steadily up to a place called Eagle's Nest that was at a height of 2,900 meters. It then descended for a distance, and then there was another steep climb up the next range, up to the Bomdila pass, which was dominated by higher mountains on both sides, and again down to a place called Dirang Dzong that was in the valley. From Dirang Dzong, the road climbed to Senge Dzong and Se La pass, which was at a height of approximately

4,270 meters. On the way to Se La, the road passed through Nykmadong, a junction where several tracks that went around Se La met. Between Se La and Towang chu, the road passed through Nuranang (approx 3,660 meters) and Jang (approx 1,525 meters). From the Towang Chu, there was another 37-km drive up the hills to Towang (see Map 3).

Map 3: Kameng Frotier Division

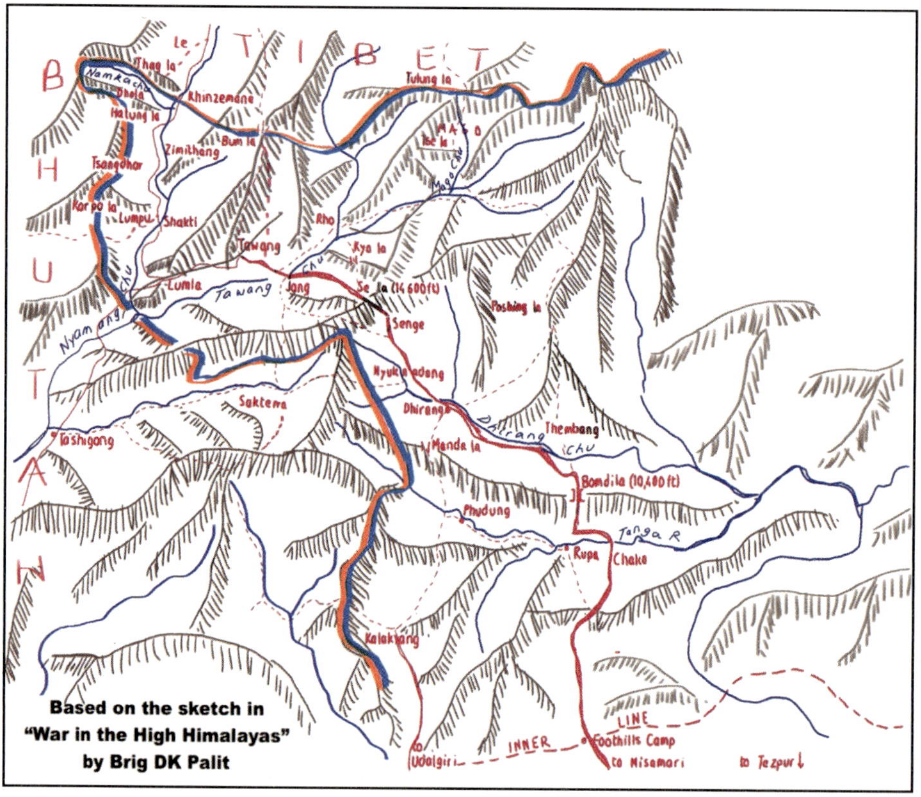

Towang, it may be recalled, was a politically important town in this division that housed an ancient monastery from where Major Bob Khating of Assam Rifles had asserted India's control over NEFA in 1951. The town is an important seat of Mahayana Buddhism. The 5th Dalai Lama was said to have been born here. Topographically, Towang was ideally suited for positional defence, being perched high above the river valleys surrounding it. To attack Towang from the north, an invading force would have to first capture Jang, which dominated the junction of valleys of the rivers Towang Chu and Nyamjang Chu, along either of which any troops from the north would approach.

The Subansiri and Siang frontier divisions are both named after the two major rivers that run through them. Both the divisions are bound by the McMahon Line to their north, and high mountain ranges separate them from the Kameng division in the west and Lohit division in the east.

The Lohit frontier division is also named after the principal river running through it (Lohit, but it is better known as Brahmaputra), which enters India about 6 kilometres north of a place called Kibithoo, and is separated from Burma in the east by the Patkoi mountain range. The McMahon Line runs along the entire northern edge of the division, and the junction between the line and the border with Burma lies at about 4,000 meters at a point called the tri-junction. Walong is an important town in the Lohit division, despite being poorly connected to the point of being nearly inaccessible. It was connected to the nearest road, which ended at Lohitpur, by a mule track over 170 kilometres. Even this track could not take sustained movement, and troops being inducted into Walong had to be airlifted.

The focus of defence of NEFA was on the western sector for reasons described. Brig DK Palit, who was the commander of 7 Brigade during the induction, had carried out a detailed reconnaissance of the Kameng frontier division on foot immediately after arrival. He had evaluated that Manda La – Bomdila area was the Division's vital ground, protection of which was crucial to defending the Kameng division of NEFA. He did not recommend deploying troops further north in strength due to the lack of any road communications. However, his plan was overruled by the Divisional Commander. 7 Inf Bde was ordered to move up to Towang and hold it in strength in view of its political importance.

Movement on the jeep track that existed up to Bomdila when the brigade was inducted was also possible only during good weather. Since winter had already set in by the time 4th Division arrived in NEFA, only one infantry company of 1/9 Gurkha Rifles (1/9 GR), one of the battalions of 7 Infantry Brigade, could be moved forward to Bomdila. This company moved on foot and carried its heavy stores on mules. Movement beyond Bomdila up to the border was even more difficult, as there were only footpaths and mule tracks traversing through the high rugged mountains and leading to the passes on the Border. So having rushed off to "defend NEFA," bulk of the troops had to remain camped in the foothills through the winter of 1959. In February 1960, the company of 1/9 GR was pushed forward up to Towang, to establish a base for the rest of the battalion. By August, the strength at Towang had been built up to a full battalion, with the Brigade headquarters at Bomdila, and the other two battalions strung along between Misamari in the foothills up to Bomdila.

The hardships undergone by the troops at this time have been recorded in many accounts, including the detailed one by the then brigade commander Brig Palit himself in his book *War in the High Himalayas*. He recounts that everything was in short supply. There was no infrastructure, no accommodation, and no snow clothing to fend off the biting cold. The troops improvised as best as they could, and not only survived, but also continued to establish themselves further and further forward. In April 1961, the Brigade headquarters had moved up to Bomdila. Brigadier Ranbir Sing, MC, had taken over command of the brigade earlier, but Brig Palit continued to play a crucial role in this narrative as he had moved to Delhi on posting as the Director Military Operations (DMO). This appointment is held by a Lt Gen today and has been re-designated as DGMO. Brig Ranbir's tenure was short lived as he had to be evacuated due to asthma, and Brig JP Dalvi took over from him. Interestingly, he had been the DMO before Brig Palit.

Defence of NEFA – Thorat Line

In October 1959, soon after the orders for induction of regular troops into NEFA, Gen Thorat, who was commanding the Eastern Command responsible for defence of NEFA, carried out an appreciation of the task of defending NEFA. Based on this, he had come up with a plan that entailed a three-tier defence. The first and outermost tier would be a line of small outposts close to the McMahon Line, situated along the possible enemy routes of approach. The task of these would be merely to provide an early warning of enemy approach, and not to actually fight and defend those posts. They were to fall back, and if possible, shadow the enemy columns to provide intelligence about their progress. The second tier would be sited at chosen locations behind the first line, on dominating (high) features from where they would be able to delay the enemy advance. These would be so sited that it would be essential for the enemy to stop and attack these features to advance any further. In the mountainous terrain, where there are limited routes along which large bodies of troops can move and be supplied, it is very easy for a smaller force sited on such key terrain features to delay an advancing enemy for a considerable period of time. Apart from delaying and causing casualties to the enemy, these would also force them to re-group and wait for replenishments, evacuation of casualties.

The bulk of our forces would be deployed along the third tier, which would be based on strong positions with adequate communications to the rear to enable replenishment and reinforcement. It was from these strong positions that the main battle would be fought. The early warning provided by the first tier, and the delay imposed by the second, would help in strengthening the third-tier posts in the specific area where the enemy was advancing by thinning away troops from areas where there was no enemy presence detected. Another advantage of this would be that by allowing the enemy to move in a few kilometres into our territory, we would be extending his supply lines, while shortening our own. We would thus be giving him battle on ground of our own choosing, instead of fighting him where he was at a greater advantage. It was envisaged that this strong third tier would be able to halt the enemy advance completely, and after that we could cut off his lines of communications in the rear and either destroy the cut off enemy forces or push them back beyond the border. In this manner, the territory lost due to the initial ingress of the enemy would be recovered.

Militarily sound though this plan was, it was not palatable to the political leadership or their advisors, neither of whom were familiar with military tactics. To them it amounted to surrendering territory to the enemy without giving a fight at the border itself. As BN Mullik writes in his book *The Chinese Betrayal*, "*There was reluctance on the part of the Army to occupy any posts north of this "Thorat Line" and defend it. ... Battles are fought on the frontier, be they suitable or not. One army is always superior to another and on this score no country would meekly allow its frontiers to be overrun by the enemy and choose a battle-ground hundreds of miles to the interior* (This hundreds of miles, was in fact, a gross exaggeration consideration of the actual distances involved). *Defeat at the frontier is always a possibility but the position can be retrieved later but on that account no country gives up the frontier without a fight.*" It was ironic that people with no military knowledge or experience whatsoever were overruling the experts based on political expediency. As a military correspondent of the *Statesman* wrote, "*They* (Politicians) *know nothing of military affairs and are not prepared to learn. This applies equally to the nabobs of the Ministry of External Affairs and Defence. Hence the gap between the civilian and soldier.*"

According to Gen Thorat, his plan was not put up to the Prime Minister, who only learnt about it in October 1962 after the initial attacks by Chinese forces. In his book *Reveille to Retreat*, Gen Thorat writes, "*I do not know how many read it but I do know that it was not shown to the Prime Minister. He saw it for the first time in October 1962 when he sent for me after the debacle in NEFA, and was very annoyed that it had not been shown to him before. An important paper concerning national security written by an Army Commander and supported by the Chief should have been shown to him, but Mr Krishna Menon had conveniently overlooked this aspect.*"

Even Menon later conceded to this blunder in an interview in November 1967 to the same newspaper. He said, "*It might have been useful to let them come into Indian territory in depth before giving them a fight. But this is the kind of thing which we were unable to persuade our public opinion to accept then and perhaps would be equally difficult to do so today or for some time to come.*" Yet he was still not willing to admit that the decisions that impacted the tactical battle plan, like deployment on the front, were something that had to be taken by the field commanders on ground. "*But whether we should defend a particular area … it is the government which tells the military command the objectives that it must try to achieve, and it is the military command which decides upon operational matters. The government can only say you must hold this or you can give up that.*" It appears from this statement that Menon was still not clear about the difference between laying down broad objectives (as the government needs to do) and dictating to the army which positions to occupy to achieve those objectives.

Forward Policy

In 1960, an operation called "Operation Onkar" was launched in NEFA on advice of the IB. This envisaged a large-scale expansion of Assam Rifles, with units deployed all along the frontier including in areas not occupied so far. Though manned by the Assam Rifles, under the supervision of the Army, the siting of the exact location of these posts would be decided by the IB and not the Army. This possibly was an outcome of the divergence in thinking between the Army and IB as obvious from Gen Thorat's plan and Mullik's views on it described earlier. It seems Mullik's view prevailed as he was amongst Nehru's close advisors at that time. By this time, 4 Div, mainly its 7 Brigade, had already moved into NEFA and were in the process of preparing their defences best as they could under the severe shortages and limitations of communications.

The government apparently rested assured that they had done enough to secure our borders. Defence Minister Menon told the Parliament on 11 April 1961, "*As a result of the violation of our territories and intrusion of Chinese elements into our soil and failure to get adjustment of this matter . . . there has been deployment of troops of this country in such a way that incursions into our territory are impossible."*

In September 1961, the IB presented a paper on its analysis of the situation and recommendations on further actions. Its reading of Chinese tactics was that they were advancing in areas where we were not occupying positions, but kept away where even a small outpost of ours was present. It surmised that the Chinese would like to advance right up to their 1960 claim line in Ladakh, but only in unoccupied areas. Furthermore, their reactions to our setting up posts in the disputed territory would be restricted to lodging protest, not taking any assertive action to confront our troops. The paper recommended that the army should be pushed forward to fill in the gaps in the areas where Chinese had not yet moved up, failing which they were bound to occupy it themselves. The IB went on to recommend the specific positions to be held by the army and the areas to be patrolled. Brig Palit's commented on this in his book as follows:

> *. . . this formed the turning point of our border policy. From a simple statement of fact – that the Chinese have so far kept away from our posts – it was but a short step to the assumption that they would always keep away; but that short step crossed a dividing line none was able to see.*
>
> *Furthermore, now the IB was laying down tactical policy. From then onward AHQ was always made to feel as if it was dragging its steps – not deploying far enough forward or in sufficient strength.*

Any reservations expressed by field commanders because of tactial unviability or logistical difficulties were viewed as "dragging steps", by the political leadership and civilian bureaucracy. Unfortunately, the military leadership at Army HQ were either unable to see the sense in the assertions of their field commanders or were incapable of convincing the government of the same. Either ways, the outcome was that the deployment proceeded as dictated by non-military considerations.

An important meeting, chaired by Nehru, was held on 2 November 1961. The Prime Minister was updated on the current deployments in Ladakh and North East, and he directed that the army should dominate the entire frontier from Ladakh to NEFA, either by setting up posts or through effective patrolling. Chinese, he said, should not be allowed to encroach any further of our territories. The troops were, however, ordered not to fire except in self-defence. This was in line with the recommendations of the IB, confirming Brig Palit's observation that they were laying down the tactical policy – something that should have been best left to the army to decide.

Although the border had been handed over to the army in 1959, the direct orders from the Prime Minister speeded up the deployment. The pattern of deployment in Ladakh and NEFA, ordered by the politicians based on the advice of IB, became to be known as the "Forward Policy". The change of leadership at the helm in Army HQ was instrumental in the government being able to push this controversial policy through. Gen Thimayya had strongly resisted implementing any unviable or impractical orders by the government, based on the army's existing force levels and shortages of airlift efforts required to maintain the outposts. His replacement Gen Thapar was more amenable to carrying them out. Gen Kaul, who had taken over as the CGS, was even enthusiastic about it. Brig Palit writes, "*In the matter of implementing the forward policy Bijji Kaul did appear to suffer from such a mental block. My own appraisal was that he firmly believed that his live wire personality and drive could help overcome logistical problems to establish forward posts and pickets, even if these were only established on a tenuous basis. If the bureaucrats in the ministries were willing to take the risk, it would not be he who would cry halt. Central to his inhibitions was the fear of being regarded operationally unenterprising. I suspect that he hoped, however irrationally, that forceful pursuit of the forward policy would establish an operational reputation for him despite his lack of combat experience.*"

All the commentators of the saga of 1962 have uniformly criticised the ill-conceived and flawed "Forward Policy" that, as per many, was one of the key factors that precipitated the Chinese attack in 1962. Interestingly, various people who were party to decision making at that time have disowned responsibility for the policy in the books they have subsequently written. In fact, it was never an officially declared policy, but a series of decisions and actions that, taken collectively in retrospect, began to be referred to as such. Bruce Riedel writes, "*The Forward Policy was never formally reviewed and approved as such by the Indian government; rather it grew from a series of incremental decisions and events. It was more of a statement of political resolve than a military strategy: The Indian army was never given the means to effectively implement it. ... For Nehru and Menon the Forward Policy was not a military challenge to a far stronger power, but the necessary physical extension of a subtle diplomatic game.*"

All through 1960, Indian policy had been conservative and restrained. The government's instructions to the army were to maintain *status quo* regarding the disputed areas, and even patrols were permitted only up to the frontier claimed by China. However, reports received indicated that the Chinese were, in contrast, establishing new posts and rapidly constructing roads to link them with the main highways in Tibet. At the same time, Nehru was facing flak from the media and the opposition about his apparent failure to take any assertive action against Chinese continuing to consolidate their hold on Indian territory illegally occupied by them. The Forward Policy was possibly more an attempt to answer this criticism rather than an effective counter to Chinese advance. It was based on the belief that Nehru, the MEA, Menon and even the Army HQ held at that time – that a full-fledged war with China was not a possibility.

Secure in this false belief, the government decided a more proactive approach by establishing posts further and further forward towards the boundary line claimed by India. Seen from the Chinese perspective, since Indian troops and patrols were crossing the Chinese claim lines with impunity, it was therefore not unjustified if it crossed Indian claim lines, which included the McMahon Line.

The posts set up by under the Forward Policy were more like police checkpoints than defensive positions usually taken up by the army. They consisted of a handful of troops with just their rifles and no heavy weapons to support them. The posts were also not stocked with any reserve rations or even ammunition to cater for a prolonged engagement with the enemy. There were also no plans to reinforce any post if it came under attack. Neither were these posts tactically sited. That is to say, their locations were neither chosen keeping any specific defence strategy, nor keeping the defence potential of the location in mind. So, for instance, posts were sited in the valley along the rivers instead of on the mountain heights dominating it. Thus, the terrain or lay of the land was not taken advantage to bolster the already weak position of Indian troops given their lower numbers and shortfall of weapons, equipment and ammunition. Besides, they were not sited in mutual support of each other, that is, the fire from one could not support another if it was under attack. The whole exercise was therefore one of political expedience rather than military prudence. Brig Palit writes, "*Eventually, by an unwritten understanding, the advance into unoccupied territory in the Aksai Chin came to be regarded as a political requirement of the government – and that also under an intelligence assurance that the Chinese were not likely to go to war over this issue. That we had no business to accept such an assurance is another matter; the fact is that we did and were, to that extent, at fault.*"

Diplomacy Continues

Simultaneously with pushing troops forward, Indian government was trying to find a diplomatic solution to the problem through lengthy negotiations and voluminous correspondence. But things seemed to be going round in circles with very little outcome, since both sides were firmly stuck on their respective stances. Accusations and counter-accusations were hurled, raising the temperature of the exchanges occasionally. Then there would be a reconciliatory offer, which would be unacceptable to the other side. A border incident would then bring forth another round of accusing each other.

The Indian side of the diplomatic negations was very confident in its stance, since it felt that it had provided adequate and substantiated legal and historical proofs to prove its stance beyond doubt. Neither they, nor Nehru, realised the little heed the Chinese side paid to such documents or assertions. Knowing that they were negotiating from a position of military strength added to Chinese confidence, and the misplaced belief in peaceful doctrines and diplomacy lulled the Indian side into a false sense of security.

After India made its "Official Report" detailing the proceedings of the talks with the Chinese public, they were under the impression that Chinese would now have no option but to adopt a more reasonable stance. Instead, in a strongly worded note in March 1962, the Chinese accused Indian government of refusal to hold negotiations and continued occupation of Chinese territory. Indian government replied, refuting their charges and asked them to restore "status quo" as it existed before 1957, as a step to create a "favourable climate" for negotiations. Chinese called this a "summary rejection of their offer for peaceful settlement." In their view, status quo implied continuation of Chinese possession of Aksai Chin, and once this was accepted, they were willing to negotiate further. Back and forth, back and forth went the letters, repeating respective stances in the floweriest of diplomatic language, each side professing its honest intention of peaceful settlement to the problem, but only one side willing, and having the capability, to fight to enforce it.

In May 1962, India made a "generous" offer of modifying its stance to allow "pending negotiations and settlement of the boundary question, the continued use of the Aksai Chin road for Chinese civilian traffic". It is, in retrospect, silly to expect the Chinese to consider Indian permission *with conditions*, for using a road that they were already in possession of, as a concession. They replied, "*How can one assume that the Chinese Government would accept unilaterally imposed submissive terms? Is China a defeated country?*" It said it was willing to consider such a proposal only if India withdrew from NEFA – thus laying down a condition that would obviously be unacceptable to India. Exchanges along such lines continued ad nauseam.

6

Disaster at Thag La

While Gens Thimayya and Thorat were in command at AHQ and Eastern Command, respectively, they steadfastly refused pressure to move troops beyond Bomdila. The reason for their refusal was unwillingness to bow down to political pressure and allotting a task to the men under their command without the wherewithal to provide adequate resources for fulfilment of the task. This attitude came under criticism from the civilian and political leadership, with insinuations of shirking from carrying out their assigned tasks. Mullik writes, "... *till the beginning of 1961, the attitude of the Army Headquarters had been to avoid any quarrel with China so far as Ladakh was concerned even if it meant allowing the Chinese to push forward their claimed border of 1960.*" Here, Mullik was thinking of posts from a border police perspective, while Gen Thimayya had a military perspective about the viability of posts based on their fighting potential and the logistics setup. Unfortunately, it was Mullik who had Nehru's ear and it was his view that prevailed.

But in May 1961, Gen Thimayya had retired, Gen Thorat had resigned, and Generals Thapar and Kaul were calling the shots at Army HQ. On 5 December 1961, Army HQ passed on the government's orders to Eastern and Western Command HQs to establish additional posts to prevent Chinese troops from advancing any further, and also carry out aggressive patrolling to cover areas not covered by these posts.

The commanders in the field, like GOC 4 Div and Commanders 7 Brigade and 114 Brigade, or even the Army and Corps Commanders, who had a greater understanding of the overwhelming challenges in carrying out the forward policy on ground, protested the orders as being militarily unsound. In the absence of senior officers in Army HQ with adequate combat experience to understand the consequences of implementing such unsound orders and the moral courage to convey the same to the political leadership, the protests by field commanders were of little avail. They were, in fact, viewed by the Army HQ and political leadership as timidness on part of the field commanders. Gen Kaul flew down to Gauhati to personally push for the deployment to be carried out as ordered. In his book *The Untold Story* he writes,

> *In connection with some difficulties which GOC 33 Corps had raised, I went to Gauhati in February 1962 and held a conference attended by senior civil and military officials who were dealing with this question in NEFA. I told them why it was important for us to establish posts all along our border and that failure on our part to do so would result in the Chinese establishing posts there instead. In view of the extreme shortage of manpower, labour, supply dropping equipment and the inaccessibility of certain areas, many of which were not easy to identify, and unreliable maps, Lt Gen K Umrao Singh, Commander 33 Corps, apprehended it might be difficult to fully implement this policy. After some discussion, it was agreed by all present that it was imperative in the national interests of defence to establish as many posts along our borders in NEFA as possible, despite our difficulties.*

But Brig Dalvi, who had replaced Brig Palit as commander 7 Brigade, writes in his book *Himalayan Blunder*, "*To my knowledge Kaul had gone there to brow-beat and bully the doubtful generals who had misgivings about the whole idea of setting up forward posts. I know that from Corps Commander down to myself as the Brigade Commander we had grave reservations about the wisdom of the new policy.*"

Brig Dalvi was briefed by the GOC and his staff, gist of which was that his main problem in the coming months would be setting up new posts under Operation Onkar. On logistics, he was told that his priority was to return the supply dropping equipment that was lying with forward posts. Essential supplies were air dropped to forward posts where moving them forward by ground route was next to impossible. Since the supply dropping equipment was, like everything else, in short supply, the troops were supposed to retrieve these and return them back via the same tenuous land route so that they could be re-used. A lot of time and energy of the troops was spent in doing this. Another major problem was that the terrain configuration was such that most of the dropping zones were not of desired dimensions, since flat areas of requisite size were not available amidst the rugged mountains. Because of this, a lot of supplies, along with the supply drop equipment, drifted away and landed on top of high mountains or in deep valleys from where they could not be recovered.

Brig Dalvi arrived at his headquarters at Towang traversing the tenuous route that was to be the lifeline for his brigade in the trying times ahead. He describes it as, "*The route from the foothills to Towang was incredible. There was a steep climb to a place called Eagle's Nest (9,000 feet); a further climb to Bomdilla at 10,000 feet; a drop to Dirang (5,500 feet); the ascent to Sela Pass (13,500 feet); the vertical drop to Jang (5,000 feet); and the final climb to Towang at 10,000 feet. The whole road had been aligned across the grain of the southern slopes of the Himalayas and was subject to frequent landslides*" (See Map 3). He made this journey in a vehicle up to Sela, where heavy snowfall made further passage of the vehicle impossible, and he trekked the rest of the way on foot. He found Towang to have "*Primitive living conditions*" even after two years of the army moving in there.

He immediately got down to taking stock of the operational preparedness of his brigade to carry out the tasks allotted to it. He realised that the men were employed to carry out jobs like constructing living huts and helipads and collecting supply drops instead of training. The biggest lacuna he found in the arrangements was that the number of troops available to him was dependent, not on the task he was allotted, but on the capability of the Air Force to carry out maintenance drops for. Thus, out of his authorised complement of 3,500 men, only 2,400 were at Towang and beyond, while the rest were strung along and line of communication right down to Misamari, for which his brigade was also responsible. A fair weather road capable of taking one-ton vehicles had been constructed by the border roads up to Towang; the brigade had to provide its own staging facilities for transit troops, right from Misamari to Towang. Another major problem was that the brigade lacked the bare minimum stocks of stores, equipment, ammunition and rations, let alone any reserves for war or to cater for induction of additional troops.

The command and control arrangements of the Assam Rifles units manning the posts along the borders were also complicated. They were under the operational command of 7 Brigade, but dependent for their administration on the IG Assam Rifles located at Shillong. Also, there were no intercommunication arrangements between army and Assam Rifles units. Messages between them therefore had to be passed through their respective HQs. Lack of any worthwhile intelligence was another handicap the brigade functioned under.

Shortly after arriving in Towang, Brig Dalvi set out for a personal reconnaissance of the forward area to gain firsthand knowledge about it. He traversed the rugged terrain right up to the McMahon Line, interacting with the headmen of the villages that fell in his route. He went up to Ziminthaung, the furthest Assam Rifles post in the area, and visited Khenzemane and Lumpu – areas that were to be scenes of intense battles in the days to come. He followed this up with another reconnaissance along the Bumla – Towang axis. He got to understand firsthand the problems in maintaining any large body of troops in these far-flung areas with the non-existent communications. Unfortunately, there was no way of making those sitting in Delhi – in uniform or civvies – understand this.

Based on his reconnaissance, Brig Palit tried to work out an operational plan to carry out the role allotted to him, i.e. defending Towang against a Chinese attack, in consultation with Major General Niranjan Prasad who had taken over as the GOC 4 Infantry Division. They had finalised a plan by August 1962, when Brigadier Palit, the DMO visited the Div HQ and assured them that as per the assessment of the government and Army HQ, war was not a possibility for the next few years.

Yet, 4 Div issued orders for re-deployment of troops of 7 Brigade to establish additional posts ahead of Towang. This was a part of the game of chess that was being controlled from Delhi in implementation of its forward policy. At no point, as per Brig Dalvi, was the possibility of these posts having to face a full-fledged attack by the Chinese mentioned. As per the orders issued to the Division and Brigade, the deployment was to be completed over two summers, clearly indicating that there was no anticipation of an immediate crisis on the horizon.

Dhola Post

As part of the Forward Policy or Op Onkar, one of the posts 7 Brigade was tasked to assist Assam Rifles in establishing was called Dhola. Close to the Tri-Junction of the borders between Bhutan, India and Tibet, this post was intended to be established to emphasise India's claim over a feature called Thag La ridge. Establishment of this post was what many believe the final spark that caused the ultimate attack by the Chinese. Captain Mahabir Prasad, and officer from 1 Sikh, a battalion part of the 7 Infantry Brigade, were ordered to lead the platoon of Assam Rifles to "site" the post – which means select the exact area the troops were to occupy, and their dispositions on ground within that.

In the map that Capt Mahabir Prasad carried, the McMahon Line was marked south of the Himalayan crest line of which Thag La ridge formed a part, and on the southern bank of Namka Chu, a stream flowing along the lower slopes to the Thag La ridge (see Map 2). The political officer's representative accompanying Capt Mahabir had insisted that the Thag La ridge itself was the watershed border and that was where our post should be. However, Capt Mahabir decided to go along with the border marked on the map. Accordingly, he established a post on the southern bank of the Namka Chu. He called it Dhola post, though in actual fact the site was known as Tsedong. Actually Dho La was a pass on the ridge three kilometres to the south. The post was established in June 1962, and Captain Mahabir returned leaving it under the charge of a Junior Commissioned Officer (JCO) from Assam Rifles.

On his return, Capt Mahabir had reported the ambiguity in the border as indicated by the political officer vis-à-vis as marked on his map. HQ 4 Div raised this issue with HQ 33 Corps asking them to confirm the actual alignment of the border. If it did lay along the Thag La ridge, it would have been logical to re-site the post tactically on the crest of the ridge rather than the valley below.

Although the matter of the exact alignment of the border became moot as the Chinese occupied Thag La ridge before a reply could be received, the following passage from Brig DK Palit's book is interesting as it is illuminating about the extent of confusion, adhocism and uncertainty prevailed during those critical days. The query about the alignment of the border, forwarded by 4 Div to 33 Corps must have found its way upwards to Army HQ, but no reply had been received. Brig Palit, during a visit to 4 Div, was apprised of this by Gen Niranjan Prasad, and he promised to send a clarification on his return to Delhi. He describes his efforts to get the accurate alignment of the border from the designated authorities:

> *I referred the Thag-la dilemma to the Director of Military Survey. The latter commented that as the existing maps of the area were "sketchy and inaccurate, having been compiled from unreliable sources," the map coordinates of the new post quoted by the patrol leader were of doubtful accuracy. He confirmed that the recognised border was the watershed, but qualified this statement by adding "the exact alignment of (this) will depend on the accuracy of survey." This, he added would take two to three years of survey.*
>
> *That was not greatly enlightening so I sent the file to the MEA. The Historical Section of which replied: "we may permit the army to extend the jurisdiction, if they have not already done so, up to the line suggested by them." I went to see Dr S Gopal, Director of the Historical Section in order to double check before I passed on this decision to HQ 4th Div. Gopal explained that at the time of the boundary talks with the Chinese, the government of India had been aware that the actual terrain in the area of the tri-junction was different from that depicted on the quarter inch scale map sheet. The Chinese were therefore given*

the reference in northings and southings. He noted on the file: "This point was further north of the tri-junction shown on our maps and nearer the point now suggested by AHQ. Furthermore the Chinese had been told that the alignment of McMahon line followed Thag-la ridge, which is also the ridge shown by the AHQ in the sketch." What Gopal had not told me – and I found out only later – was that the Chinese had not accepted our arguments and had counter claimed Thag la ridge, as well as the valley at Khinzemane, as Chinese territory.

I passed on Gopal's remarks to HQ Eastern Command for onward transmission to 4 Infantry Division, but by then it was mid September and events in that remote region on the border of Bhutan and Tibet had already reached a critical state.

As is apparent from the discussions described above, this area remained disputed on a matter of detail without prejudice to the larger issue of the legality of the McMahon Line. Therefore, setting up a post here without the military force to sustain our interpretation of the line, by force if necessary, was unwise to say the least.

The Chinese reactions to Indian troops occupying positions in this area were sharp and swift. By the end of August 1961, they had concentrated their troops in strength on Thag La ridge. The post at Thag La reported the presence of a full Chinese battalion. It was on 8 September that the actual trouble began. The sentry on duty at Dhola noticed Chinese troops, who had been restricted to the Thag La feature hithertofore, were now crossing the Namka Chu. Within a few hours, a large number of troops (600, as reported by the post in their frantic messages rearwards) had surrounded the post. The closest army troops were a detachment of 9 Punjab located at Longju, and the CO also happened to be present at this location at this time. He assured the post commander at Dhola that he was dispatching reinforcements immediately.

Brig Dalvi, who was spending the night at Tezpur, on his way home for a few days of leave, learnt of this development at 6:30 pm when his staff officer Major Pereira passed him this message from Towang:

"The post commander at Dhola has been sending frantic messages that about 600 Chinese soldiers crossed Thag La ridge at 8 am and had come down to Dhola post. They had cut one of the log bridges on the supply route to the post, and they were threatening their water supply. The post commander wanted immediate help."

By late that evening Brig Palit had discussed the developments with the GOC, Gen Prasad, who passed him orders to the effect that

(a) *Dhola post would be ordered to hold on to their positions. There was to be no withdrawal.*
(b) *The detachments of 9 Punjab at Shakti and Lumpu were to move ahead to reinforce Dhola after opening a line of communication. Rest of the battalion, which was located at Towang, would stage forward to Lumpu to reinforce Dhola if required (see Map 2).*
(c) *Brig Dalvi was, of course, to cancel his leave and return to his headquarters and take charge of the situation.*

The news of the developments at Dhola was communicated to Army HQ, and on 9 September, a high-level conference was held in Defence Minister Krishna Menon's office. The COAS Gen Thapar, GOC-in-C Eastern Command Lt Gen LP Sen, Cabinet Secretary and Director IB were amongst those who attended. At this meeting, a decision was taken to evict the Chinese from south of the Thag La ridge. The decision was accepted by the COAS without any apparent reservations, although he is bound to have been aware of the ground realities – that the task was not possible to carry out given the existing shortage of troops, supporting weapons and logistical support. Orders were nevertheless issued to initiate this operation under the code-named "Operation Leghorn." As per the consequent directions passed by Army HQ to HQ Eastern Command, the nearest battalion was to move immediately to Dhola (this was 9 Punjab which had a company at Lumpu). Within the next 48 hours, 7 Brigade was also to build up in the area, prepared for battle, and to encircle the Chinese troops who had surrounded Dhola.

This order was met with a stiff resistance from Gen Umrao Singh and Gen Niranjan Prasad. They were aware that the task was beyond the capability of the troops at their disposal and the tenuous supply lines and stocking situation made it next to impossible to sustain any offensive even if additional troops could be rushed in from anywhere. On 12 September, Gen Sen flew down to Tezpur in an attempt to overcome the objections of the Corps and Division commanders. However, they perhaps managed to make him realise the near impossibility of launching the envisaged offensive with the limited resources at hand, against an obviously superior enemy force. The COAS accordingly "*warned the government of consequences of any armed action in NEFA in view of deficiencies there.*" This failed to cut any ice with the government, as an official release on the same day announced, "*Indian troops have moved up in strength towards the Thag La ridge. Our post in NEFA (Dhola) has been strengthened and the Eastern Command is continuing its efforts to deal with the situation.*" From the public posturing by the government, it is apparent that they still viewed it more as a contest of wills rather than a military operation – that seeing India's stated resolve, the Chinese government would order its troops to pull back.

The disposition of 7 Brigade at this time was as follows (refer to Map 3 to correlate places). 9 Punjab was concentrated at Lumpu, and was in the process of moving to the Dhola post to relive the Assam Rifles platoon and take over the defences there. They were moving on a self-contained basis, which meant that the only supplies and ammunition they had was what each man carried. The latter amounted to just 50 rounds per man. They were clad in winter uniform, which was sufficient for the winters in the plains, but not for the snowy peaks they were operating in, which required additional snow clothing. 1 Sikh was at Dirang Dzong, below the Se La pass and 1/9 GR was at the foothills in Misamari, having completed their tenure at NEFA and awaiting to move out to a peace station. 4 Grenadiers, the battalion that was to relive 1/9 GR had also arrived at Misamari on 11 September. Another battalion, 2 Rajput, which was being de-inducted after completing its tenure in Walong, had been placed under 7 Brigade and was moving towards Dirang and onwards to Towang. The battalion had been carrying out pre-induction training for their new role in a mechanized formation. They had already handed over equipment like radio sets and digging tools to the battalion that had relived them. After being relieved, they had also sent a large number of men on leave with orders to re-join at Mathura, where they were moving to. Hence, the battalion was inducted into a battle zone at high altitude with no notice, no acclimatization, deficient of equipment and without their complete complement of manpower. Nevertheless, the unit reached Lumpu by 24 September. 1/9 GR, which had also been ordered to re-join 7 Brigade, also arrived at Lumpu by 29 September.

The tactical headquarters of 4 Div had been established at Towang by 17 September, with the main headquarters still at Tezpur. 33 Corps had also staged forward its advance headquarters to Tezpur. The headquarters of 4 Artillery Brigade was also ordered up from Tezpur to Towang to take over the responsibility of local defence of Towang. Such a task is normally not allotted to an Artillery Brigade HQ, whose role is to control and coordinate artillery fire support to the entire division. But in this case, the division had no option as the only infantry brigade available to it had been staged forward to Lumpu. Besides, the meagre artillery resources available in the forward areas were distributed in penny packets, making the task of the artillery brigade carrying out any coordination or exercising any command and control impossible. The artillery brigade had an assortment of troops including 1 Sikh (of 7 Brigade but left behind at Towang) and elements of 5 Assam Rifles placed under it for this task.

Meanwhile, on 13 September the Chinese had forwarded a proposal to commence negotiations after withdrawal of forces of both sides 20 kilometres behind the borders to ease the ongoing tensions. In retrospect, it would appear that the action at Dhola was an attempt to enforce their earlier proposal that had been made by Chou En-lai during his visit to Delhi in April 1961, and had been rejected outright by India at that time. This proposal too was rejected on 19 September, with the remarks that "*it leaves the aggressor in possession of the fruits of his aggression.*" In fact, in a meeting in the Defence Ministry on 15 September, army had been ordered to establish posts at Karpo La II and Yumtso La (both were features on the Thag La ridge, west of the Thag La feature itself, and lay on the north of Namka Chu). While the Defence Ministry instructions carried the caveat "If possible", the Army HQ turned this ill-advised and futile order as a diktat down the line. The government spokesperson even made an announcement to the press that army had been ordered to throw the Chinese out, one day before India formally informed China about rejecting its proposal.

Back in NEFA, hectic activities were on. Brig Dalvi, after cancelling his leave returned to Towang from Misamari, moved forward on reconnaissance and met up with Lt Col RN Misra, CO 9 Punjab at Namka Chu on 19 September. It was here that he learnt about the orders for Operation Leghorn, which had been addressed directly from Army HQ to 9 Punjab. Passing of orders by the Army HQ directly to a battalion, bypassing all the formations in the chain of command, was an unusual step to say the least. The gist of the orders was that 9 Punjab was ordered to "*capture Thag La, contain Yumtsola and Karpola II by 19th September.*" The CO updated Brig Dalvi on the actions by his battalion over the past few days and their current deployment. When they had arrived at Namka Chu on 15 September, they had found Chinese troops on both sides of the river near one of the log bridges labelled as Bridge 2. The Chinese also had a civilian official, probably a political officer, along with them. The Chinese shouted across to the Punjabi troops that this area was Chinese territory, and they wished no ill will or harm to Indians, and asked the troops to send their local civil officers to discuss the exact location of the borders. Of course, the battalion had its orders and such things were way beyond their purview.

Col Misra had ignored the Chinese and deployed his battalion along the river line, bypassing the Chinese blocking their path. This included the erstwhile

Assam Rifles post at Dhola, which was at another of the log bridges, Bridge 3. This company was virtually face to face with the Chinese. One platoon of this company was deployed at the Tsangdhar feature, which dominated the river. Thus, the task of relieving the Assam Rifles post at Dhola had been accomplished.

By now it was clear that more than a battalion strength of enemy was dug in on the southern slopes of Thag La ridge, and the river had become the de facto border between troops of both the sides. It would require much more strength than was available at Dhola to evict the Chinese. Considerable amount of time would be required to build up the troops and more importantly, the logistics required to launch an attack to evict the enemy nestled on dominating ground across the river. The order to evict them by 19 September passed down by Army HQ was thus plainly unimplementable within the timeframe, and Brig Dalvi termed it as a "*Political Slogan*". He informed the Div HQ about the impossibility of it, with detailed reasons why. The GOC was in agreement with Brig Palit's argument, as was Gen Umaro Singh, GOC 33 Corps.

Despite his reasonable protestations, Brig Palit was not very optimistic about their resulting in the Army HQ changing its orders. He therefore began preparations for carrying them out within the severe constraints he had highlighted. As a first step, he ordered the entire brigade to stage forward to Lumpu to increase the force level in the Namka Chu area. After passing this order, he went forward to carry out a detailed reconnaissance of the area, walking along the length of the deployment of 9 Punjab to get a firsthand assessment of the challenges that faced him.

There was no suitable position for a complete battalion to form up for an attack on the Chinese position at Thag La as they had been ordered to. Forming up in the river valley would expose the troops to deadly fire from the dominating heights of Thag La ridge. The Chinese positions were sited in three tiers and were well prepared, as was plainly visible. The standard military practice while attacking such positions is to first subject them to heavy artillery bombardment, in order to "soften" the defences and reduce the resistance that the assaulting infantry would have to face. Without even basic artillery support, attacking such positions would be nothing short of foolhardiness.

He also knew that Dhola post, located in the river valley, was indefensible and virtually a trap for the troops deployed there. Two routes that led out of the valley, via Hathungla and Karpola, needed more than one battalion to defend. The dropping zone for receiving supplies, located at Lumpu, was also vulnerable to enemy interference – an eventuality that would completely cut off even their limited logistic support. He needed to re-deploy his defences to provide a better firm base to the attack on Thag La that the Army HQ was insisting on. It had to be a strongly defended position, which could withstand any counter-action by the Chinese as a consequence of their attack.

He found the Tsangdahr feature, which was well south of the river and dominated the river valley below, to be a better location for this purpose. This feature had a flat area on top that made it suitable to receive air drops as well. At present, the supplies had to be carted to Dhola from the dropping zone at Lumpu, which was a two-day march. With no porters available, the soldiers had to undertake this themselves, thus adding to their hardships. While air dropping at Tsangdhar would cut down a lot of inconvenience to the forward troops, it was suitable only for dropping by smaller aircraft. Later, in their rush to build up logistics in the forward zone, the Army HQ used this as a full-fledged dropping zone for larger aircraft, resulting in large parts of the goods being dropped drifting away into the valley and getting lost. Besides, the drops were clearly visible to the Chinese on the other side of the river, who assumed we were preparing for a massive assault. As intelligence reports revealed later, the Chinese had subsequently built up their strength opposite Dhola from a battalion to a brigade, possibly spurred on by this assumption. Brig Dalvi came to the conclusion that it made tactical sense to pull back the troops deployed in the valley to the heights behind. However, it was no longer a matter of a few square kilometres of territory, as it seemed the politicians in Delhi had taken Dhola to be a prestige issue. Brig Palit was not allowed to vacate Dhola in order to carry out this redeployment.

On the night of 20 September, the Chinese struck at the Dhola post. Two Chinese soldiers approached the post undetected and threw grenades at it. In the ensuing melee, Indian troops saw a large number of Chinese assembled not very far from the post. Firing broke out from both sides, and continued sporadically through the night. However, there was no escalation from either side.

Exchange of fire continued on an almost daily basis, and the Chinese started using heavier weapons including automatics and 3-inch mortars. They also used loudspeakers to make announcements in Hindi on a regular basis, in an attempt to demoralise our troops. By 30 September, 1/9 GR and 2nd Rajputs had started moving up to occupy defences in Dhola area. Their move forward had been besotted with problems, as the usual complement of units that assist such moves along a line of communication were not available. The units had to cover major part of the way on foot in the absence of sufficient transport (or roads to ply them on), and the unacclimatised troops fell ill in large numbers. Continuous rain and freezing temperatures made the 15-day ordeal of the soldiers, clad only in summer uniforms, unimaginable.

Because of the limited capacity of traffic and even movement by foot that the roads and tracks in the forward area could take, the main Brigade HQ was still at Towang. The Brigade Commander himself, along with his tactical HQ, was well forward though. Since he was convinced that a full-fledged offensive to dislodge the Chinese from Thag La was impossible with the resources available to him, Brig Palit made a realistic plan to undertake a limited offensive action that he thought was within his force's capabilities. This entailed capturing Tseng-jong, a feature on the west of Thag La, and then progress towards the Chinese positions eastwards. Even to put this plan into action, he projected the need for setting up the requisite logistics within the next 15 days. Gen Prasad approved this plan, and it was put forth before Gen Umrao Singh, who arrived at Lumpu by helicopter on 26 September. Having seen the situation on ground and studying the plan, he realised the impossibility of the task allotted to 7 Brigade without building up their strength and resources first.

Gen Umrao met the Army Commander Gen Sen on 29 September and put forth his objections about the feasibility of the operations with the existing resources and capabilities. His objections were overruled, and in order to make his stance clear, Gen Umrao set forth his objections in a letter and sent them to Gen Sen on 30 September.

Gen Umrao's continued insistence that the task allotted to his troops was not within their capability was a great inconvenience to the Army HQ. Instead of paying heed to his advice about the envisaged operation, the government chose to replace the Corps Commander rendering this inconvenient advice. Since it would be imprudent to "sack" Gen Umrao at such a critical juncture (especially since his stance was completely justifiable), a way around was found by taking 4 Div away from under his command. A new Corps HQ was raised, designated as 4 Corps, and Gen Kaul was appointed as its Corps Commander, with 4 Div being placed under its command. It was a complete farcical move, since in effect the only troops 4 Corps had under its command were two brigades of 4 Infantry Div. Brig Palit called the creation of 4 Corps HQ a "*political gimmick*".

Gen Kaul, who had been on leave in Kashmir while all this was going on, took off for his new assignment immediately on being appointed the Corps

Commander, to take charge of the situation personally. After he arrived in Tezpur, where 33 Corps had set up its tactical HQ for operations in NEFA, Gen Sen and Gen Umrao updated him on the situation, specially the difficulties with building up adequate logistics to undertake Operation Leghorn. Kaul took several decisions, including commandeering a large number of labourers from the BRO as porters, and also ordering 1/9 GR and 2 Rajput forward from Lumpu to Tsangdhar and 7 Brigade HQ to Dhola. He also ordered 4 Garhwal Rifles, a battalion of 62 Brigade, to move to Towang. This brigade had arrived at Misamari in the middle of September and was located at Charudhar. In Brig Palit's words, "*Instead of allowing himself time to get into the operational picture he strode into the scene like the God of War, ridiculed the tardiness of his superiors and subordinates and expressed his avowed intention to get everyone … cracking.*"

The troops and commanders at the frontline, meanwhile, were doing their best to deal with the situation they had been thrown into. Patrols had earlier been sent out from 9 Punjab to probe towards Tseng-jong from an area called Tsangle, which was prominently marked on the map but consisted of just a couple of shepherd huts. It was on the other side of Namka Chu. The patrol, under Major MS Chaudhary, had reported back that the entire area in the west had no Chinese presence. They found that the river could be crossed by small parties easily, though the water was freezing cold. Two routes were reconnoitred, one along the southern bank of the river, and the other through Tsangdhar. The first was found to be extremely difficult, while the second, though longer, was easier to traverse. 9 Punjab was ordered to send a company to occupy Tsangle, using the longer route via Tsangdhar, and they had set out for this on 3 October. Now Brig Dalvi received an order through Gen Prasad to move to Tsandhar himself, and set up his headquarters there. Gen Kaul would, he was told, be arriving at Tsangdhar on 7 October. Despite his misgivings, Brig Dalvi moved to Tsangdhar, albeit with his tactical headquarters only, as moving the main headquarters would be logistically impossible.

Gen Kaul's enthusiasm for his first operational command was immense, and after having "gingered up" things from the rear, he took off for the tactical headquarters of 7 Infantry Brigade to personally direct Operation Leghorn. Arriving by helicopter at Lumpu on 5 October, Gen Kaul was furious to find that the main brigade headquarters had not moved up to Tsangdhar, and he ordered the Brigade Major to start moving immediately. All arguments about absence of stocking at Tsangdhar to cater for the additional strength, non-availability of snow clothing and other necessities, fell on deaf ears.

The untold confusion, misery and hardships caused by the orders passed by Gen Kaul without heeding to advice or objections are given in this one paragraph which Maj KC Parwal records in his book *Red Eagles* (which is the formation sign of 4th Infantry Division, and the book is the semi-official history of the division):

> *It would be pertinent here to see the result of the move ordered by General Kaul at Lumpu on October 5. ... The two infantry battalions, the brigade headquarters (less the DAA and QMG who was left behind to supervise despatch of stores and equipment), company (less platoon) of 6 Mahar and 34 Heavy Mortar Battery reached Tsangdhar around 5 pm on October 7. They had marched, as per orders, by way of Karpo La I (5,250 meters) on "hard scales," each man carrying 30 to 35 kilograms of weight. Only a few porters could be given to each unit, barely sufficient to carry the cooking utensils. Every man, including officers and JCOs, had to carry one blanket, three days rations, one hundred rounds per rifleman, two grenades, one entrenching tool (if available), share of LMG magazines and 2-inch mortar bombs. On arrival at Tsandhar (4,790 meters) the men bivouacked in the open in freezing cold, with groups of three sleeping under two ground sheets. The exposure brought a good deal of sickness: pulmonary disorders, chilblains, frostbite. Two men of 1/9 GR died of pulmonary oedema on October 8.*

Many more suffered later and had to be evacuated.

This one paragraph exemplifies the tragedy that the whole episode was, caused by nothing but one man's desire to prove himself as a capable operational commander. Brig Palit calls the premature move of 7 Brigade to Namka Chu, with vague assurances that the heavy weapons and clothing would fetch up later as a "military blunder." He writes, "*Of what use was an infantry formation without its tools of war? 7 Brigade moved without basic winter clothing; with only three days rations on the man; no reserves; without mortars and ammunition; without rocket launchers and ammunition; without defence stores and with only personal items of kit. This meant that the battle worthiness of the battalions would be negligible till these caught up with them.*" The military leadership at Army HQ had taken the path of least resistance, passing on the orders of the political leadership. The political leadership, in turn, with no understanding of tactics or strategy, were going through the charade of "throwing the Chinese out" to fend off accusations of inaction from the opposition and the media. And in Gens Thapar and Kaul, they had found willing tools.

It is interesting to note the mismatch between the accounts that Kaul himself relates in his own book *The Untold Story*, and those described by others in their respective books. There is also a frequent mismatch between his thoughts he himself describes in his book and the actions that he actually took on ground. For instance, Kaul claims that he had received intelligence inputs from an agent in Ziminthang about the substantial strength of Chinese troops at Thag La, and that he had sent a signal to Army HQ predicting a "national disaster" if the situation wasn't retrieved speedily. However, his actions of pushing more and more troops forward without any provision for supplying them seem to be accelerating the very disaster he claims to have been waring against.

By 7 October, Kaul himself had reached Dhola. He had ordered an improvised helipad to be constructed at Serkhim by the Engineers of 7 Brigade overnight, and from there walked the last part of the journey over the formidable Hathung La pass. He summoned the Brigade Commander and Commanding Officers of 2 Rajput and 1/9 GR to Che Dong. Kaul started the meeting with the grandiose announcement that he had been handpicked by the government to throw the Chinese out from this area and insisted that Operation Leghorn – the attack on Thag La – would go in on 10 October. He told the two battalion commanders to work out their plans and brief him the next morning.

All through his stay at the forward area over the next few days, Gen Kaul took time out to send long-winded signals back to AHQ. The story of the journey of these signals is also interesting. He would dictate these to be written out in long hand at night. The next day they would be sent by a "runner" to Lumpu – a full day's march. From there, the contents would be dictated on phone to Zimingthang, where the signal would be encoded and transmitted. Apparently, when the first of the signals reached Menon in Delhi, he wanted to sack the Chief Signals Officer of Eastern Command for the delay in communications – little realising the difficult conditions it had travelled through before it actually reached the signals network. In the signals, Kaul talked at length about the great hardships faced by him and his troops, but their determination to carry out the assigned task nonetheless. Even at this late stage, having seen the situation on ground for himself, Kaul did not realise the bleakness of the situation that confronted the ill-equipped troops trapped in a tactically unviable location thanks to the insistence of senior leadership.

The Corps Commander's conference began on the morning of 8 October near one of the bridges on Namka Chu. During this conference, which was interrupted once by random firing by Chinese troops from across the river, Kaul unveiled a fantastic plan. He ignored protestations by Brig Dalvi about the requisite logistic supplies not having built up, and reiterated that the operations to capture Thag La must commence on 10 October.

Having seen the Chinese in action across the river with his own eyes and realising that it was impossible to dislodge them by physically attacking them (as had been ordered by Army HQ all along), his plan was to occupy peaks to the west of enemy's position at Thag La to make a "positional warfare manoeuvre". He ordered 2 Rajput and 1/9 GR to move to Yumtsola to outflank the Chinese and get behind their position. The order was met with disbelief by Brig Dalvi and the Commanding Officers of the battalions, because it completely disregarded the basic percepts of tactics. It involved both the battalions moving along the river over a long distance, exposed to the entire Chinese arsenal on the heights across. Thereafter, they were to cross the river over a defile, which any sensible enemy would turn into a massacre by heavy bombardment by artillery. If they survived that, they would be required to move from the valley to a peak almost 16,000 feet high, without any warm clothing, without any artillery support. It was apparent to the brigade commander and the COs that this was a suicidal plan not likely to achieve anything even if they managed to carry it out against all odds. If, by superhuman effort, they were even successful in capturing the objectives, holding on to them against Chinese counter-attacks would be impossible. But Kaul would not listen to any reason and brushed all objections aside.

Instead, he sent out another long-winded signal to Army HQ assuring them that everything was being done to carry out their orders of throwing the Chinese out. From his communications, two things emerge. First, that he was still grandstanding, and trying to showcase the fact that it was his personal efforts and interventions that ensured launching of the operation. "*By my bold and speedy tactics, taking the enemy by surprise, I have been able to compensate for the manifold disadvantages under which my forces suffered and have made a good start to the task of clearing Thag La ridge of the enemy,*" read the signal. Of course, the only step he had taken to "compensate for the manifold disadvantages" was simply to disregard them, pushing the troops to the edge of their resilience. Second, he was expecting a huge "national effort" to back up his operations once his troops went into their initial assault. The signal said that he was "*already facing much heavier odds than could be coped with the resources available to him in the theatre*" and presumed that Army HQ would be taking suitable steps to meet the subsequent threats by "*marshalling of all military and air resources.*" As the CGS, he ought to have been aware that no such contingency plan existed, so either he was expecting one to be drawn up now at the eleventh hour and executed immediately, or was merely resorting to rhetoric.

He used promises of future resources to fend off the objections made by the brigade commander and commanding officers about the shortages to undertake the immediate operations. For instance, when they represented about the lack of winter gear or shortfall of artillery support, he assured them that snow clothing was being flown in from Canada, or that artillery guns were being flown in from Agra. This was cold comfort to those commanding the troops who would be undertaking operations without the benefit of these future assets. After a great deal of arguing, Brig Dalvi persuaded Gen Kaul to first send a patrol of smaller strength to gauge enemy's reaction before committing a larger force across the Namka Chu river.

Map 4: Dhola Area

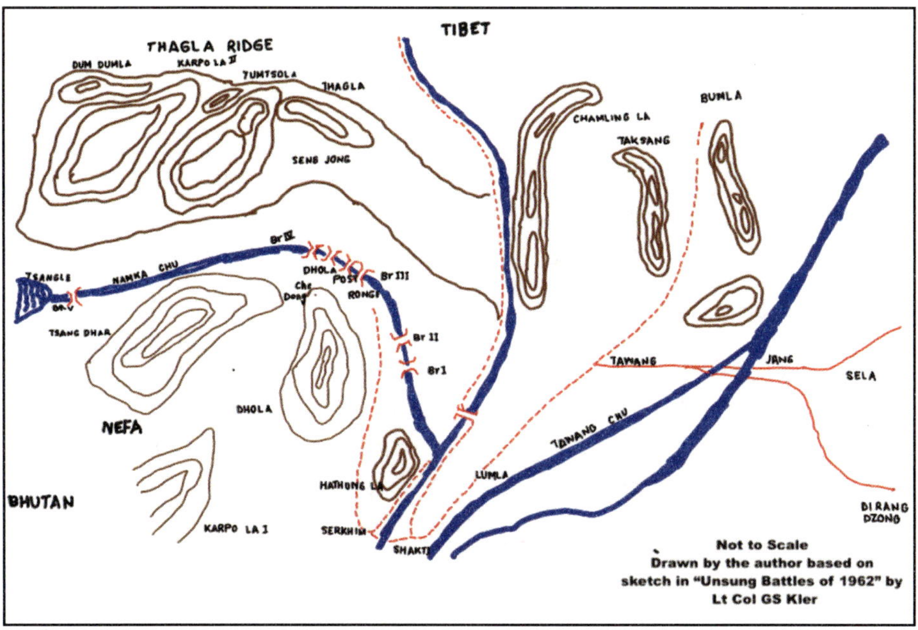

Not to Scale
Drawn by the author based on sketch in "Unsung Battles of 1962" by Lt Col GS Kier

Accordingly, a patrol of 50 men from 9 Punjab led by Major Chaudhary was sent out, and it reached Tseng Jong on 9 October evening, having crossed the river over two temporary log bridges. They occupied a position, creating makeshift defences out of rocks (referred to as "*Sangars*") as the ground was too hard and rocky to enable digging of trenches. The next morning, one company of 2 Rajput was poised to cross the river to build up on the Punjabi patrol, and rest of the battalion was moving along the river to follow them. But before the Rajput company could cross, the Chinese reacted with a dawn attack on the 9 Punjab patrol by about 800 men with artillery guns bringing down heavy fire in support of this attack. The patrol held fast, supported by one section that Major Chaudhary had earlier detached and positioned on a nearby peak. From there, this section could engage the attacking Chinese from a flank and beat them back inflicting heavy casualties. But the enemy re-grouped and attacked from three directions now, wounding Major Chaudhary and killing six men. The surviving troops were ordered to extricate and return but Dalvi was unable to provide them the artillery support they requested for since the area was out of effective range, and he did not want to provoke the Chinese further and escalate the already tense situation. These troops came under repeated enemy attack and shelling and extricated themselves with great difficulty after losing 22 men including 6 dead, 11 wounded and 5 missing.

Major Chaudhary led his men in the brave fight back heroically and managed to extricate his patrol thanks to a daredevil rearguard action by Havildar Malkiat Singh and Naik Chain Singh. Major Chaudhary and Naik Chain Singh were awarded the Maha Vir Chakra, while Hav Malkiat Singh received the Vir Chakra. Naik Chain Singh had laid down his life in this battle, and both the Major and the Havildar died fighting in the subsequent battle a few days later. In a broadcast on Peking radio, the Chinese officially admitted to 77 of their soldiers having died and 100 wounded in this action.

While this action was going on, rest of 2 Rajput was moving along the southern bank of Namka Chu on their way towards Yumtso La for their attack. They were ordered to halt by Gen Kaul, who finally realised that "*the strength of the enemy immediately opposite us was far beyond our capacity to take on.*" Brig Palit writes, "*The swift and massive retribution for our attempt to disturb the de-facto boundary shook Gen Kaul, who saw the first Chinese attack develop. His first reaction was one of disbelief, shock and disillusionment. 'Oh my God', he cried, 'You are right, they mean business'... His moment of 'challenging grandeur' had turned into disaster.*" Up until this moment, he shared the misplaced belief of everyone in Delhi Prime Minister downwards, that China will never actually attack us. All his posturing, playacting and bravado so far had been in keeping with this belief. This was now shattered, along with all his bravado. After passing orders for the brigade to get back into defensive positions along the Namka Chu river, and "ensure not an inch of territory is lost", he unceremoniously "handed back" the battle to Brig Dalvi and left. His intention was to go back to

Delhi and put before the COAS and the government a firsthand account of the situation, having "*fully understood the implications of our predicament.*"

Even at this stage, after he had seen the intention and capabilities of the Chinese, had Gen Kaul taken the decision to re-deploy 7 Brigade to positions that were tactically more defensible, the disaster that was to come could have been averted. But he did not want to return to Delhi only to inform the Prime Minister that he had ordered a "withdrawal" from Dhola. He therefore left orders for the current positions to be held.

After the smoke settled from the days' battle, Brig Dalvi had no option but to follow Gen Kaul's orders to deploy his troops to hold the river line, despite the fact that all these positions were dominated by the enemy located at Thag La. It was in these indefensible positions that Kaul had left 7 Infantry Brigade to fend for itself.

Ironically, Gen Kaul had written in an article in the *USI Journal* three years earlier in 1959, "*The test of a leader comes in a crisis. And the biggest crisis of all is war. It is a tempest which blows through our lives and challenges every institution of our society. It is in war that we are exposed mercilessly and emerging from it as good or bad leaders of men. ... A leader may succeed for sometime in persuading his superiors that he is a good commander but he will never be able to persuade his subordinates unless he has the real qualities of leadership.*" Gen Kaul being entrusted with the command of 4 Corps in the middle of a crisis meant that he had succeeded in persuading his superiors, but the subsequent unequivocal opinions of his subordinates in battle proved that he couldn't convince them.

Although many of the accounts attribute the action across Namka Chu on 9 October as the final trigger for the Chinese attack, as per Bruce Riedel, the decision to go to war had already been taken by Mao in a meeting with his senior generals on 6 October. Reminding them of the PLA's victories over the Nationalists during the revolution, Japan and the US in Korea, he said now "*Nehru sticks his head out and insists on us fighting him; for us not to fight with him would not be friendly enough. Courtesy demands reciprocity.*" The PLA was accordingly ordered to impose "*a fierce and painful*" blow on India expel Indians from the Chinese claimed territories. Apparently, the Chinese Foreign Ministry informed the Soviet ambassador about the imminent attack by China on 8 October. However, the Russians had their own preoccupations because of the Cuban missile crisis and took no action or notice of this.

Meanwhile, Gen Kaul returned to Delhi on 11 October, suffering from symptoms of high-altitude sickness because of his rapid ascent to heights above 12,000 feet and equally rapid descent during the past few days. At the airport itself he received a message to join a meeting at the Prime Minister's residence. Present at the meeting, chaired by Nehru himself, were Menon, the Army and Air Chiefs and the Cabinet, Defence and Foreign secretaries. Kaul gave an account of the past few days' events, and the situation as it prevailed at the Namka Chu front. As per his own description of the proceedings in his book, he says that the three alternative courses of action he presented before the gathering was to continue building up this sector for a subsequent attack on Chinese despite their obvious superiority, cancel orders for attack and hold on to present positions, or to hold a more advantageous position elsewhere. He says that while he personally favoured the third option, Thapar and Sen recommended the second. Nehru concurred to their advice, and accordingly formal orders were passed to 7 Infantry Brigade through 4 Corps to hold on to their present positions.

The next day Nehru was leaving for Colombo, and when questioned by reporters at the airport, told them that he had instructed the army to "free our country", but had left the time and methodology to them. His remarks were sensationalised by the media, and the headlines spoke of the Prime Minister having instructed the Army to "throw the Chinese out". Bruce Riedel writes, "*The Indian and international media interpreted Nehru's remarks ... as an ultimatum to China. The New York Herald Tribune headline was "NEHRU DECLARES WAR ON CHINA." The People's Daily in Beijing reported 'A massive invasion of Chinese territory by Indian troops seemed imminent.' It urged Nehru to pull back from the brink of the precipice.*" Nehru's statement, meant merely to deflect domestic criticism on inaction, conveyed an unintended message to the Chinese government that India had offensive designs. This would have consolidated Mao's resolve to teach India a lesson, and removed any lingering doubts about his decision to attack.

By 13 October Kaul had returned to his HQ in Tezpur, though he was still suffering from the effects of his illness. Meanwhile, Namka Chu (which was "no longer a place but a principle" as per Kaul) had become the de facto line between the two opposing forces in eyeball confrontation with each other. An uneasy calm prevailed, broken only by occasional loudspeaker broadcasts by the Chinese in Hindi, aimed at demoralising our troops. The forward posts also reported hectic activities on the Chinese side, including the movement of a jeep and a visit by "*an elderly officer, with an impressive fur hat being treated with great deference – obviously a general.*" The observation posts also reported large-scale dumping of ammunition. As per the battle indicators taught in every military school of instruction, these observations added up to the conclusion that Chinese were preparing for an attack.

7 Brigade, which had received two additional companies of 4 Grenadiers on 11 October, was deployed along the river on a 12-mile front from Bridge I to Tsangle – it took five days to march between these two points. Most of the troops were deployed around the bridges on Namka Chu. These were numbered from 1 to 5 from west to east, but were nothing more than a couple of logs thrown across the river. One company of 9 Punjab continued to be at Tsangle across the river. One platoon of 1/9 GR was at Tsangdhar, which was a makeshift maintenance base with the helipad and dropping zone for air dropped supplies. The brigade's mortars were also located here. Besides these troops under 7 Brigade, 4 Grenadiers minus the two companies it had detached to 7 Brigade, and one company of 4 Garhwal were deployed between Khinzemane near the boundary and Ziminthang where the tactical headquarters of 4 Infantry division was deployed.

There were adequate gaps along the widely dispersed deployment of troops where the Chinese could infiltrate easily. The troops continued to be ill clad for the high-altitude terrain they were operating in, and there was a shortfall of everything that could be named. There was no depth provided to the brigade, nor were there any visible plans of doing so in the near future.

Attempts were made to build up stocks of ration, ammunition and other warlike stores of 7 Infantry Brigade through air drops at Tsandhar over the next few days. However, as this area was far from suited as a dropping zone, more stores were lost down the precipitous slopes into the surrounding valleys than were recovered. As per Brig Palit's estimate, only 30 percent of the stores dropped reached the troops. Four para-field guns were also air dropped, but two of them were damaged. The two undamaged guns were deployed along with the mortars at Tsangdhar. A limited stock of ammunition, barely enough for a day's engagement, was built up for these. Preparation of defences on the Indian side was also hampered by the complete lack of axes, saws, cutting tools and defence stores. The breakneck pace at which the troops had been rushed forward, placing a full brigade right on the boundary itself, had resulted in these shortages all round. While it was possible to push forward the troops along non-existent lines of communications, maintaining them and stocking them up to fight an intense battle within a short timeframe was not physically possible.

Movement of casualties – injured or ill soldiers – rearwards was another challenge. As per Brig Dalvi, "*Prompt evacuation of casualties was well nigh impossible, as the only method was by helicopter – and the only helicopter available was one two-seater Bell. The normal channel was from the Namka Chu by unit stretcher bearers to Tsangdhar; thence by the Bell to Ziminthaung: and to Tezpur in a larger helicopter. Each casualty required eight men as stretcher bearers and the men had to be found by the units themselves, as the Brigade had no stretcher bearer units. … The wounded and sick had to be carried up steep and treacherous paths from about 10,500 feet to 14,500 feet, for over eight hours. This was an ordeal as the stretcher was constantly tilted or put down as the bearers tumbled, slipped or got tired. The same men would be required to carry heavy stores from the dropping zone to their units, on the return journey.*" Similar problems were faced in every facet of logistics, whether it was supply of rations or repairing damaged weapons. It speaks volumes for the indomitable spirit of the soldiers and officers that they continued to face these odds as bravely as they faced the enemy.

Brig Dalvi writes that on 16 October, Gen Prasad dropped another bombshell with the news that "*Gen Kaul had not been able to convince the 'higher authorities' of the impossibility of evicting the Chinese. The Defence Minister had now given the 1st of November as the last date acceptable to the Cabinet.*" It is incredible that the decision makers sitting in Delhi were so out of touch with the reality of the situation at the front that they believed such an operation was possible. "*I began to realise that my troops were likely to be sacrificed through the stubbornness of others.*"

On 17 October, the Defence Minister, COAS and GOC-in-C Eastern Command had flown to Tezpur, and had emphasised to Kaul the importance of holding on to Tsangle, since it was close to the Tri-junction of Bhutan, India and Tibet. The brigade was therefore ordered to send another company there to reinforce the one already present.

On 18 October, the Chinese across the Namka Chu could be seen preparing for an attack. The forward troops could observe their guides and parties for marking forming up places moving up. That night, there were reports of some Chinese troops having crossed the river and infiltrated between the two Indian battalion positions. Attempts at apprehending the infiltrators by sending out patrols were unsuccessful, though there was no clash. By 19 it was clear that an attack by Chinese could come anytime. Chinese units could be seen moving into the locations they had reconnoitred and marked the previous day. These activities were reported back to 4 Div, but this was of no use. The lack of a division's usual component of artillery rendered the divisional commander helpless at taking action against the enemy preparing for attack in open sight of his frontline troops. Amidst these ominous developments on the front, Gen Kaul had been taken ill once again and evacuated to Delhi the previous evening. And in this scenario, the entire formation was now without the only person who had any powers to take decisions. In a long telephone conversation with Gen Prasad, Brig Dalvi implored him to assume command in the absence of Gen Kaul and take charge of the situation. Finally, he lost his cool and offered to resign his commission, and an equally emotional Prasad offered to come forward the next day and "*stay and die with the brigade if necessary.*"

Early morning on 20 October, the Chinese attack commenced with heavy artillery and mortar fire on the 7 Brigade positions all along the front except in the eastern end. After almost an hour-long barrage of fire, the infantry assault was launched on the companies of 2 Rajput and 1/9 GR. While these two battalions were under frontal attacks, Chinese columns that had infiltrated through the wide gaps over the previous nights were heading for Tsandhar and Hathungla in the rear. By his own admission, Brig Dalvi had lost all hopes and the Brigade had lost all cohesion within a few minutes of the Chinese attacks. There were no hopes of reinforcements, as no reserves were available. The communication lines with the battalions had been cut within a few minutes by enemy artillery shelling. The wireless operators had to leave their radio sets unattended and pick up their rifles to fend off the Chinese. Chinese infiltrating columns had cut off the battalions from each other by getting into the gaps between them. The Indian troops were soon under heavy fire from all sides, having been surrounded by the Chinese. Instead of a coordinated brigade defence, the battle was reduced to company, or even platoon-level actions, as in the absence of communications it was impossible for commanders to coordinate the fighting. The men fought back bravely, with their officers leading from the front. Tales of individual gallantry abound, and there is no doubt that everyone, from the junior most soldier to the commanding officers of the battalions, put up the fiercest fight possible. But the odds against them were overwhelming to say the least.

2 Rajput had first borne the full brunt of the debilitating artillery shelling and soon afterwards it was attacked from the rear by a column that had infiltrated behind them. The enemy advanced upon them in wave after waves, till their resistance crumbled as their limited stock of ammunition ran out, leaving them helpless in the face of a well-armed enemy. Most of their officers were killed in

this action. The commanding officer Lt Col MS Rikh was wounded, and the second in command, Major Gurdial Singh, who was instrumental in rallying the men to fight back, was captured. For his role in the gallant fight back by the battalion, he was awarded the Maha Vir Chakra, which was announced while he was still in captivity. Out of a strength of 513 of the battalion, four officers, six JCOs and 272 other ranks were killed; 81 all ranks were wounded and 90 captured.

Similar fate befell 1/9 GR as the Chinese infiltrated and attacked them from both their flanks and the rear. The battalion also fought back tenaciously, but they too had soon fired the entire limited stock of ammunition they had. The battalion suffered heavy casualties and Lt Col BS Ahluwalia, the commanding officer, was taken prisoner by the Chinese.

Within three hours, all the positions in Dhola sector had been overrun. Troops in the Khinzemane area had also faced simultaneous shelling and attack, and despite putting up an equally brave fight, met with the same fate. Tsangdhar also came under attack by 9:00 am, and a helicopter about to land there was shot down along with the pilot and another officer on board. It was a providential escape for Maj Gen Niranjan Prasad, the GOC of 4 Div, as he narrowly missed being on this helicopter. When the news of the fighting had reached the Div HQ, Gen Prasad wanted to fly down and see the situation for himself. But fate intervened in the form of Major Ram Singh, the second in command of the Signal Regiment, who volunteered to fly in first and take stock instead and report back to the GOC.

The entire Indian frontline in the sector had collapsed by the afternoon of 20 October. The Brigade headquarters was ordered to fall back to Tsangdhar to try and muster the troops against the expected Chinese attack there. But the enemy infiltrating columns reached there before, and Tsangdhar also fell. Brig Dalvi witnessed the gunners of 17 Para Field Regiment putting up a tough fight before being overrun at about 1600 hours. He marched rearwards for a couple of days along with an ad hoc party of officers and men who had accompanied him, hoping to run into one of the rear positions. But the Chinese preceded him everywhere, and even the Divisional headquarters had beaten a hasty retreat to Towang on 21 October. Brig Dalvi was ultimately captured by the Chinese and made a Prisoner of War. He remained in Chinese captivity in Tibet and China for 7 months till he was finally repatriated in May 1963.

The Chinese issued a carefully worded statement that altered the reality to suit their narrative. It read, "*At 7 o'clock (Peking time) in the morning of 20th*

October the aggressive Indian forces, under cover of fierce artillery fire launched massive attacks against the Chinese Frontier Guards all along the Kachileng River (Chinese name for Namka Chu) *and in the Khenzemane area."*

The Chinese resumed their attack the next day, even as the troops of 7 Infantry Brigade were falling back without any command and control in position. With the impending fall of the positions at Hathungla and Serkhin, the Divisional headquarters also beat a hasty retreat from Zimithang. From all accounts, this was not an orderly, planned withdrawal. They fell back to Towang via Lumla in small parties without any coordination, command and control. As per Brig Palit, "... *7 Infantry Brigade had virtually ceased to exist; even the two battalions on the eastern flank of the Namka Chu line found themselves encircled and cut off. Many were killed in the running battles that ensued. Those who managed to slip out of the noose scattered over the inhospitable ranges of Bhutan Himalayas. Thus the whole of the Nyamjang valley and the western approach to Towang fell under enemy control....*"

7

Fall of NEFA

Towang Falls

When 7 Brigade had been hurriedly ordered to move forward to Namka Chu in September, the responsibility for the defence of Towang had been passed on to an ad hoc brigade under the command of Commander 4 Artillery Brigade Brig Kalyan Singh. An assortment of units and sub-units was placed under his command for this task. This included two infantry battalions: 1 Sikh and 4 Garhwal. 1 Sikh was deployed in companies spread up to Bum La covering the tracks leading on to Towang from the north. 4 Garhwal was deployed between Towang and Jang, with the battalion headquarters and one company at Towang itself for its protection. It also had a platoon each of 5 Assam Rifles deployed at Bum La pass and at Sulla on to its left. The artillery units were positioned in and around Towang itself.

62 Brigade was located at Charduar as Corps reserves. This was allotted to 4 Div and ordered to move up to Towang to take over its defence from 4 Artillery Brigade. One battalion of 11 Brigade (which was looking after the defence of the Lohit sector), 13 Dogra, had also been ordered to move to Towang. Two companies of 13 Dogra and a part of 62 Brigade had reached Towang on the night of 21–22 October. By this time, 7 Brigade had disintegrated and the threat of a Chinese attack at Towang had become very real. Having run over the defences at Namka Chu, Chinese were now advancing towards Towang in three columns – from Khinzemane via Samatso, from Bumla via Tongpeng La, and the third outflanking from the southeast towards Jang. At about 11 pm on 22 Oct, 62 Brigade received a Top-Secret Flash message directly from Army HQ, with the information that Chinese were likely to attack Towang the next morning.

On 23 October, the Assam Rifles platoon at Bumla was attacked and beaten back by the Chinese. The next post to come under attack was the 1 Sikh platoon on IB ridge commanded by Subedar Joginder Singh. The Chinese attacked with a strength of about 200, almost six times of what Subedar Joginder had under his command. The platoon fought back three successive attacks, holding on to their positions bravely, urged all along by Subedar Joginder. Despite being wounded, the brave JCO moved from bunker to bunker inspiring his men to keep fighting back. Finally, when the Chinese kept coming and their ammunition was running out, Subedar Joginder ordered his men to fix bayonets and charge at the attacking Chinese troops. This brave but futile act ended up with almost the entire platoon being wiped out or taken prisoner. Subedar Joginder Singh was awarded the Param Vir Chakra, the nation's highest gallantry award, for this brave stand. Another epic battle was fought by the 1 Sikh company under Lieutenant Haripal Kaushik at Milakteng La. They too fought back several waves of Chinese before falling back to Milakteng La.

Subedar Joginder Singh's citation for Param Vir Chakra reads as follows:

> *Subedar Joginder Singh was the commander of a platoon of a Sikh Regiment holding a defensive position at a ridge near Tongpen La in NEFA. At 0530 hours on 23 October 1962, the Chinese opened a very heavy attack on the Bum La axis with the intention of breaking through to Towang. The leading battalion of the enemy attacked the ridge in three waves, each about 200 strong. Subedar Joginder Singh and his men mowed down the first wave, and the enemy was temporarily halted by the heavy losses it suffered. Within a few minutes, a second wave came over and was dealt with similarly. But the platoon had by then lost half its men. Subedar Joginder Singh was wounded in the thigh but refused to be evacuated. Under his inspiring leadership, the platoon stubbornly held its ground and would not withdraw.*
>
> *Meanwhile, the position was attacked for the third time. Subedar Joginder Singh himself manned a light machine gun and shot down a number of the enemy. The Chinese, however, continued to advance despite heavy losses. When the situation became untenable, Subedar Joginder Singh and the few men emerged from their position with fixed bayonets and charged the advancing Chinese, bayoneting a number of them before he and his comrades were overpowered.*
>
> *Throughout this action, Subedar Joginder Singh displayed devotion to duty, inspiring leadership and bravery of the highest order, and finally made the supreme sacrifice.*

While these fierce battles were raging north of Towang, the garrison at

Towang itself was preparing to withdraw. The Army Commander Gen Sen himself was present in Towang. He had arrived the previous evening and had ordered Gen Prasad to hold on to Towang at all costs. He had promised two more brigades to be inducted shortly. But in the morning, hearing the reports of the Chinese advance on Towang and the reverses suffered by own troops defending the approaches to it, he changed his mind. He didn't want the Chinese outflanking Towang and cutting off its retreat and therefore he ordered the Towang garrison to fall back. After this, he boarded his helicopter and flew out of Towang. Towang was thus abandoned by 4 Div without a single bullet being fired in its defence, let alone putting up a tough fight. After the Chinese occupied Towang, there was a pause in their advance as they consolidated their gains and waited for their logistics to build up.

Meanwhile reinforcements were being rushed into the East from other parts of the country in a delayed effort to stem the Chinese tide. A new infantry division (2 Infantry Division) was raised to take over Subansiri and Siang frontier divisions that were under the responsibility of 5 Brigade, and Lohit frontier division, being looked after by 11 Brigade. In a move that the Army HQ thought would raise the morale of the troops, all the senior commanders of 4 Division, including the GOC, were replaced by officers who had received gallantry awards in previous wars. Maj Gen AS Pathania, MVC, MC, was placed as the GOC instead of Maj Gen Niranjan Prasad. The latter was under a cloud for the defeat at Namka Chu, though it's not clear what more he could have done to avoid the debacle given his constraints. Brig Hoshiar Singh, IOM, IDSM, replaced Brig Lal as the commander of 62 Brigade, and Brig AS Cheema took over as commander 65 Brigade from Brig GM Sayeed. Since Gen Kaul was still sick and at Delhi, Lt Gen Harbaksh Singh, VrC, was brought in as GOC 4 Corps in his place. His command, though, was short lived as within a few days, the moment he became a little better, Gen Kaul was back to resume his duties. All the new commanders were briefed at the Corps HQ at Tezpur by Gen Sen. Gen Pathania then took off to Dirang Dzong, to take over command of the division from Gen Prasad.

Gen Pathania, the new GOC 4 Division worked out the deployment for the task given to him: defence of Se La – Dirang Dzong – Bomdila area. He planned to guard the three main approaches leading to the area and estimated that he would need a total of 17 infantry battalions for this. Of these, he wanted to deploy five battalions at Se La, three around Nyumkmadong, three at Bomdila, two near Nagakuri Remba – Kalaktang and one guarding the Poshing La approach. Two battalions he intended to keep in reserve along with the Div HQ at Dirang Dzong. This decision to locate his headquarters in a valley and hold back two battalions to provide it extra protection when a full complement of battalions to defend the approaches wasn't available was unwise, as we shall see later. He was allotted three brigades: 62, 48 and 65 Infantry Brigades. A fourth brigade, 67, which was to be inducted shortly, was also promised to him on arrival. 4 Div was also allotted one squadron of tanks of 7th Cavalry. Of these, one troop was located at Bomdila, and one troop with the Squadron HQ at Dirang Dzong. The third troop was to be at Se La, but the tanks could not make it up the steep climb.

62 Brigade headquarters, which had fallen back from Towang to Jang on 23 October, was ordered to take up defences at Se La, with additional troops that were on their way. Brig NK Lal, the commander of 62 Brigade, carried out reconnaissance of Se La for deploying his brigade. Additional battalions flown in from other formations outside Eastern Command were allotted and by 28 Oct, five battalions with other units of supporting arms were concentrated for the defence of Se La.

The situation regarding supplies, however, had not improved much. The troops that had fallen back from Towang area had lost much of their stores and equipment. The new units being inducted were also short of clothing, entrenchment tools and radio sets. Stores to prepare defences were in short supply all around, as were anti-personnel mines. However, the troops dug in and prepared the defences, making do with the resources available. Stocking and maintenance was still by air, and the dropping zone was at Senge Dzong.

Besides preparing their defences, units sent out regular patrols along the approaches they were guarding to ensure early warning of any Chinese activities. These patrols would regularly run into Chinese patrols, which indicated that they were probing forward. Occasional clashes with Chinese patrols also took place. One of the patrols reported that blasting noises could be heard from Bumla – Towang area. Around 3 November, the covering troops of 4 Garhwal deployed in the Nuranang area saw a large number of Chinese troops building up opposite them. Patrols from Sikh LI were ambushed on 6 November, and the next day another patrol reported seeing about one battalion of enemy in the Dzalung La area.

Gen Kaul, who was back in command of 4 Corps after the short-lived tenure of Gen Harbaksh Singh, visited the Div HQ at Dirang Dzong on 7 November. He expressed his satisfaction with the deployment, and Gen Pathania requested him for additional troops, which he dutifully passed on up the chain of command.

On 9 November, observation posts of 4 Garhwal reported a large column of pack animals moving from Rho to Melling. The next day, a Chinese patrol infiltrated the position of 1 Sikh, which was deployed on the right shoulder of Se La. They engaged the rear company of the unit and retreated after a fierce fire fight lasting an hour. On 11 November, about a thousand Chinese were reported moving towards Melling. By all such indications, the Chinese would not remain content with the territory they had already captured, as these signs meant they were preparing for further attacks.

By 15 November, the defences had been occupied as best could be within the constraints, and stocks had been built up to some extent. The units had two first line of small arms ammunition (a "first line" is the amount of ammunition a unit is expected to use in one day's operations. So they had enough ammunition for two days' worth of fighting) and about one week worth of rations. Since rations are replenished regularly on an ongoing basis, this reserve was in case the supplies get disrupted for some reason, like being cut off by the Chinese. Grenades and mortar ammunition were in short supply. Artillery also had about only one and a half days' worth of ammunition.

On 17 November, the forward company of 4 Garhwal in the Nuranang area came under heavy Chinese attack at 0500 hours. The Chinese had apparently advanced dressed as locals to avoid early detection. The brave Garhwalis beat back successive attacks on their position, but the Chinese were able to get their mortars on to the flanks and started shelling the defensive positions. They had also got two of their medium machine guns forward, which were causing heavy casualties by their relentless fire. Rifleman Jaswant Singh, one of the brave Garhwali soldiers, rushed at the enemy machine gun and grabbed it. He was cut down by enemy fire while he was running back with it. He was awarded the Maha Vir Chakra for this gallant action. The battle raged on till the afternoon, but the Garhwalis were vastly outnumbered, and soon they ran out of ammunition. By 1700 hours, the position at Nuranang was ordered to fall back to Se La. Covering troops of 4 Sikh LI were also ordered to fall back to the main defences.

That evening, Gen Pathania received inputs that about a battalion worth of Chinese troops had bypassed Se La and established a road block between Dirang Dzong and Bomdila near kilometre stone 6. Since the defences of Se La were still intact, the Brigade Commander Brig Hoshiar Singh informed Gen Pathania that they could easily hold the position for a week despite being cut off, and longer if air supply continued. Hence, the cutting off of the road did not warrant any panic with regard to Se La. The GOC, however, wanted 62 Brigade to withdraw that night itself and join 65 Brigade and the Div headquarters. Brig Hoshiar Singh was insistent that withdrawing that night would create panic, and if withdrawal was necessary, it could be carried out the next night, on 18 November. Detailed orders for an organised withdrawal were drawn up by the brigade staff that night itself.

From accounts, it emerged later that Gen Pathania was extremely jittery and many of his actions were not taken with the best of tactical prudence. This could partially be attributed to the fact that command of a division had been thrust upon him in the middle of a war at a time when he was awaiting retirement from a peaceful appointment in the National Cadet Corps. On taking over command, he had preferred to site his Div headquarters down in the valley at Dirang Dzong instead of a tactically better position on the mountain top. He had pleaded that he was suffering from high-altitude sickness as the reason for this, and Gen Kaul had readily agreed. However, as per Brig Palit, the decision was more to do with the availability of comfortable (relatively) BRO hutments in the valley. The decision to withdraw 62 Brigade from Se La without even a full-fledged battle was also taken more out of concern for the safety of the Div HQ and himself rather than the fighting potential of defences at Se La.

The communication lines from the Brigade to the battalions were cut that night – possibly by a Chinese patrol. The Brigade commander had left his headquarters early in the morning for the location of the forward troops to have a look at their withdrawal himself, and pass orders about their positions after withdrawal. On his way, he found 1 Sikh position in complete confusion. 1 Sikh troops had not been informed about the withdrawal of Sikh LI troops from the covering positions ahead of the main defences, and seeing their rearwards move, 1 Sikh troops also started withdrawing. A Chinese column was closely shadowing the withdrawing the Sikh LI troops, and now they opened up fire with small arms and mortars, leading to even more chaos in 1 Sikh location.

Since the Chinese column had already infiltrated and taken control of one side of the Se La defences, the remaining troops were open to attack from three sides. The Brigade commander therefore decided to order the immediate withdrawal of troops at Se La instead of waiting for the night as earlier planned. They were to concentrate at Senge Dzong. The withdrawing columns, most of them marching on foot, came under enemy fire around 1100 hours. Fire fights broke out between the Chinese and the columns leading the withdrawal, which created much chaos amongst the columns following. Initial columns on reaching close to Dirang Dzong found that it had been abandoned by the Div and enemy was already present there in large strength. The long column stretched out between Se La and Dirang Dzong in complete disarray. The chaos was multiplied as soon as darkness fell, and the organised columns disintegrated into parties of a few men each trying to evade the Chinese en route and reach Dirang Dzong or Bomdila on their own. As per Gen Kaul, "*No one knew what was happening. There were orders and counter orders. Many abandoned their arms, ammunition and wireless sets and seemed to be for themselves, some escaping into the adjoining hills. … Pathania, in asking them to abandon Se La hastily, had put them in this situation.*"

By the night of 18 November, 62 Brigade had all but ceased to exist as a fighting formation. As per Brig Palit, the withdrawal was "*not carried out as an operation of war. It was a panicky flight, and the Chinese took every tactical advantage…*" The withdrawing column of the units of 62 Brigade came under enemy attack, and the CO of 4 Garhwal, Lt Col BM Bhattacharjea was captured. The Brigade Commander, Brig Hoshiar Singh, was killed in a Chinese ambush during this withdrawal. As per the official Chinese version, they treated his body with utmost honour and gave him a ceremonial burial.

48 Brigade at Bomdila, commanded by Brig Gurbaksh Singh, had suffered a near similar fate. The brigade was taking up defences at Bomdila between 7 and 11 November. This brigade, which was on loan from 17th Infantry Division, had under its command 1 Sikh LI, 1 Madras and 5 Guards. The GOC 4 Div ordered the brigade to push one battalion forward to Pohsing La – Changla area. This was held by two platoons of Assam Rifles, but the GOC was apprehensive that the Chinese could use this axis to bypass our defences. 5 Guards was detailed to take up this position, and were tasked to initially send a strong patrol on test waters. The patrol, under Captain Amarjeet Singh, reached Changla on 8 November and carried out further reconnaissance of Poshing La for suitable areas to deploy. The battalion started building up on the patrol, and stocking of rations and ammunition also commenced. However, on 15 November, a large Chinese column attacked a patrol from this position that was exploring the area Topgey for further advance, and Captain Amarjeet was killed in this action, along with 16 others. The Chinese pushed past this patrol and attacked the position at Poshing La, which also fell. The Brigade commander ordered 5 Guards to withdraw to Bomdila, but the withdrawing battalion column

ran into a strong enemy force en route. The unit disintegrated into small parties, some of which found their way to Misamari over the next weeks.

The opposition that 5 Guards had run into was a large roadblock that the Chinese had established at kilometre 9 on the road Bomdila – Se La. The Brigade commander had learnt of this and was informed that the Chinese strength at this roadblock was estimated to be 400 troops. Being out of communication with the Div HQ, he spoke directly to Gen Kaul on 17 November and informed him of the tight situation they were in. The Corps Commander ordered him to attack the roadblock that very night. This was neither prudent nor possible with the limited strength of six companies available at Bomdila. Gen Kaul assured him that two battalions would be dispatched as reinforcements next morning. These were 3 Jammu and Kashmir Rifles (3 JAK Rif) and 6/8 GR, part of 67 Brigade, which had arrived at Dirang Dzong on 17 November while the Division itself was preparing to withdraw.

Next morning the advance party of 3 JAK Rif under its commanding officer had reached Bomdila and was ordered to occupy the position vacated by 5 Guards. 6/8 GR couldn't make it beyond Chako. A mobile column comprising two companies of 1 Sikh LI and two tanks of 7 Cavalry was dispatched from Bomdila to open the roadblock and link up with Dirang Dzong. Meanwhile, around 1230 hours, the positions vacated by the 1 Sikh LI companies came under attack. Although held by only a small party of cooks, sentries and a section of medium machine guns, they managed to beat back the attack. The positions were reinforced by newly arrived troops of 3 JAK Rif and the Sikh LI companies sent out for road opening were ordered to fall back. Chinese attacked again with greater determination at around 1330 hours, but with the help of accurate artillery fire, this too was repulsed. When the Sikh LI companies returned and were re-occupying their defences, they came under a much heavier attack around 1445 hours and were unable to hold on. The situation at Bomdila was now critical, and by 1630 hours, the brigade commander ordered the brigade to fall back to Rupa, 14 kilometres to the south. These orders were not received by the CO 1 Madras, whose battalion came under Chinese attack around the same time the brigade was pulling out. When he couldn't establish communication with the Brigade HQ, he too took a decision to withdraw his battalion too. The battalion was ambushed during their withdrawal, and was scattered into small parties, some of which subsequently found their way back to the plains. 3 JAK Rif was also unaware of the withdrawal, and when the main body of the battalion reached Bomdila around 1700 hours, they found the defences empty. The CO promptly ordered the battalion to take up positions around the Dropping Zone.

The next day Brig Gurbaksh Singh went back to Bomdila, and ordered the troops remaining there to withdraw to Rupa and join up with the rest of the remnants of 48 Brigade. Meanwhile Rupa also came under enemy attack and the troops there withdrew to Tenga. Troops withdrawing from Bomdila also ultimately made their way to Tenga.

Headquarters of 65 Brigade was located near Dirang Dzong, with one of its primary tasks being the protection of the Div HQ. Two of its battalions – 4 Rajput and 17 Maratha – were deployed to cover the approaches leading to the Div HQ. These battalions had sent out several patrols on 15 and 16 November, but these were ambushed by the enemy. By the 17th evening, the Div HQ was out of communication with the forward brigades, and there was a near sense of panic at being cut off. On the 18th morning, when the GOC was in conference with his staff officers and the commander of 65 Brigade, he received news from a patrol of 19 Madras that the Chinese had established a road block at Kilometre 31 on Bomdila – Dirang Dzong road. Another unconfirmed report spoke of two Chinese battalions closing in on Dirang Dzong. Gen Pathania, accompanied by a couple of his staff officers, took off in a jeep, which they later abandoned and headed for the plains on foot. He was found and picked by Gen Kaul who was flying over the area in a helicopter after the ceasefire on 22 November. Commander 65 Brigade also took off in his jeep, virtually abandoning his brigade.

If the debacle at Namka Chu was unfortunate, the abandoning of Towang and subsequently Se La – Bomdila, by the Div HQ and four brigades, without a single pitched battle from a prepared position, was downright tragic. The entire 4 Division, including its Div HQ and additional brigades allotted to it, had virtually disintegrated by 19 November. As per Gen Kaul, this was purely due to the insecurity of the GOC 4 Div. He writes, "*It was not Hoshiar Singh pressing Pathania but Pathania pressing Hoshiar Singh to withdraw from Se La. Actually Pathania, advised by one of his staff officers, was itching to give up his strong position at Se La, only to reinforce his own at Dirang Dzong. In the process he fell between two stools He lost his heart, Se La, Dirang Dzong and Bomdila, all in a row.*"

By the time the Chinese announced a unilateral ceasefire, 4 Div and all its brigades had been reduced to small groups of men without any command and control, trying to find their way back to the plains. Parties of stragglers falling back from Se La, Dirang Dzong and Bomdila continued to arrive at Misamari, Charudhar and Tezpur for many days after the ceasefire.

Fighting at Walong

While most of the fighting in NEFA took place in the Kameng division under 4 Div, Walong in Lohit frontier division also came under Chinese attack during those fateful days. Walong was then a small village located on the banks of Lohit river near the trijunction of the borders of NEFA, Tibet and Burma. If the communications in the Kameng division were under-developed, they were almost non-existent in the Lohit division. The area was bisected by Lohit river, and movement across this wide river was possible only over one existing bridge. Switching of troops from one side to the other for the attackers or the defenders was therefore not possible. Di Chu and Tho Chu are the other two rivers in this division, both of which are tributaries of the Lohit.

An earthquake in 1951 and subsequent floods had resulted in the virtual isolation of this area. Because of the almost complete lack of roads and even viable tracks, the only mode of maintaining troops in this area was through air supply. There was only a foot track leading to Walong from Tezu, which was also the location of an airfield used for air supplies to Walong. There was a small airstrip at Walong, which was usable only by small aircraft like the Otter of the Indian Air Force. From Walong, two tracks led towards the McMahon Line along either banks of Lohit river. One led along the western bank to Kibithoo, a tiny village two miles south of the McMahon line, crossed the McMahon Line, and went onwards to a big village in Tibet called Rima. The second, along the eastern bank passed through small villages called Tinai, Dong and Kahao. Both were foot tracks, but the one through Kibithoo could take limited movement of pack animals. From Kibithoo, another track ran rearwards to Hayuliang along the thickly forested bank of river Dau.

In July 1961, as a part of the forward policy, troops from 2 Rajput of 5 Brigade, 4 Div, were pushed forward to Walong. The battalion minus one company was located at Walong, while one company was at Tezu along with one troop of heavy mortars from 44 heavy mortar regiment. In April 1962, 2 Rajput was relieved by 6 Kumaon under Lt Col CN Madiah. 2 Rajput, as the reader would recall, was subsequently rushed to 7 Infantry Brigade instead of carrying on to its designated peace station, and took an active part in the battle of Namka Chu.

In September 1962, two more battalions were allotted to 5 Brigade: 4 Sikh and 2/8 GR. Of these, 4 Sikh was allocated to this sector. As a result, two companies of 6 Kumaon, along with its battalion headquarters, were pushed forward to Kibithoo, while two companies of 4 Sikh took over the defences of Walong. The other two companies of this battalion were moved to Chabua.

The reorganised defences in the Lohit division were divided into three sub-sectors: Dirang Valley, Kibithoo and Walong. By 18 October 1962, the deployment in these was as follows:

- 2 Assam Rifles was deployed in the Dibang Valley sub-sector.
- 6 Kumaon was deployed in the Kibithoo sub-sector, with the tactical headquarters at Kibithoo and its administrative base at Walong. One company each was deployed at Dichu, East Ridge, Kibithoo and Thapa Dropping Zone near the ladders area. There were also six platoons of 2 Assam Rifles: 2 at Jachep with one section at Chu Pass, 1 at Hot Spring, 2 at Kibithoo and 1 at Tangkhal/Du Dakhru. In the Walong sub-sector, Battalion headquarters of 4 Sikh was at Walong; one of its companies was in Dong along with a mortar section and the other company was deployed at Maling. One platoon of this company was at Ladders.

As per the scanty intelligence available, the Chinese had carried out improvement of roads on their side of the McMahon Line, and about six battalions were located opposite the Lohit frontier division.

The first sign of trouble in this sector became apparent in Kibithoo on 18 October 1962. A reconnaissance patrol observed the presence of Chinese soldiers, presumably a patrol, on a feature on the own side of McMahon Line, known as Hundred Hill. A platoon of Assam Rifles from a nearby post was dispatched to Hundred Hill the next day to occupy it before the Chinese could do so. Simultaneously, one platoon of 6 Kumaon was ordered to move forward and deploy on a feature called McMahon Ridge, lying squarely on the McMahon Line. This position was beefed up shortly, bringing the strength up to a full company. Another platoon was moved forward along Di Chu river on the ingress route from Taluk Pass.

The Chinese attacked on the night of 21–22 October. The McMahon Ridge position came under artillery and machine gun fire. This was swiftly followed by a battalion worth of Chinese attacking the position. The first attack was beaten back, thanks to the fire support of mortars deployed nearby. The Chinese regrouped and came in for another attack, but the determined Kumaonis beat them back again. The company was withdrawn to Kibithoo the next morning, as it was pointless giving a pitched battle at the boundary itself, defending a position that could not be reinforced.

Several developments took place on 22 October. 5 Brigade was placed directly under the command of 4 Corps, which passed orders for the defences to be reorganised. 6 Kumaon and 4 Sikh were ordered to deploy close to Walong for the protection of Walong airfield. Troops at Kibithoo were to be withdrawn, as these positions were no longer tenable in view of the enemy advance. A number of twine ropeways that had been set up across the Lohit river at Kibithooto to facilitate crossing of own troops were also ordered to be cut to delay enemy advance. Assam Rifles were also re-deployed to cover Walong from the west, withdrawing their posts from forward locations at Hot Spring, Jachep, Chu Pass and Du Dakhru.

6 Kumaon withdrew from Kibithoo that night after destroying everything that couldn't be carried, and also the ropeway as ordered. The battalion closed in at Walong between 23 and 25 October. Two companies of 2/8 GR were also flown in to reinforce Walong and one company each was placed under command 6 Kumaon and 4 Sikh. Dichu Ridge and Kibithoo were occupied by the Chinese shortly afterwards.

The Chinese attacked a 4 Sikh position on the Mithun track on the early morning of 27 October. The men put up a stout defence, and the enemy attack was foiled. Sep Kewal Singh was awarded the Maha Vir Chakra in this action.

GOC 2 Infantry Division, Major General MS Pathania (not to be confused with GOC 4 Div Major General Anant Pathania, who was his cousin) reached Walong on 26 October for reconnaissance. The sector was now to be under an Independent Infantry Brigade as exercise of direct control from the Divisional Headquarters was difficult. 11 Infantry Brigade, commanded by Brig NC Rawlley, MC, located at Nagaland, was earmarked. Brig Rawlley reached Walong on 31 October. Besides the existing troops in the sector, 11 Brigade had under its command one company of 3/3 GR and one troop of 62 Para Field Battery.

The Chinese, meanwhile, kept our troops at Mithun and Ladder positions constantly engaged by regular firing and probing attacks, which were all beaten back. However, this was apparently to divert our attention from their activities in the area of Green Pimple, where they were busy constructing a track and building up strength. A patrol consisting of an OP party from the mortar battery and a platoon of Assam Rifles, under 2/Lt PS Bhandari of artillery, discovered enemy presence in this area. They had a short but sharp engagement before returning. 2/Lt PS Bhandari and Subedar Jagandhoy Limbu of 2 Assam Rifles were awarded Vir Chakras for this action.

Map 5: Walong Area

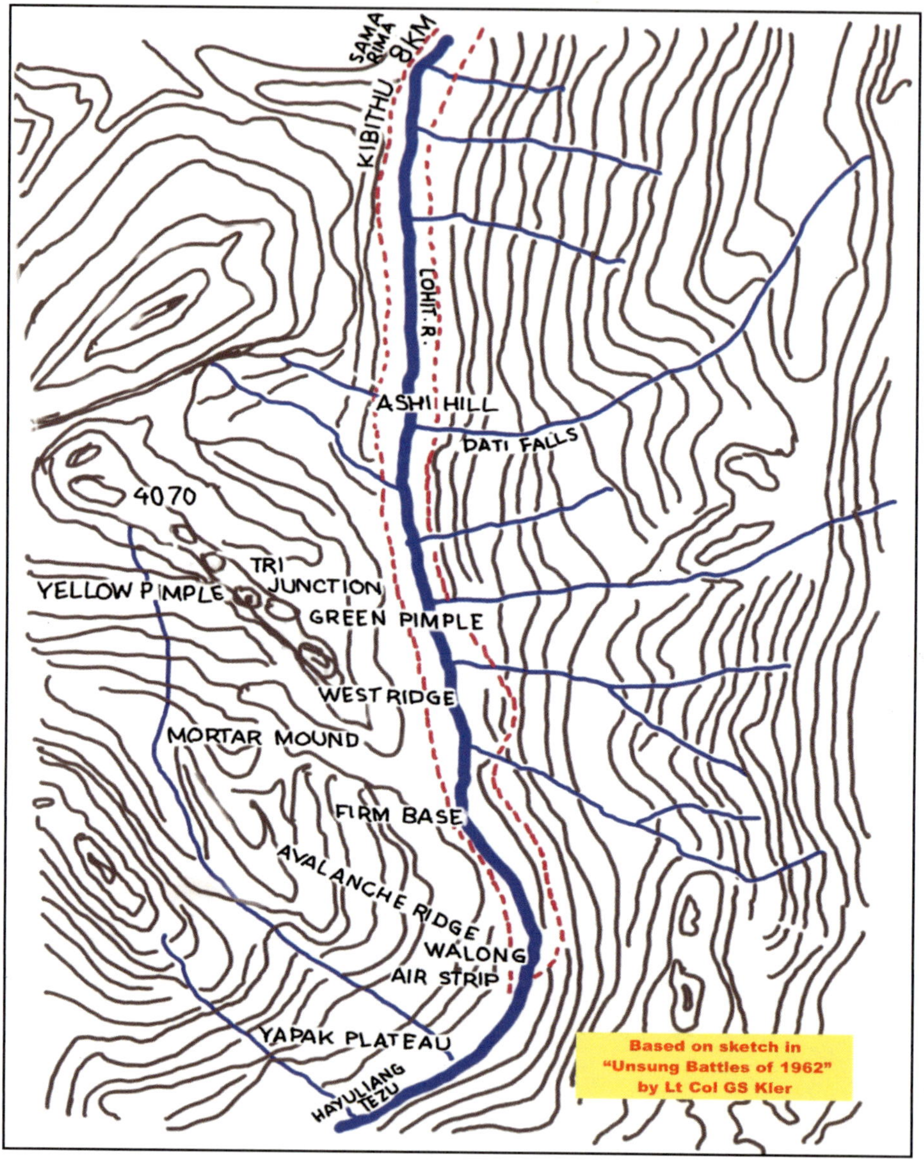

Since the enemy presence in this area was a potential threat to the airstrip and dropping zone, which were the lifelines of the troops in Walong, it was decided to evict the enemy from Green Pimple. One company of 6 Kumaon under Captain RK Mathur was assigned this task, and artillery support was allotted from the heavy mortar battery. The attack, launched on 6 November, was successful in pushing the Chinese back from their forward defences. Since their ammunition was running short, the Kumaon company could not press on with the attack and had to pull back and take defensive positions near the Tri-Junction area dominating the enemy route of advance towards Walong. Captain RK Mathur was awarded the Vir Chakra for this action.

On 12 November, Gen Kaul visited Walong and saw the fighting at the 4 Sikh position first hand. As was his habit, he sent lengthy signals back to Army HQ from there, making demands like helicopters for the evacuation of casualties from forward posts and replenishing them with ammunition. Having been the CGS only over a month ago, the impossibility of allocation of such resources due to their non-availability must have been known to him.

Fresh troops from 4 Sikh were brought in for another attack on Yellow Pimple on 14 November. The enemy defences at Yellow Pimple and adjoining Ashi Hill were bombarded by own artillery before the attack was pressed in. This was undertaken by two companies, with one more company in reserve, while a fourth company was to engage Green Pimple to ensure the enemy could not send reinforcements from it to Yellow Pimple. The attack on Yellow Pimple was launched at 0930 hours, and pressed on with determination despite heavy enemy artillery fire. However, the heavy resistance by well dug in Chinese, who had not been affected by the heavy artillery bombardment we had unleashed before the attack, brought this attack to a standstill. The reserves were brought in at about 1200 hours in the form of two platoons of 6 Kumaon under Subedar Govind Singh and Subedar Surendra Chand. The enemy LMG post that was holding up the Indian attack was swiftly dealt with and the attack made some progress. The Indian troops were ordered to hold on to the ground captured so far, and try to advance further after nightfall. However, the Chinese reinforced the position meanwhile, and launched a counterattack. After a fierce fight, the Indians had to give up the gains made and fall back to Tri-Junction after suffering heavy casualties. Only 90 of the 200 men who had gone into the attack returned.

The next morning, the Chinese attacked Tri-Junction with preponderance of force. The remnants of two companies who were located there put up a brave fight under Capt Bhatia and 2/Lt Khatri, both of whom were wounded, but the attack was repulsed. Both received Vir Chakras for this action. 4 Dogra was ordered to reinforce Tri-Junction, but the Chinese outflanked the post and cut off the route leading up to Tri-Junction. About a platoon strength of Dogras still managed to get past and reach Tri-Junction.

The enemy put in repeated attacks on Tri-Junction on the night of 15 November and early in the morning of 16 November, but the determined troops held fast and beat the enemy back, undeterred by the heavy shelling they were subject to. By now, communications with the Brigade HQ had been cut off, and it was clear that no further reinforcements were possible. Continuing to fight there would be futile, given the overwhelming strength of Chinese. The CO 6 Kumaon therefore decided to pull back, and Tri-Junction was abandoned at 0900 hours on 16 November.

One company of 4 Sikh was deployed at a place called "Patrol Base" near the Yellow and Green Pimples. As obvious from its name, the post served as a base for patrols operating towards Chinese positions at Green and Yellow Pimples to interfere in their route of supplies. This base was set up on 13 November, and one of the patrols interdicted an enemy column on the same day.

On the night of 15 November, the Chinese retaliated by launching an attack on the base. The attack began at 2100 hours, but was soon beaten back with the help of artillery fire. There were several more attacks that night, but all were unsuccessful. As the post was running out of ammunition, and the Chinese had cut off the route for replenishment, the Quarter Master of 4 Sikh Captain Inderjit Kumar personally led a replenishment column that fought its way into the base and delivered much needed ammunition. The base continued to fight through the night, and the next morning they were ordered to withdraw to an area between Mithun and Ladders.

One of the companies of 3/3 GR, which was under the command of 4 Sikhs, was holding the Ladders position. This company came under heavy attack by the Chinese on 16 November morning, just as the troops from patrol base were falling back. Major NB Chand, the company commander, led his men to fight back despite the heavy casualties suffered. In the absence of reinforcements and replenishment of ammunition, as neither were available with the battalion, the company commander ordered his company to pull out when the ammunition was about to run out. While ensuring that his men could withdraw successfully, Maj Chand himself succumbed to enemy fire.

The positions at Maha Plateau, Lachhman Ridge and Mithun also came under attack on 15 and 16 November. These were being held by one company of 3/3 GR and one company of 4 Sikh. In beating back the initial attacks, the Indian troops took heavy casualties. The positions were overrun by the Chinese and both the company commanders were captured.

The next position to come under attack was West Ridge. The initial attack was beaten back by the 6 Kumaon platoons deployed there. The Chinese then launched a multidirectional attack supported by machine gun and artillery fire. Lt Bikram Singh, who was the company commander at this post, was ordered to hold the position at all costs till 1100 hours. The loss of this post would have posed a direct threat to Walong, and hence this was imperative. The post held on as ordered, thanks to the inspirational leadership and courage of Lt Bikram Singh. Finally, when withdrawal was ordered, only 1 JCO and 17 other ranks could extricate while rest of the troops, including Lt Bikram Singh, laid down their lives defending this post.

The troops deployed on the eastern bank of Lohit river, which included two companies of 3/3 GR and one company of 4 Sikh under the battalion headquarters of 3/3 GR, also came under attack on 16 November. They were soon surrounded by the Chinese and cut off.

Gen Kaul flew in again on the 16th morning, literally breathing down the brigade commanders' neck while the battle raged. There was no purpose served by the presence of the Corps commander to supervise a brigade battle, except perhaps giving bragging rights to Gen Kaul himself, who had always been sensitive about his lack of combat experience. He made sure that his presence did not go unnoticed by his superiors. He writes in his book: "*I sent a message through signals to the Army Chief and Army Commander at 0945 hours giving them the latest situation, I could hear the enemy advancing towards the Brigade Headquarters where I stood. I told them in my signal that the enemy was assaulting us with a Division. I requested for reinforcements and additional weapons and got back a reply from the Army Chief to say I had his full support and wishing me luck in the battle.*" Both, his requests and the Chief's assurance were meaningless, given that there weren't any troops available to reinforce. And even if there had been some available, there was no way they could be inducted into Walong within a reasonable timeframe.

Gen Kaul left Walong at 1100 hours on 16, after instructing Commander 11 Brigade to hold on to the sector till as long as possible, and then fall back taking a series of delaying positions if necessary. Such vague and generic orders were standard for the prevailing situation and leadership. All forward troops were ordered to withdraw and fall back to Walong. With almost all of them having suffered heavily in the battles for the past 24 to 48 hours, there was very little cohesion left in companies and platoons. A large number of all ranks – 832 – had been killed, wounded or taken prisoner.

The Brigade commander issued orders for withdrawal from Walong to Tezu, and the men trickled in from the forward localities into Walong and onwards to Tezu, in small parties. They had to cover the long distance on foot, carrying the wounded, often subsisting on limited or no supplies. The men were still trickling in when the Chinese declared the ceasefire on 21 November, and continued to do so almost till December.

Subansiri Frontier Division

Before the implementation of the forward policy, 9 Assam Rifles was responsible for the Subansiri frontier division. Two posts were set up, at Longju and Takaing. The Chinese had protested the setting up of the posts, and considerable correspondence was exchanged between both sides on this. In August 1959, Chinese crossed over into the Indian side of McMahon Line and fired on the Longju post. Encircled, and outnumbered, the Indian post was forced to withdraw. This post was not re-occupied after the Chinese left, based on an agreement at political level. However, a post at Maja nearby was set up instead.

After the induction of 4 Infantry Division, this area came under the responsibility of 5 Infantry Brigade. One of its battalions, 1/5 GR (Frontier Force) was located at Salonighat. In May 1962, it was relieved by 2 JAK Rif, and the location was between Daporijo and North Lakhimpur. Between January and August 1962, a number of Assam Rifles posts were set up under Op Onkar. These were on or very close the McMahon Line, and included Asaphila, Potrang, Tamala, Sagamla, Kashongla, Pagak, Dharmu, and Vatey.

Operationally, the area was divided into Kamla Valley sub-sector under 9 Assam Rifles and Subansiri sub-sector under 2 JAK Rif. One wing of 9 Assam Rifles was located at Ziro with its eight platoons deployed as above. Battalion HQ of 2 JAK Rif was at Daporijo, along with one company. The other three companies were at Takaing, Taliha and Lemeking, where the tactical headquarters of the battalion was also located. On 22 October, Taliha was reinforced from the troops at Daporijo.

After the attack on Namka Chu on 20 October, since 4 Div was completely embroiled in the battle in Kameng frontier division, control of 5 Brigade was taken away from it and paced directly under 4 Corps HQ.

The Chinese had been building up their forces opposite Longju area in this sector, and had also considerably improved the roads leading up to the border. On 23 October, they attacked our forward posts at Asaphila, Sagamla, Tamala and Potrang. Asaphila was the first to come under attack, and took heavy casualties. The surviving troops fell back to Takaing. Troops from the other three posts also withdrew and reached Takaing the next day. On 24 October, Takaing itself came under heavy shelling, and was abandoned. It was occupied by the Chinese on 25 October. The troops from Maja had also been withdrawn in the face of the heavy Chinese buildup, and this post was occupied by Chinese on 25 October. The withdrawing troops were engaged at Reding. The defences all along the frontier were pushed back by the Chinese, who consolidated their hold over the positions vacated by Indians.

With the raising of 2 Infantry Div under Major General MS Pathania, 5 Brigade came under its command. The responsibility of Lohit and Siang frontier divisions was taken away from the brigade, and it was now tasked exclusively for the defence of Subansiri frontier division. Defences were now readjusted, and defences at Lemeking were strengthened with the existing troops available with 5 Brigade. It was also promised additional troops to man posts at Taliha, Sarli and Huri, forming a viable brigade-defended sector or battalion-defended areas. Artillery support was to be augmented, and logistics, especially ammunition stocks, were to be built up.

In November, 1/4 GR from 192 Brigade was placed under command 5 Brigade. This battalion reached Daporijo by 14 November, and was deployed in the North Lakhimpur sub-sector. By 18 November, the Brigade HQ was at North Lakhimpur, with the battalion HQ of 1/4 GR along with two companies at Daporijo, and the other two companies along with rest of the administrative elements were at Taliha, along with the battalion HQ and two companies of 2 JAK Rif, a mortar battery and Medium Machine Gun platoon. The other two companies of this battalion were at Lemeking along with the tactical headquarters of the battalion and one detachment from the Medium Machine Gun platoon.

The lull in the battle was shattered when a protective patrol deployed ahead of Lemeking spotted a strong Chinese force and engaged them with Light Machine Gun, mortar and rifle fire. They kept the fire going till they ran out of ammunition, causing substantial casualties on the enemy. Thereafter, they withdrew to Lemeking. While the brigade ordered a withdrawal of troops from the forward areas on 20 November, these orders were countermanded by the Army HQ. The issue became irrelevant and there was no further engagement in this sector as the ceasefire announced by the Chinese came into effect.

Siang Frontier Division

Lying between the Subansiri and Lohit frontier divisions, Siang division had its headquarters at Along. Gelling, Korbo, Jidu Tuting and Menchuka were prominent villages close to McMahon Line, while Lo La, Dom La, Shoka La, Lamdo La and Lusha La were the passes on the border through which ingress into the area was possible. The tracks leading from the border converged at Along, which made it a vital hub from the defence point of view. Two of the most important amongst these tracks were from Kepang La – Gelling – Tuting – Pasighat and from Tuting to Along.

The area was held by 11 Assam Rifles prior to the induction of regular army in 1959. When the responsibility of this area came under 5 Brigade, 2 Madras along with 3 wings of 11 Assam Rifles were located here. A company each of 2 Madras was deployed at Tuting and Menchuka, while the battalion headquarters with the other two companies were at Along. Its rear HQ was located at Lakhimpur. The battalion headquarters of 11 Assam and one of its wings were at Along, while the other two wings were at Menchukha – Manigong and Pashighat – Tuting.

In February 1962, as part of Op Onkar, a forward post was established at Gelling, which was 6 kilometres short of the border. Several additional Assam Rifles posts were also established by September 1962. Subsequently, under Op Leghorn, the tactical headquarters of 2 Madras was moved up to Tuting on 20 September 1962. After the induction of additional troops into NEFA, 2/8 GR was also allotted to 5 Brigade for this sector. Now the defences in Siang were reorganised and divided into three sub-sectors.

The Menchukha sub-sector under Lt Col DA Taylor, CO 2/8 GR comprised Menchuka, Nisangong and Lamang. Besides the battalion headquarters and one company plus of 2/8 GR, it had one company of 2 Madras, and a wing of 11 Assam Rifles. For fire support, they had one section of 3-inch mortars and two sections of Medium Machine Guns. The Manigong sub-sector was commanded by the CO 11 Assam Rifles Lt Col RP Gautam. Under him, he had one wing of his battalion and a section each of 3-inch mortars and Medium Machine Gun. The Tuting sub-sector was commanded by Lt Col SK Mushran, CO 2 Madras. He was responsible for Tuting – Gelling and the routes connecting these. Being the biggest and most threatened sub-sector, he had his entire battalion minus the company deployed in Menchuka, two wings of Assam Rifles and a heavy mortar battery. Battalion headquarters of 11 Assam Rifles with four platoons was in Along – Pashighat area. There was an acute shortage of ammunition, and no reserves were stocked at the forward posts. The entire area was maintained by aircraft of a private airlines, owned by Mr Biju Patnaik. He was a former RIAF pilot, and prominent politician who later became the Chief Minister of Orissa, and the father of Mr Naveen Patnaik, who currently holds the same post.

Chinese activities opposite this area had been reported by Tibetan refugees. Some incursions in the Lo La area were reported, and an Assam Rifles patrol sent to investigate in August 1962 lost two jawans. It was believed they had been taken prisoner by the Chinese. It was estimated that the Chinese had about five battalions deployed against this area, poised to launch attack.

On 21 October 1962, an Indian patrol reported a company of Chinese had occupied Lo La pass and Lasam which lay opposite the Indian post at Lamang manned by Assam Rifles. On 23 October, the Chinese launched an attack on Lamang, and after a brief firefight, the post was ordered to withdraw to Menchukha. Between 21 and 23 October, Indian patrols in the Manigong sub-sector also reported that Chinese had occupied the passes. The Corps HQ passed orders for the forward posts to be withdrawn, but due to a breakdown in communications, these orders could not reach the posts. As a result, the Chinese attacked the post near Gingtung and pushed it back to Henkar. The post between Dom La and Henkar was also attacked and pushed back. The troops fell back to Manigong, except one platoon that was tasked to hold on to Papikrong. But the enemy bypassed this position on 26 October, and captured Manigong on 28 October.

In the Tuting sub-sector, the post at Lamdo La was attacked on 24 October. The troops from all the forward posts were withdrawn to Tuting and Ogong. By the end of the month Chinese had advanced up to Lamang, Manigong and Jorging.

Meanwhile, the responsibility for the Siang frontier division was handed over to 192 Infantry Brigade under 2 Infantry Division. Since its battalions were diverted to Subansiri frontier division as mentioned earlier, just the headquarters was available, and it took over the command of troops already located here. Two companies of 2/8 GR, which had been loaned to Lohit frontier division, were also to re-join their battalion here. The area was reorganised into two sub-sectors instead of three: Menchukha and Tuting. By 16 November, the deployment was as follows:

Brigade headquarters and two companies of 2/8 GR were at Along. Battalion headquarters of 2/8 GR, along with a company of 2 Madras, one platoon of 3-inch mortars and a section of Medium Machine Gun were in the Menchukha sub-sector. The two companies of 2/8 GR were planned to be pushed in here on arrival from Walong. Battalion headquarters and three companies of 2 Madras, 10 platoons of 11 Assam Rifles and a platoon of Medium Machine Guns less one section were located in the Tuting sub-sector.

On 17 November, an engagement with a Chinese column of approximately two companies strength was reported near Nisangong in the Menchuka sub sector. Since the induction of the 2/8 GR companies had been delayed due to the bad weather, the sub-sector was acutely short of troops. Subsequently, since the planned induction of the two companies was cancelled because of the greater threat perception in Walong, the GOC 2 Infantry Division ordered the unviable Menchuka sector to be vacated. The withdrawal was to take place over two nights: November 18/19 and 19/20, occupying an interim position at Rego.

However, as soon as the withdrawal began, the 2 Madras troops at Saung came under heavy enemy mortar fire. It appeared that the enemy was trying to cut off the route of withdrawal from Menchukha. The CO 2/8 GR therefore decided to expedite the withdrawal, and he personally set off to reconnaissance an alternate withdrawal route along with a platoon strength while the main body under Major SN Dar continued along the planned route. This party was ambushed by the enemy and were scattered, some of the troops making it back over snow-clad mountains to Tato, only to find that the Chinese had preceded them there. The CO Lt Col Taylor, and two more officers of 2/8 GR, and another officer of 2 Madras succumbed to the cold and exhaustion. 39 other ranks also lost their lives in this withdrawal. A large number were also reportedly taken prisoner by the Chinese.

The troops at the Tuting sub-sector also withdrew without giving battle to the enemy, falling back to Along after destroying the bridge on Siang river near Jidu. This withdrawal was apparently carried out prematurely, without waiting for the deadline given by the brigade headquarters to allow for withdrawal of heavy equipment.

8

The War in Ladakh

Ladakh is the largely uninhabited expanse of snowy desert in the north east part of Jammu and Kashmir covering about 98,000 square kilometres. The average height of mountains here is over 5,000 meters, with Nubra, the highest peak being 7,500 meters high. The terrain in Ladakh, while as rugged as in NEFA, was by and large devoid of vegetation in contrast with the heavily forested north east. The plateau of Ladakh has the Karakoram mountains to its north, with a branch running south and east. To its east lies the Ladakh range. Further east lies the flat area of Aksai Chin, the primary bone of contention between China and India. The sparse habitation of the area is spread along the four main valleys: Leh, Nubra, Chushul and Demchok. Indus and Nubra are the major rivers flowing through these valleys, with other minor tributaries flowing into them. Pangong Tso is a high-altitude saltwater lake 64 kilometres long and 3 to 6 kilometres wide. While constructing roads in the mountainous terrain on the Indian side is extremely difficult, the flat open terrain on the Chinese side makes it much easier.

Leh is the only important town in this region, which has been a trade centre right up to the Chinese invasion of Tibet in 1951, after which trade had come to a virtual halt. The town is also a significant centre of Buddhism, with its ancient monasteries and predominantly Buddhist population.

The border in this area runs from the Karakoram Pass along the watershed between the rivers Shyok and Yarkand, through the Qaraqash river and down the KunLun Mountains, along the crest and thence through Lanak Pass, Kone

Pass and Kepsang Pass. It then runs along the southern bank of Chumesang and eastern bank of Chang Lung Lungpa, skirts along the Pangong Tso, across the eastern part of Spanggur Lake, along the watershed of Indus through Chang Pass up to Jara Pass. It then turns south west, crosses the Indus southeast of Demchok, through Charding Pass, Imis Pass and Kyungzing Pass. It then turns westward and crosses Pare river south of Chumar and goes on to Gya peak.

Map 6: Ladakh – Aksai Chin

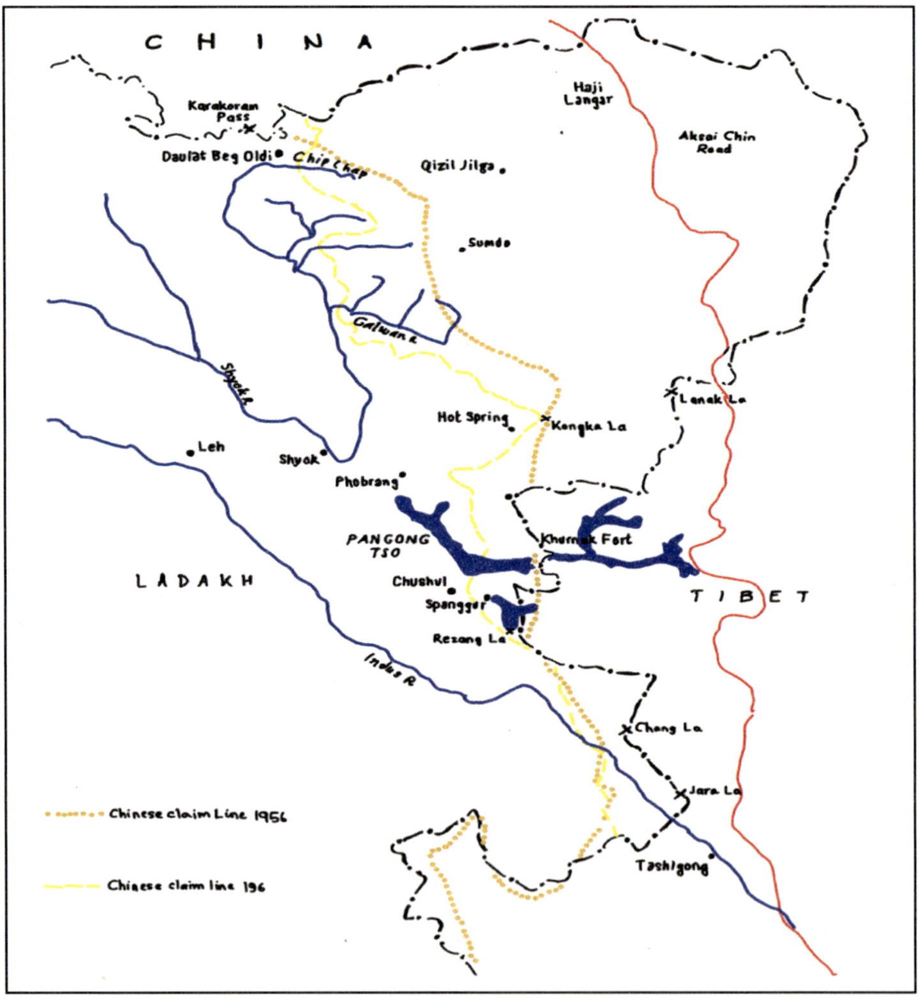

Map not to scale

Based on the geographical features, the area was divided into four sectors for military deployment: Daulat Beg Oldi (DBO), Changchemno-Galwan valley, Chushul and Indus valley sectors. The terrain did not permit lateral communications across sectors, except between Chushul and Indus valley. This meant that switching of forces between sectors was almost impossible. Troops in each sector would have to per force fight an isolated battle with little help or support from neighbouring sectors. The siting of the posts was also based on administrative considerations. Since all the posts were air maintained, and the dropping zones were in the flat valleys rather than on mountain tops, the posts had to be located closer to these instead of occupying the dominating heights as dictated by tactics.

The road, which earlier ended at Leh, was extended by constructing a jeepable track up to Chushul via Dunti in 1962 by the BRO. It ran along the Indus valley, and the going on it was extremely slow due to the rough terrain. From Dunti, another track was constructed to connect the post at Demchok. Besides, there were a few mule tracks that connected Leh to Shyok, DBO and Karakoram Pass.

In April 1960, 114 Infantry Brigade under Brig DS Garewal was inducted into Ladakh in compliance with the order of Army taking over the border there as well. It had two Jammu and Kashmir Militia battalions and 1/8 GR under command. In 1961-62, DBO was set up as a supply base with a landing strip where aircraft carrying supplies could land. Several new posts were opened, including Charding La and Chang La, to protect either sides of Demchok. The area of responsibility was divided between the three battalions, with 14 Jammu and Kashmir Militia responsible for area north of Galwan river, 1/8 GR for the area between Galwan river and Chushul, and 7 Jammu and Kashmir Militia to the south of Chushul.

Despite the massive communications and logistics difficulties, the brigade established posts in the forward areas. Notable amongst these were Thoise Panamik, Point 16550, Shyok and DBO in DBO sector; Hot Spring, Chushul and Rezangla in Changchenmo/Chushul sector and Dungti, Demchok, Dumchek and Chang La in Indus Valley sector. An improvised landing ground was established at DBO for landing of supplies, and this became an important administrative base for the entire forward area. In order to provide protection to this base, two posts called Charding La and Chang La were set up on its either flanks.

Setting up these posts was a herculean task, given the poor state of communications up to these far-flung areas. When a platoon of 14 Jammu and Kashmir Militia first set out to establish the post at DBO as ordered, it was equipped with adequate rations and fodder for 10 days. They were expected to be maintained by air once they reached DBO. They ran into rough weather en route, and lost many of their pack animals. The last leg of their journey was touch and go with the limited rations they could carry on the surviving mules. But the platoon managed to reach DBO with just one casualty, and were soon replenished by air drops.

Based on the directions received by the Army HQ regarding the forward policy in 1961, they instructed HQ Western Command "*to patrol as far forward as possible from our present positions towards the international border as recognised by us. This will be done with a view to establishing additional posts located to prevent the Chinese from advancing further and also to dominate any Chinese posts already established in our territory. This forward policy will be carried out without getting involved in a clash with the Chinese unless it becomes necessary in self defence.*"

One additional battalion, 5 Jat, was allotted to 114 Brigade – a meagre resource to implement the humongous task envisaged by the forward policy. But because of the onset of winters, even this battalion could only be moved forward for deployment in May 1962. Troops from DBO set up posts in Chip Chap Valley, perilously close to the Chinese positions there. The distance between the Indian posts was such that just like in NEFA, they were neither mutually supporting nor geared up to give a pitched battle to any attacking enemy. But the decisions makers in Delhi were not expecting any attacks and viewed this as a merely a game of who could occupy more territory by setting up posts.

Thus, like in NEFA, the checkposts were aimed merely at showing the flag and claiming territory rather than tactical defence. The idea was to "leapfrog" into the Chinese occupied territory by establishing these tiny posts advancing successively eastwards. The line of such Indian posts thus slowly advanced towards the international border as defined by India. But the Chinese were in a much better position than us to play this game of high-altitude chess. They had constructed roads emanating eastwards from the Aksai Chin Highway all along the border. Thus they could set up and maintain posts with roads running almost up to them, making their task so much easier. In our case, every kilogram of supplies – whether it was rations or ammunition or any other kind of essential store required for setting up defences – had to be carted on animals like Yaks, mules or ponies, over the narrow tracks for hundreds of kilometres. The animals had to carry their own fodder in addition to the stores loaded on them, and thus the turnaround distance of these animals was also limited.

In a letter addressed to the CGS, Western Command had written in August 1962 that while as early as 1959, the minimum requirement assessed by Western Command for defence of Ladakh was five battalions, to date only four battalions had been allotted to it. In the absence of adequate logistics support, even the deployment of these four battalions served no military purpose, and these were merely occupying ground and showing the flag. Their fighting capability was severely restricted based on their scattered deployment on posts that were not tactically sited. The letter also pointed out that the Chinese capacity to induct and maintain troops far exceeded ours. The increasing number of clashes indicated that the Chinese were reacting to the establishment of forward posts by India. It highlighted that in Ladakh, four Indian battalions were faced with an estimated strength of a full division, with its complement of supporting weapons. The communication systems connecting the Chinese posts were far better, with vehicular movement possible on their side right up to their posts. The Command HQ recommended that India should focus on defending Leh instead of scattering its limited troops in penny packets all along the border. It advised building up communications and strength on our side before taking up the forward policy in earnest.

In its reply, the Army HQ blamed the Command of being alarmist, and reiterated that the Chinese had no intention of using force to vacate Indian posts. They cited the incident at Galwan post, where the Chinese troops had surrounded the Indian post but not opened fire, to support their argument. It therefore summarily rejected the contentions and recommendations made by the Command Headquarters in its letter.

Brig TN Raina (who later rose to become the COAS) took over the command of the brigade from Brig Garewal (who received the Param Vishisht Seva Medal for his role in Ladakh). After the induction of 5 Jat, the deployment of 114 Brigade was as follows.

Map 7: Ladakh

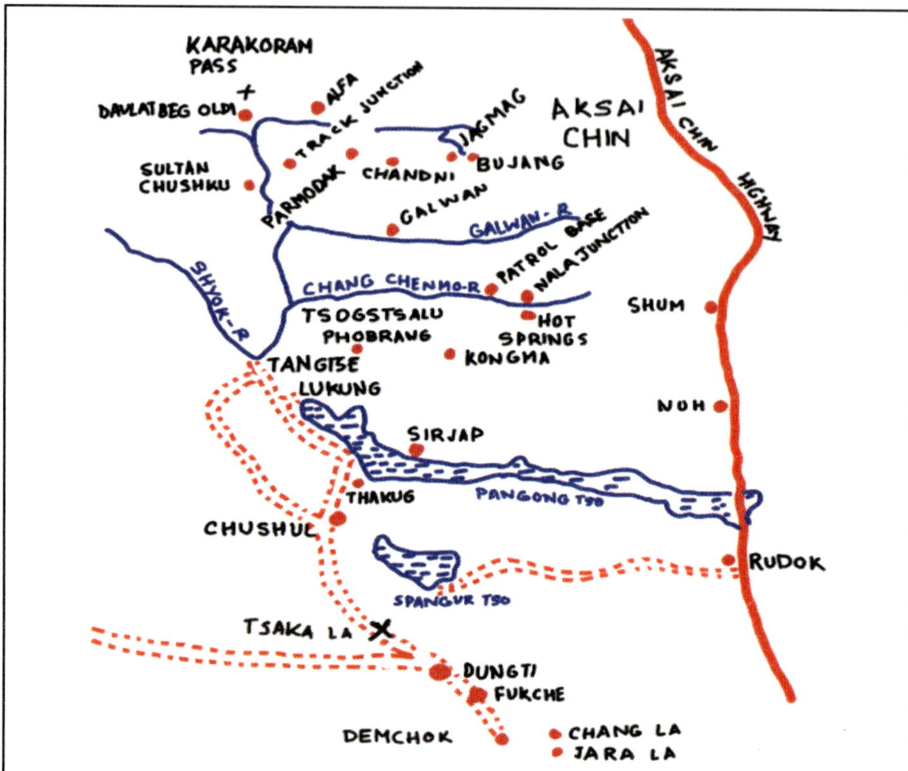

Not to Scale
Drawn by the author based on sketch in "The Saga of Ladakh" by Maj Gen Jagjit SinghDBO Sector

DBO Sector

14 Jammu and Kashmir Militia with an additional company from 5 Jat was deployed in the DBO Sector. This was the north most sector, with DBO as its hub. This was an ancient village through which four tracks, including the traditional silk route passed. The village was named after a Yarkandi merchant called Daulat Beg who was said to have been caught in a blizzard and died here while traversing over the old silk route, which crossed the Karakoram Pass and carried on towards Sinkiang. There was another track that went eastwards, following the Chip Chap river, which led to the disputed Aksai Chin over which the Chinese had built the controversial highway. It passed through a village called Qizil Jilga. The third track connected DBO with Leh via a place called Track Junction, along the Chip Chap river, through the Depsang plains,

crossed the Shyok river and past Shyok village and then followed the Indus down to Leh. It was about 200 km from Leh to DBO and took about 12 days to cover this distance over the difficult terrain. The fourth track, which was only usable during the summer months, also went to Leh. It crossed the Shyok river at Saser Brangsa, went through the Saser La pass on the Karakoram range, along the Nubra valley, and crossed over the Shyok river again, through the Khardung La pass on Ladakh range onwards to Leh.

14 Jammu and Kashmir Militia was deployed with the Battalion HQ at DBO and the five companies (including one from 5 Jat) holding the two approaches to it. There were 10 posts located along the Chip Chap river, and four along the approach from south. These posts did not have any name, as they were not based around any known geographical features. They had local nicknames like "Alpha" and "Chandni" and were also numbered from 1 to 14 for ease of reference. Some of the troops were deployed on the track from Leh, covering the replenishment route, spread between Murgo and Track Junction. Except for DBO, which had about a company's strength, all the other posts had either a section or a platoon's strength. The largest weapons available with these posts were Light Machine Guns, except Post 1 along Chip Chap valley, which had a section of 3-inch mortars. All the posts were isolated, without any mutual support between them. None of them were stocked adequately for a prolonged battle.

Changchenmo – Galwan Sector

The Changchenmo valley lies about 10 kilometres south of the Galwan river, and 5 Jat less one company was deployed in this sector along these two valleys. It was connected to Leh by a 70-kilometre-long mule track via Chang La Pass, Tangtse valley and Phobrang. However, the posts were largely maintained by air. The Battalion HQ was located at Phobrang, which was also the base for operations in this sector. It had one company at Galwan, and a platoon each at Patrol Base, Hot Springs and Nala Junction. These posts had been established by 1/8 GR, and were taken over by 5 Jat, whose company had been airlifted to relieve 1/8 GR.

Chushul Sector

The Karkoram range continues into the Chushul sector south of the Changchenmo valley, running up to the Pangong Tso. Towards the south of the Pangong Tso lies another lake, called Spanggur. There is a wide gap in the mountains south of Spanggur Lake, called the Spanggur gap, and Chushul is a small village on the west of this gap. Like at DBO, a makeshift airfield had been set up near Chushul. Chushul had also been connected to Leh by a road, which traversed along the Indus river through Dungti and Tska La pass. A mule track also ran from Leh to Chushul via Changla, Dorbuk, Tangtse and Tartar. Two companies of 1/8 GR were deployed at Chushul, with one company less a platoon at Srijap, north of Pangong Tso. One company was deployed in the south of Pangong Tso in a group of three posts called Yula complex. Heights on the north and south of the Spanggur gap had a post each, called Gurung hill and Magar hill, respectively, and one post was in the gap itself.

Indus Valley Sector

This was the southernmost sector of Ladakh. Three roads run into this sector – from Leh to the west, Chushul to the north and Demchok from the south. All these converged at a place called Dungti, making it an important communication hub. This was the only sector where roads on our side were better developed than on the Chinese side. 7 Jammu and Kashmir Militia was deployed in this sector, with its battalion headquarters and one company located at Koyul. Another company was at Dungti. Two companies were scattered in penny packets along the border to man passes and routes of ingress.

Preliminary Encounters

In May 1962, one of the posts about 24 kilometres north east of DBO, called "Post Alpha," which was being held by a strength of 14 men under a JCO, reported that about 100 Chinese soldiers were advancing towards it. The post was ordered to stay firm and neither open fire nor withdraw. The brigade headquarters was monitoring the situation, and had also informed the Corps, who had passed along orders from Army headquarters not to allow the post to withdraw, but to fight it out. Had the Chinese actually attacked the post, it was doubtful if 14 men with just rifles and no heavy weapons would have been able to hold out for long against 100 enemy soldiers. But fortunately, the Chinese did not actually attack.

Shortly after this incident, 114 Brigade was ordered to set up a platoon post in the Galwan valley at a location specified by New Delhi. This was a departure from the past, when the strength and location of the posts was left to the brigade commander to decide. Setting up an isolated post in an area with hardly any defence potential was not militarily sound, but the decision had been taken at Delhi during a meeting held on 26 September 1961, attended by the Foreign Secretary, CGS and Director IB. The IB recommended the setting up of this post in view of the substantial advance to our territorial claim this post would signify. Accordingly, the order was passed by the Army HQ through HQ Western Command to the brigade. The incident at "Alpha post" had probably given an indication to the decision makers in Delhi that tactical siting of the posts was not really required, as the Chinese did not intend to aggressively assert their claims. But contrary to this belief, the Chinese reaction to the setting up of this post was swift.

In July 1962, a strong Chinese force of approximately a battalion's strength surrounded the post and cut it off from its route of maintenance. Any attempts to reinforce the post by supply columns met with a strong show of force, though the Chinese did not actually resort to firing. Frantic queries from the brigade headquarters up the chain of command about the course of action received no reply. After maintaining a close cordon around the post for a few days, they withdrew from south and southeast of the post, giving the Indian troops the opportunity to withdraw. The Indian troops of 1/8 GR stood firm, even though the Chinese continued to build pressure on them without actually firing. They set up loudspeakers near the posts and made threatening announcements in Hindi to demoralise our beleaguered jawans. A relief column under Major VP Bhasin made its way to the post, which held out for two months, before they were finally relieved by troops of 5 Jat, the relief taking place by air in helicopters in view of the continuing siege of Galwan by the Chinese. Ultimately, the Chinese troops were pulled back after a strong diplomatic protest was lodged by India.

Instead of setting off alarm bells about Chinese intentions, the Galwan incident further helped reinforce the belief held by Indian decision makers in Delhi that China did not intend to push forward its claims forcefully by resorting to confrontation. While the standoff was underway in Ladakh, Prime Minister Nehru was holidaying in the more salubrious parts of Kashmir along with his sister, daughter and two grandsons. When questioned about the situation at Galwan by reporters at the airport when he returned from his holiday on 12 July, Nehru confessed to not knowing much about the situation. Two days later, he left for another holiday to Nandi Hills in Mysore. No one in the government was taking the Chinese threat seriously despite clear evidence of hostile intent.

Occasional notes written by Chinese government to the MEA, asserting their reluctance for a conflict and willingness for compromise, were taken by the Indian side at face value, further bolstering this belief. All indications that went contrary to this belief – like the continued buildup of Chinese troops in all the sectors, and the improvements carried out in roads, were blindly ignored.

Shortly after the Galwan incident, there was a firefight between an Indian patrol from 14 Jammu and Kashmir Militia and the Chinese near the DBO camp. Several other patrol clashes took place across the sector, and the Indian side suffered some casualties in these. These clashes were accompanied by several instances of Indian air space violation by Chinese aircraft. As a result of all these incidents, tension was slowly building up. Patrols and intelligence sources reported buildup of Chinese forces and communications across the length of the front. The Indian post commanders were now given permission to open fire if they felt their posts were threatened, instead of the earlier order to fire only if actually fired upon. The Chinese incursions in the Thag La area in September 1962, followed by the massive attack on it on 10 October, gave the Indian side a clear indication of the seriousness of the Chinese intent, and their willingness to fight to enforce their assertions.

First Wave in Ladakh

The first serious action in Ladakh coincided with massive attack across the McMahon Line in NEFA on 20 October. On the 19th night, all the Indian posts in the Chip Chap valley were surrounded by Chinese. It was estimated that two battalions worth of troops were used by the Chinese in this sector. The first attacks took placed on the posts numbers 5 and 9 that night. These posts, which had two sections worth of troops combined between them, were subject to heavy mortar and medium machine gun fire from standoff range. Having makeshift defences with no overhead cover, the posts were not geared to face such fierce attacks. The posts were in communication with the company headquarters where their company commander, Major Randhawa was located. They held fast under enemy fire for the first few hours, without being able to retaliate with their rifles with limited range. A little before morning, the posts went out of communication, and there were very few survivors who could make their way back. Havildar (Hav) Tulsi Ram, who was commanding the 5 men at Post 5 (locally known as Post Parmodak within the unit), was the lone survivor here, holding on to the post by himself and continuously firing the Light Machine Gun till the ammunition ran out. He was awarded the Vir Chakra for this action. Post 9 (Bishan) was commanded by Company Hav Maj Anant Ram, who extricated his men after giving a tough fight and beating back two Chinese attacks. He too was awarded a Vir Chakra. By occupying these posts, the Chinese had cut off all the other posts deployed to the south and east.

The other posts along Chip Chap valley suffered a similar fate and were withdrawn after suffering casualties. Only post no. 1, which was referred to as "Chandni," held by a platoon of 14 Jammu and Kashmir Militia, remained. It was located on a high ground that was difficult to attack at night. The Chinese continued to shell it throughout the night, and in the morning they launched an attack. After fighting back for some time, this post also fell, opening up the approach to DBO. The post commander, Subedar Sonam Stopdhan, who laid down his life defending his post, was awarded the Maha Vir Chakra, while two of the men received the Vir Chakra.

By the evening of 20 October, posts 1 to 5 and 9 had fallen, while the others were still holding on. That night, most of the remaining posts came under attack again, and by the morning of 21st, the remaining posts were ordered to fall back to DBO. Now the posts in the rear along the track to Leh were also under Chinese threat. Lt Col Nihal Singh, CO 14 Jammu and Kashmir Militia had reached DBO, and attempted to send reinforcements to the post in the rear at Track Junction, but they met with heavy Chinese resistance en route and had to fall back. DBO was thus surrounded from all sides, and the post at Track Junction also stood isolated.

On the evening of 22 October, 114 Brigade ordered all the troops to withdraw from this sector after destroying all stores and weapons that could not be carried. The injured men were loaded in the few vehicles available at DBO, but these could not make it beyond a few kilometres due to poor road conditions. It was a tough, long march back, but because of the effective command and control exercised by the CO and officers, it remained orderly. The withdrawing column was air supplied twice en route, and some of the serious casualties were also evacuated by helicopter.

Changchenmo – Galwan Sector

In the Changchenmo – Galwan sector, 5 Jat had taken over the posts from 1/8 GR in the first week of October. The post at Galwan had been under siege by the Chinese right since July as mentioned earlier, and the land route for relief of troops was blocked by them. A company of 5 Jat was therefore brought in for the relief by helicopters. In contrast to the Chinese posts, which had motor able roads connecting them to the Aksai Chin Highway, Indian posts in this area had to be maintained by air.

On 20 October, the Galwan post had also come under heavy attack during the early hours of the morning. This post had a strength of 60 men, commanded by Major SS Hasabnis. The Chinese attacked the post with a strength of about 600 men, after prolonged firing by artillery, mortars and automatics. In the tough fight, half the strength of the post, including the medical officer Captain Paul, succumbed. Soon, their wireless communications also shut down. The next day, a helicopter sortie was sent to try and establish communication with the post. The helicopters had to retreat under fire from the Chinese surrounding Galwan, but the pilot who flew over the post reported no sign of life there.

The story about fighting at Galwan was pieced together later from the accounts of the survivors who managed to make it back. The makeshift shelters of the post were destroyed in the intense artillery shelling that had been on since morning. The Chinese assaulted the post in strength, running over the forward section. The men at Galwan fought back three successive attacks, but by the evening were overwhelmed by the preponderance of strength and firepower of repeated Chinese attacks. Almost half the strength of the post was wiped out, and with the retreat of this post, Indian presence in the Galwan valley no longer existed.

The Chinese now targeted the Indian posts in the Changchenmo Valley – Patrol Base, Nala Junction and Hot Spring. All three of these came under heavy artillery fire on 21 October. The platoon at Patrol Base was commanded by Subedar Amar Singh. He received orders to pull back to Nala Junction, as this post became redundant after the fall of Galwan. A section was ordered to be left behind to provide early warning of any Chinese movement towards Hot Springs. Subedar Amar Singh took the decision to stay back with this section instead of leaving with the rest of his platoon. The next morning, the post was engaged by enemy artillery, followed by a physical assault on the forward observation post. Soon the entire post was under attack. They stood and fought till they could, and Subedar Amar Singh laid down his life along with most of the men of this section.

The 5 Jat platoons at Ane La and Kongma to the south of the Changchenmo valley came under attack in the afternoon of 22 October. In a repetition of the sequence of the battles everywhere else, after beating back initial attacks, the posts also fell to superior Chinese fighting potential. The post commander at Kongma, Subedar Surjit Singh, also laid down his life there. With the fall of these two posts, the Chinese were in a position to cut off the route to Nala Junction, Hot Spring. Rather than allow these posts to be isolated and then destroyed piecemeal, they were ordered to withdraw to Tsogatsalu. While the withdrawal was in progress, the troops at Tsogatsalu were also ordered to withdraw to Phobrang. After a tough march through snow-covered terrain along the northern bank of the Changchenmo river, the men staggered back to Pobrang, suffering from cold injuries and chilblains. After the situation had stabilised, 5 Jat re-occupied the Nala Junction. There were no further clashes in this sector till the end of the war.

Chushul Sector

The attack in the Chushul sector began with heavy shelling of Sirijap I and II early in the morning on 21 October. The Chinese had also brought up their tanks to attack this post. In fact, the *Times of India* had carried a report on 10 June about the Chinese having inducted tanks in Ladakh. When questioned about this in parliament, Defence Minister Menon had professed no knowledge of such induction. Consequently, troops there had no anti-tank weapons and were completely defenceless. They fought back nevertheless, instead of abandoning their post. The post had gone out of communication after intense fighting, and a patrol sent out to link up with them reported that the entire post, including the post commander Maj Dhan Singh Thapa, had succumbed in the attack. By 22 October, the Chinese had occupied the northern bank of Pangong Tso, cutting off the Yula posts that had no land route to the rear and were maintained by boats over the lake. Troops from there were ordered to Gurung Hill.

Aerial reconnaissance indicated a large column of Chinese vehicles moving towards the Spanggur gap. Fearing threat to the vital Chushul area, 13 Kumaon, which had recently arrived in the formation and was located at Leh, was ordered to move to Chushul. A medium machine gun platoon of 1 Mahar was allotted to them. Simultaneously, one artillery battery was also flown into Chushul. However, the anticipated attack on Chushul did not materialise at this time.

Indus Sector

Chinese attacks in this sector began on 27 October, and the outlying posts were soon overwhelmed. The Chinese troops then infiltrated between Fuckche and Demchok, making it difficult to hold on to these locations. One of the notable battles in this sector was at Changla post, held by half a platoon strength commanded by a JCO. The Chinese attacked this post with vehicle-mounted machine guns raining deadly fire. The defenders responded with mortar fire, setting a few of the vehicles on fire. The post held on for over three hours of fierce fighting, before the post commander ordered withdrawal. He himself stayed back with a small party to cover the withdrawal of the rest of the troops, and was killed with all the men of the covering party. The forward troops, withdrawing from their beleaguered posts, converged at Koyul. The decision on withdrawing from Koyul was left on the CO of 7 Jammu and Kashmir Militia, Lt Col RM Banon, who decided to hold on to their positions. The Chinese, who had established themselves on the hills to the east, did not advance further.

Despite the heavy odds they were pitted against, the troops and officers displayed amazing courage, resourcefulness and resilience throughout these operations. The sheer staying power, of being able to fight back even with the knowledge of its futility and that the enemy will keep coming no matter how many you kill, was commendable. Many battles were fought to the last man last round, which was not merely a cliché. The Chinese were successful in coming up to their 1960 claim line, but this was because it was physically impossible for the limited forces allotted for the sector to defend it against heavy odds of superior strength, coupled with lack of heavy firepower on own side.

Reorganisation

While fierce and desperate battles were ranging in the further reaches of Ladakh, a new Division headquarters was raised to take control of the area. The 3rd (Himalayan) Division (3 Div) came into being on 26 October 1962 at Leh under the command of Major General Budh Singh, MC. 114 Brigade, which had been responsible for the whole area till now, was moved forward to Chushul, to defend Chushul and Phobrang sectors. Indus valley was now the responsibility of the newly inducted 70 Brigade under the command of Brig RS Grewal, MC. An ad hoc headquarters, Delta sector, was raised at Thoise within the existing resources and was given the responsibility for the northern sector. The third brigade allotted to 3 Div was 163 Brigade, which was located at Leh itself and tasked for its local protection. Artillery firepower was also strengthened with the induction of a battery of 25 pounder field guns at Dungti and another at Leh and a 4.2-inch heavy mortar battery at Dungti. Hectic road building was also in progress to improve the connectivity to the posts. A troop of AMX-13 tanks of 20th Lancers was also airlifted to Chushul on 25 October, while the fighting had already commenced.

Airlifting of tanks to the altitude of 14,230 feet required special preparations.

Maj Gen AK Dewan, who led the two troops airlifted as a young Capt then, recounted in an article in the *Asian Age*:

> *The first problem was to avoid the tank slipping on the aluminium floor of the AN-12 aircraft. Our CO, Lt. Col. Gurbachan Singh — popularly known as "Butch" (who later in service rose to be an Army Commander) — overcame this problem by getting hold of carpenters in Chandigarh and got a platform made of the same height as the aircraft floor and flush with it, along with a suitable ramp. Also, a wooden decking was also done on it. It was now easy for the tank to go up the ramp to the platform, which would absorb the thud of its dead weight, and drive slowly into the aircraft.... The next problem was that of bringing down the tank load within the aircraft restrictions of an all-up weight of 10 tonnes. Speedy preparedness for action would be highly problematical if the tanks were inducted in part knocked-down condition. The Air Force reduced the all-up weight by cutting down on fuel in the aircraft. We unloaded its ammunition, kept fuel to the minimum, and removed all detachable access plates/ equipment and stowage items. A number of other technical problems were overcome by innovativeness.*

After the reorganisation and reinforcement, the new deployment was as follows:

- 14 Jammu and Kashmir Militia was deployed in the north, in the area Saser La – Shyok – Thoise. It was directly under command the Div HQ.
- 114 Infantry Brigade was moved forward to Chushul along with additional resources allotted to it.
- 70 Infantry Brigade, along with 7 Jammu and Kashmir Militia was deployed at Demchok – Dungti area. It also had in support a field artillery battery, a mortar battery and a company of medium machine guns.
- 163 Infantry Brigade was located along with the Div HQ at Leh.

The Final Round

The battle in the second phase in Ladakh was restricted to the Chushul sector, where 114 Brigade was deployed. Now that a full brigade was available in the area, the existing posts were strengthened and new ones were opened. The brigade was allotted fresh troops to replace the Jammu and Kashmir Militia battalions. It now comprised 1 Jat, 5 Jat, 1/8 GR and 13 Kumaon.

13 Kumaon was deployed on the south of the Spanggur gap, with a company at Rezangla, two companies at Magar Hill and the battalion headquarters and

Map 8: Chushul

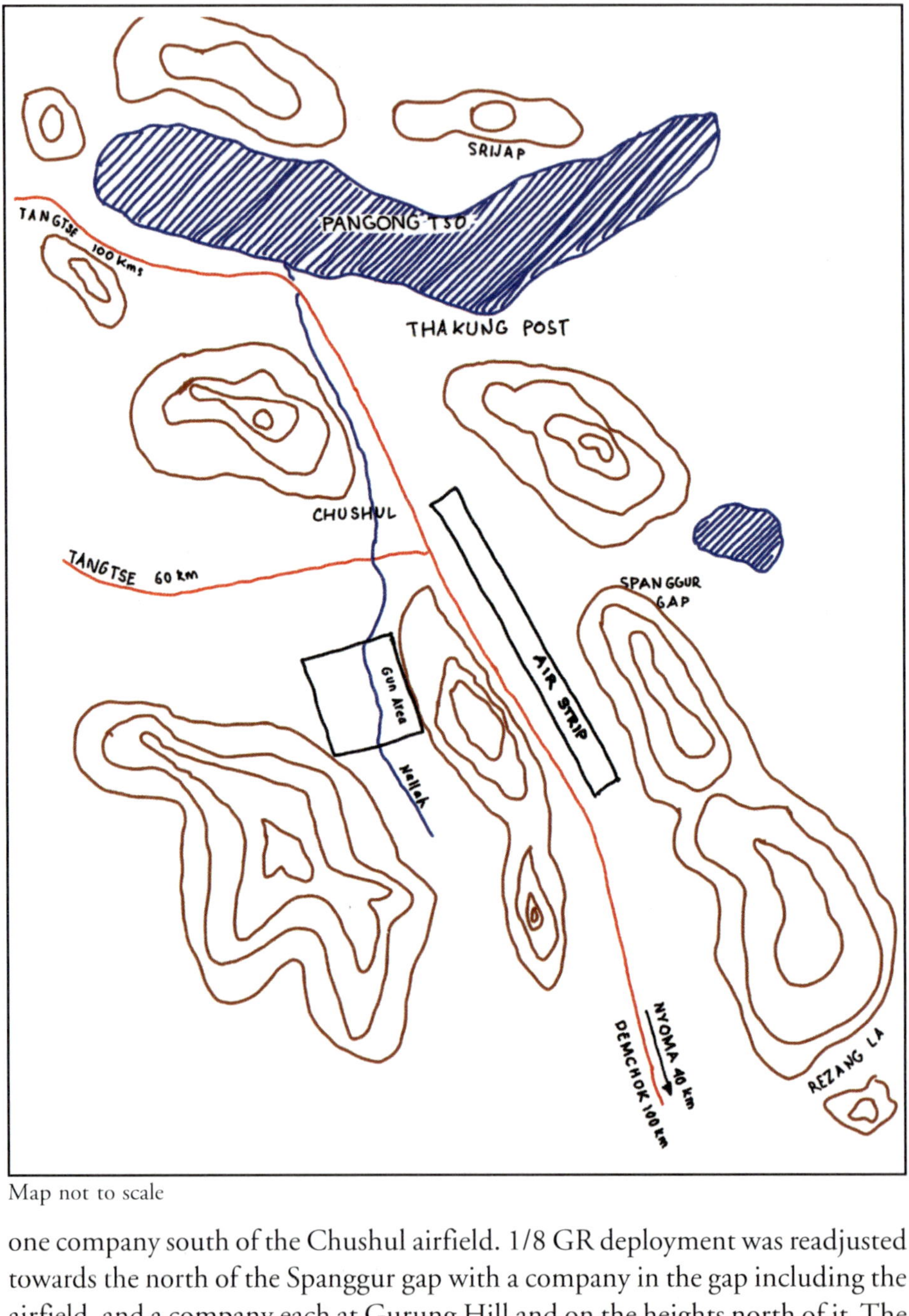

Map not to scale

one company south of the Chushul airfield. 1/8 GR deployment was readjusted towards the north of the Spanggur gap with a company in the gap including the airfield, and a company each at Gurung Hill and on the heights north of it. The battalion headquarters was located near the airfield along with an ad hoc company. One company of 5 Jat was located at Tsakala, and rest of the battalion along with its headquarters was in the Lukung defile. 1 Jat was deployed near Chushul village, with two of its companies near Thakung and on the heights north of Gurung Hill. The brigade headquarters was located near the battalion headquarters of 1 Jat behind Chushul village. The two tank troops along with the squadron headquarters was at the base of Gurung Hill. The battery of 25 pounder guns was split into two to be able to support Gurung Hill and Magar Hill positions.

The Chinese had also built up their troops, mainly concentrated opposite Gurung Hill and in the Spanggur gap itself, where they had even deployed their mortars that were under clear observation from Gurung Hill.

On 18 November, the anticipated Chinese attack on the Chushul sector commenced with a simultaneous attack on Gurung Hill and Rezangla. Gurung Hill was attacked by almost a battalion strength, rolling down from a nearby feature called Black Top hill that they had been holding. Rezangla also came under heavy artillery fire before the Chinese came in for their first of many attempts to assault it. It was critical for these two posts to hold on, because if they fell it would lay open Chushul to the Chinese.

The first indication of the attack on Rezangla came when the listening post deployed ahead of the main defences came under machine gun fire at 0400 hours, and reported approximately 400 Chinese approaching its location. The company came to stand to and prepared for the impending attack. The defences of the company were reasonably well prepared, despite the limited availability of defence stores. They had followed the basic drills required for preparing defences, including providing for crawl trenches between platoons and sections, and limited overhead protection for key positions. Because of space constraints in the area, and the need to protect a larger area, the three platoons at Rezangla were deployed in a linear fashion, thus devoid of depth or reserves.

After passing on the warning about the enemy, instead of falling back to the main defences as per its orders, the listening post decided to stick to their positions and fight the advancing enemy. This brave act gave the company additional time to prepare for the impending attack, but at a heavy cost in the lives of the brave men manning the listening post. They had gone beyond the call of duty to afford their comrades some extra time.

The company was soon enveloped by Chinese troops coming in from the south and east. Major Shaitan Singh, the company commander, ordered his troops to hold their fire till the Chinese were closer. When the entire company opened up with all their weapons, including 3-inch mortars, the approaching Chinese were caught in a defile between two of the platoons. The first attack was thus beaten back with heavy casualties to the Chinese.

Thus far, the Chinese artillery had not opened up, possibly because the Chinese intended to launch a surprise attack. But this intention was foiled by early detection by the alert observation posts. Now, as the Chinese regrouped, their artillery and mortars opened up on Rezangla. Though the shelling didn't cause many casualties, the telephone lines and radio sets were damaged, cutting off Rezangla's communication with the battalion headquarters. But the news about the fighting was relayed back to the battalion by the post at Tsakla, which had Rezangla under its observation.

Now an attack developed from the south under the cover of artillery fire. As the Chinese in large strength approached the rear platoon of Rezangla, the Kumaonis took them on with their bayonets. But soon this platoon was overrun by two companies of Chinese, with every last man fighting to his last round, last breath. The Chinese also suffered heavy casualties, especially from the deadly fire of the 3-inch mortars. Soon torrents of Chinese troops spread out all over the Rezangla post, and the brave Kumaonis grappled with them in hand-to-hand combat. Major Shaitan Singh was at the forefront of the fighting, urging his men to keep fighting. The battle raged on through the whole day, and by nightfall the entire post was strewn with bodies of soldiers from both sides. Almost the entire company, including Major Shaitan Singh, died defending Rezangla. Only 14 survivors lived to tell their tale of valour. As a tribute to the bravery of the fallen men at Rezangla, the Chinese covered the bodies of some of the fallen Indian soldiers with blankets and stuck bayonets next to them. Such a token of acknowledgement from the enemy is possibly the highest recognition of bravery a soldier can get. After the war when Indian troops returned to Rezangla, the bodies of dead soldiers were found with their fingers still on the triggers of their weapons. Many had obviously fought to their last breath. Major Shaitan Singh was awarded the Param Vir Chakra for his personal gallantry and leadership in this unparalleled action.

Citation for Param Vir Chakra to Maj Shaitan Singh:

Major Shaitan Singh was commanding a company of an infantry battalion deployed at Rezang La in the Chusul sector at a height of about 17,000 feet. The locality was isolated from the main defended sector and consisted of five platoon-defended position. On 18 November 1962, the Chinese forces subjected

> *the company position to heavy artillery, mortar and small arms fire and attacked it in overwhelming strength in several successive waves. Against heavy odds, our troops beat back successive waves of enemy attack. During the action, Major Shaitan Singh dominated the scene of operations and moved at great personal risk from one platoon post to another sustaining the morale of his hard-pressed platoon posts. While doing so he was seriously wounded but continued to encourage and lead his men, who, following his brave example fought gallantly and inflicted heavy casualties on the enemy. For every man lost to us, the enemy lost four or five. When Major Shaitan Singh fell disabled by wounds in his arms and abdomen, his men tried to evacuate him but they came under heavy machine-gun fire. Major Shaitan Singh then ordered his men to leave him to his fate in order to save their lives.*
>
> *Major Shaitan Singh's supreme courage, leadership and exemplary devotion to duty inspired his company to fight almost to the last man.*

The fighting at Gurung Hill also raged simultaneously and equally as fiercely as the one at Rezangla. But unlike Rezangla, the companies here had the advantage of being under effective range of our own artillery. Even while the Chinese troops were forming up for the attack, they came under effective fire of Indian artillery. They launched a series of unsuccessful attacks, and after the first few were beaten back, the Chinese finally got a slight foothold on a small part of the Gurung Hill. But the Gurkhas charged them with their Khukris bared and evicted the Chinese. By 1000 hours, the Chinese had been beaten back, but the companies were expecting them to regroup and be back. The second attack a while later came with even greater ferocity, and under the cover of heavy artillery. They managed to overrun the forward platoon, from which they were poised to attack further. But at this stage, the tanks of 20th Lancers, under Capt AK Dewan, came to their rescue. The Chinese were unable to stand under the deadly direct fire of the tank guns, and had to withdraw once again.

By now the Gurkhas at Gurung Hill had suffered heavy casualties, and were also out of communication with the battalion and brigade headquarters. The next attack on Gurung Hill came on the 19 November afternoon, but it was once again beaten back, thanks to the deadly artillery and tank fire adding weight to the determined Gurkhas' resolve to push them back at all costs.

All through the fighting, our positions at Magar Hill and Spanggur gap were also under heavy artillery shelling, keeping them pinned down. Since sending up reinforcements was out of question, and the threat to Chushul itself had become very real by now, the brigade decided to withdraw the posts at

Gurkha Hill, Muggar Hill and Spanggur gap to occupy pre-planned positions closer to Chushul.

The position at Chushul itself was tenuous now, because of several reasons. The airfield was under threat of closing down if Gurung Hill fell to Chinese, since any aircraft landing at Chushul would be an easy target to any Chinese located there. The land route of maintenance was also threatened after the fall of Rezangla, and Chushul would instead have to rely on the mule track from Leh, with limited capacity. With limited maintenance, it was only a matter of time before Chushul would fall to repeated Chinese attacks. Besides, if the Chinese cut off the one remaining route too, the troops at Chushul could be destroyed in detail without much effort on the Chinese part. It made sense to send back all the vehicles located at Chushul keeping these aspects in mind. The vehicles were marshalled in a convoy under one of the staff officers of the brigade and sent off back to Leh. They managed to make it without any interference from the Chinese or even any mechanical breakdown.

The withdrawal of the forward troops also took place in an orderly manner, under the cover of artillery fire. The withdrawal from Gurkha Hill was also covered by the tanks of 20th Lancers. A special mention is deserved by 2/Lt SB Goswami, the Artillery Observation Post officer who continued to direct this fire to cover the withdrawal despite being severely wounded. The officer was severely injured, and left for dead. However, when he came to his senses, he managed to make his way back to the nearest troops from where he was evacuated to the field hospital. He could never walk again, having lost both his legs, but the brave officer was awarded the Maha Vir Chakra. The Chinese did not attempt to pursue the withdrawing troops either from Gurung Hill or Magar Hill. By the morning of 20 November, all the forward troops had reached their alternate positions in the depth and occupied them.

Chushul garrison now geared up for the expected attack. However, this never came, as the unilateral ceasefire announced by the Chinese came into effect the next day. The Chinese had, however, reached up to their 1960 claim line.

While every action during those fateful days was fought with extreme courage and valour, the battle of Rezangla deserves a special mention as the epitome of the valour of Indian soldiers, and of the exemplary leadership of the officers.

9

Behind the Scenes

While the hills in NEFA and Ladakh were resounding with gunfire, and heavy battles described earlier were raging between the advancing Chinese and retreating Indian troops, confusion, chaos and indecision prevailed amongst the decision makers from Delhi to Tezpur. Some of these happenings behind the scenes have been mentioned in the passing, but it is important to cover them in detail separately. It was these meetings, visits, conversations and decisions taken during their course that directly impacted every move that was made on ground. Surprisingly, rarely any minutes of such important deliberations were kept, and according to some contemporary sources, this was intentional. Rightfully, the discussions that led to such momentous decisions affecting national security, besides costing hundreds of lives, should have been minuted. In the lack of such official documentation, books written by those present and other contemporary sources like newspaper reports have to be relied upon to piece together the occurrences.

The meteoric rise of Lt Gen BM Kaul and the appointment of General PN Thapar as the COAS to replace Gen Thimayya has been described earlier. With Gen Thapar and Kaul at the helm of affairs, the government found it easier to push through orders that were earlier resisted by Gen Thimayya. They were squarely responsible for acceptance without debate by the army of an ill-considered "forward policy", without adequate thought to either the viability of the task, our own preparedness to execute it, or the subsequent Chinese reaction or retaliation. Every subsequent decision, whether imposed by the government, or taken by Gen Kaul who was pretty much the de facto COAS by then, followed the "sunk cost" theory propounded by economists. Having already given a buy-in to the forward policy, they were sucked deeper and deeper into taking or endorsing erroneous decisions to support it.

In the absence of official minutes, the onus of the decisions taken, especially contentious ones, has been attempted to be put on each other by various players, each absolving himself of the culpability in his own book or account. BN Mullik, who was the only other principal advisor to Nehru on security matters apart from Menon, continuously asserts that the military leadership was not coerced towards accepting any decision, and all decisions were taken with their active assent. On the other hand, Gen Kaul repeatedly tries to establish how he opposed the government's ill-considered decisions at various meetings in his own book *The Untold Story*. It is therefore both interesting and important to go examine the different accounts of important meetings at Delhi or in Corps headquarters where crucial decisions were taken.

The first of these crucial meetings took place on 9 September 1962, immediately after the Assam Rifles post at Dhola reported presence of large number of Chinese troops on the crestline opposite them across the river (Thag La ridge). Chaired by Defence Minister Menon, the meeting was attended by the COAS, Gen Sen, Mullik, the cabinet secretary, and officials of Ministry of Defence. It is notable that the Prime Minister was attending the Commonwealth Summit at London, along with the Finance Minister Morarji Desai, who usually presided over cabinet meetings in Nehru's absence. The only remaining member of the Cabinet Committee on Defence, the Home Minister Lal Bahadur Shastri, though in the country, was not consulted. Interestingly, the two army officers who directly dealt with operations – the CGS Gen Kaul and the DMO Brig Palit – were also out of station. Gen Kaul was spending his annual leave in Kashmir, and returned only on 2 October, despite the crisis that was clearly building up. Brig Palit had proceeded to attend a Naval exercise on board a ship that very morning and returned on 15 September.

It is claimed by Neville Maxwell in his book *India's China War* that "*officers present at Krishna Menon's meeting on September 9th raised the issue of the siting of Dhola Post relative to the McMahon Line, pointing out that their own maps indicated that it was in Chinese territory … they were told to disregard their maps and treat the crest of Thag La ridge as the boundary.*" Menon ordered the COAS to launch an operation to throw out the Chinese and reclaim Thag La ridge. This decision was taken unilaterally by Menon in a cavalier manner, without concern about the feasibility of its execution given the strength and resources available to do so. It was a decision that was to cost the country very heavily in terms of life of soldiers and prestige of the nation in the days to come.

Although it is understandable for someone like Menon to pass orders without understanding the practicality in implementing them, it was the duty of the COAS to explain the same to him. He was expected to be familiar with the terrain and communications, and the resulting capacity to move, fight and maintain troops in the area concerned. There was no way that political leadership could override expert military advice offered with conviction. Sadly, Gen Thapar did not do any such thing. In Maxwell's words, "*He just seemed to swim with the tide, transferring his interests elsewhere, and as often as not letting his subordinate officers, especially those he thought might be able to soften Krishna Menon's temper, act as buffer between himself and the Defence Minister.*" The sordid affair of Gen Thimayya's resignation and his subsequent humiliation had served its probable purpose – of ensuring that senior military leadership tow the line and do as they were told instead of asserting themselves.

After the strong opposition to these orders by Lt Gen Umrao Singh, GOC 33 Corps, and an attempt by Gen Sen to push it through despite his misgivings, Gen Thapar made a weak attempt at resisting the government's insistence on ordering a brigade-level offensive action to evict the enemy from Thag La, at another a meeting in Delhi on 22 September.

The skirmishes ongoing at Dhola for the past few days indicated that the previous beliefs that China would not attack but merely play along with our game of chess was not true. Yet, with the Prime Minister already abroad, even Menon had proceeded abroad to attend the UN General Assembly after passing the orders on 9 September mentioned above. The two top political decision makers being out of the country at this time clearly indicates that the government was not, even at this late stage, anticipating any major military threat from the Chinese.

The meeting on 22 September was presided over by K Raghuramaiah, the Deputy Defence Minister. Gen Thapar asked the government to reconsider its decision to execute Operation Leghorn (as the envisaged operation to evict Chinese from Thag La had been named), in view of China having displayed its resolve to fight. The deputy minister, who neither in the loop for operations before now, nor probably empowered to overrule a decision taken by Menon, insisted that the order to evict the Chinese from Dhola area be implemented. As per Neville Maxwell, he spoke to Menon on phone and was instructed to go ahead with the order. Palit records the proceedings of this meeting in his book as under:

> *After giving the update position in Bhutan – Tibet – NEFA trijunction area, the COAS gave his appreciation of the Chinese reactions to our operations in Dhola area. He stated that the Chinese could do any or all of the following:*
>
> *(a) Send more reinforcements against Dhola.*
> *(b) Retaliate elsewhere in NEFA.*
> *(c) Retaliate in Ladakh.*
>
> *He considered that it was most likely that the Chinese would attack our posts in Ladakh in the area of the unchartered Chip Chap and Galwan rivers....*
>
> *The Foreign Secretary then explained the PM's instructions on the subject of our posts in Ladakh and elsewhere. He further stated that the government's view was that we must not accept any infringement of our border in NEFA. He was of the opinion that as we built up strength in the Dhola area we should evict the Chinese form our territory even at the cost of Chinese reaction in Ladakh, where owing to our weakness, we may lose further territory. He felt that in Ladakh the Chinese would probably NOT react strongly but may try and capture one or two posts.*
>
> *The COAS then asked for written instructions of the government to evict the Chinese in Dhola area. After some discussion the minister decided to issue instructions as drafted in the meeting.*

The order ran as follows:

> *The decision throughout has been as discussed at previous meetings, that the Army should prepare to throw the Chinese out as soon as possible. The COAS was accordingly directed to take action for the eviction of the Chinese in the Kameng Frontier Division of NEFA as soon as he is ready.*

From this account, it seems that Thapar did not emphasise that the order to "throw out the Chinese from Thag La" was not practically implementable given the tactical situation, as represented by the field commanders. Instead, his basis for objection was the fear of Chinese retaliation in Ladakh sector. It is not clear whether he himself believed the operation was, in fact, possible with a reasonable chance of success. Nevertheless, he did ultimately bow down to the government's wishes. Consequently, a signal went out from the Army HQ to the Eastern and Western Commands that read,

> *... (.) personal from COAS for GOC in C Eastcom (.) govt has decided that the Chinese troops who have entered the Kameng Frontier Division of NEFA will be evicted as soon as you are ready (.) all necessary arrangements required to achieve this aim will be made at top speed (.) ...*

So far, the orders passed from the government to Army HQ and onwards to Eastern Command did not specify any time by which the orders had to be executed. It was clear that the implementation was to be "as soon as you are ready." Lt Gen Umrao Singh, GOC 33 Corps, who was the senior most officer to have visited the posts so far, had understood not just the enormity, but impossibility of what 7 Brigade was being asked to carry out. Accordingly, he had expressed his views to Gen Sen during their meeting at Lucknow, the location of the Command HQ, on 29 September. Details of this meeting are not recorded, but on 30 September, Gen Umrao put down his reservations about the orders passed to him in an official letter to Gen Sen. It appears, however, that Gen Sen had by now made up his mind to push the operation through, irrespective of the inputs from his subordinate commanders, as is obvious from Brig Palit's account of their meeting in Delhi on 1 October, the very next day. He writes,

> ... *I began to realise, with something of a shock, that it was Bogey* (the nickname by which Gen Sen was known) *who was mainly responsible for promoting the idea of an offensive at Namka-chu. It also became obvious that he had little knowledge of the terrain but, uncharacteristically, he would not back down from his commitment.*

Gen Sen went on to tell Brig Palit that Gen Umrao was not "*exerting himself fully*" to carry out the orders. Furthermore, he asked for advice on replacing Gen Umrao as the Corps Commander. Brig Palit advised him that he could, under such a situation, take personal command of the troops if he was dissatisfied with the conduct of operations by Gen Umrao, but this idea was rejected. From what transpired subsequently, it is clear that Gen Sen's complaint against Gen Umrao had reached the COAS and Defence Minister, who had returned to Delhi by then, as had the Prime Minister and Gen Kaul. In a meeting with Gen Thapar and Gen Sen, Nehru is believed to have told them that "*he had good reasons to believe that the Chinese would not take any strong actions against us.*" While the basis of this belief is not clear, but it, according to Neville Maxwell, "*consigned military considerations to the waste-paper basket.*"

The decision makers at Delhi therefore found a workaround solution to Gen Umrao's insistence that the orders passed to his subordinate commanders were unimplementable. The "solution" is indicative of the ad hoc manner in which decisions were being taken and implemented even as the armies of China and India stood face to face at the border. The responsibility for operations in NEFA were to be taken away from 33 Corps, and placed with a new Corps raised specifically for this purpose: 4 Corps, with Gen Kaul as its GOC. 33 Corps, with Gen Umrao continuing as its GOC, would remain responsible for Sikkim, Nagaland and East Pakistan front. By not sacking Gen Umrao and placing Gen Kaul as GOC of 33 Corps, the government probably wanted to avoid a controversy by making it apparent that they were acting against military advice. Neville Maxwell writes,

> *If Umrao Singh were simply removed form* [*sic*] *his command, questions would inevitably be raised. If it emerged that he had been sacked because of differences with his superiors over the practicability of the promised operations against the Chinese, the cat would be out of the bag and there would be a public and political uproar with unpredictable consequences. He had to be displaced quietly, and the neatest way to do that would be to leave him as a corps commander but deprive him of responsibility for Operation Leghorn.*

On 3 October, Kaul met Nehru (both of them were back in Delhi). Bolstered by the assurance against any Chinese adverse action by Nehru, Gen Kaul, who had re-joined from leave just the previous day, took on this task enthusiastically. Here was an opportunity to rectify the absence combat experience from his resumè, something that he had been conscious about and, in his book, gone to great lengths to explain and justify his non-combat roles during the World War. There was no thought given by him or the ones who had ordered this, about the prudence of replacing an established headquarters – which is far more than just the GOC, but includes staff officers looking after every aspect of military operations and logistics. No thought was given to the fact that officers would require to be found to staff this new headquarters, and that it would take them time to get familiar with the terrain and other intricacies involved at a time when the troops it was to command were already in confrontation with the enemy. Nor was a thought given to leaving the appointment of CGS vacant – no one was appointed to replace Gen Kaul. Once again, it was probably the confidence that war wasn't an immediate possibility that engendered this kind of complacency. It was probably assumed that once the affair of evicting Chinese from Thag La is taken care of, Gen Kaul could come back and continue being the CGS.

As if this wasn't enough, the news about the raising of the new headquarters with Gen Kaul as its GOC was splashed across newspapers the next morning. It thus became common knowledge to the Chinese as well, and probably expedited their offensive plans. Whether as a consequence of this or otherwise, the Chinese issued a statement reiterating their stance that the McMahon Line was "null and void", never having the recognition of the Chinese government. The implication of this was that the Chinese were free to conduct military operations inside NEFA. In another development, on 6 October the government sanctioned a "High Altitude Allowance" for soldiers. This had been proposed a couple of years earlier by the army but was since drowning in red tape in the Ministry of Finance. God and soldiers, it is rightly said, are remembered only in times of trouble and danger.

Meanwhile in China, the newspapers and radio broadcasts were full of propaganda and abuses against India, which, as per Indian ambassador Bannerjee, rose to new heights of malicious falsehoods from the beginning of October. Since the entire media in China was tightly controlled by the government, this could only be with the approval of the government, or even under explicit instructions from them. Bannerjee writes in his book *My Peking Memoirs*,

> *The general vicious themes included (a) India was the running dog of the imperialists, headed by the United States of America. (b) Nehru, a feudal lord, had sold his country and lost his head (as emphasised in a series of ideological essays such as "More on Nehru's philosophy", "A mirror for revisionists", etc) (c) oppression and degradation of the Indian population, which was ready to overthrow the New Delhi government; (d) the tension on the Indo-China border had increased because of Indian military provocation and continual violation of the Chinese territory; (e) the Chinese believed in peace and peaceful negotiations but did not have unlimited patience and tolerance, in the face of serious and ever increasing Indian provocations.*

While the Chinese were apparently preparing grounds for the oncoming offensive, the newly appointed Corps Commander arrived at Tezpur to take charge of his command. With Gen Kaul, who had a direct line not only with the COAS and the Defence Minister, but also the Prime Minister, appearing on the scene, Gen Sen retreated into the background. In fact, a clear indication of who called the shots and in direct contravention to established protocol, Gen Sen was present at the Tezpur airfield to receive his subordinate commander. After receiving the briefings at Tezpur, Gen Kaul lost no time in taking off to the front to assess the situation for himself. His activities at the 7 Brigade location at Namka Chu and his hasty exit from there once the firing started on 10 October have been described earlier.

On his return to Delhi on 11 October, Gen Kaul rushed to the Prime Minister's residence immediately, where the Defence Minister, Army and Air chiefs, defence and foreign secretaries were already present. He gave them a firsthand account of the situation at the front – which wasn't anything different from what Gen Umrao had been asserting all along. In his own words, Gen Kaul "*told them what I had observed in the Dhola area where I had recently spent four days and seen a battle the day before. I described our various shortages and the Chinese advantages over us in many ways. I explained the unsuitability of the position we had taken up along the river Namkachu....*" At this point, Kaul's firm recommendation should have been to immediately withdraw the troops from what he himself referred to as an unsuitable position to a more defensible one, as Brig Palit had also recommended to him before he had left Dhola. Instead, he was ordered to cancel the attack, but 7 Brigade was to continue holding the current positions along the river. No one pointed out that now that active hostilities were imminent, and offensive action had been ordered, the brigade needed strongly defensible positions as firm base to launch the attack. Being spread out for miles along the river valley left them extremely vulnerable to the enemy attack instead. The political expediency of "not ceding an inch of territory" trumped the military wisdom of "trading space for time."

The next day, i.e. on 12 October, Nehru left for Colombo to attend a conference. At the airport, he gave a statement to the press that he had ordered the army to "throw the Chinese out." This was probably meant as grandstanding for the benefit of the public and opposition. But once again it would have sent a wrong signal to the Chinese, giving them an excuse to claim India was acting as the aggressor.

Gen Kaul returned to Tezpur (although he was still unwell and was running a fever) on 13 October and passed on the orders to 4 Div and 7 Brigade to hold their present positions. With winter approaching, if a brigade-sized force had to sustain itself in the Namka Chu area even without launching an offensive, stocks of supplies needed to be built up to sustain them. As a massive logistic exercise, it would involve air dropping hundreds of tons of supplies onto makeshift dropping zones. The task required detailed planning and staff work, which the understaffed makeshift Corps headquarters was just not geared for. The strength of troops in the forward area was over 3,000 now, strung along from Towang to Namka Chu, while winter clothing and tents sufficed only for about 300 people.

On 17 October, Menon, Gen Thapar and Gen Sen arrived at the 4 Corps HQ at Tezpur. During this visit, Menon instructed Kaul to hold on to Tsangle because of its political importance. This, it may be recalled, was a small position held by 9 Punjab across the Namka Chu river. It was close to the Tri-Junction of the borders between India, Bhutan and Tibet (McMahon Line). It was nothing more than a shepherd's hut and a small lake marked on the map. Tragically, the Army HQ, which would have briefed the Defence Minister, believed that Tsangle was about three miles from Dhola post. This assumption was based on a not-to-scale sketch drawn by an NCO from an initial patrol sent to this area. On ground, Tsangle was a good two-day march away, which represented enormous difficulties in maintaining a post there during winters when the turnaround time increased to five days. Oblivious to all this, Kaul passed an order to 7 Brigade to send one more company to Tsangle in view of the instructions to hold it at all costs. Another decision at this meeting was to move 65 Brigade, which was the Army HQ reserve, to Misamari. Another one, 48 Infantry Brigade of 17 Division was moved on 20 October.

By that evening, Gen Kaul's medical condition deteriorated, and the doctor at Tezpur recommended that he be evacuated to Delhi. He flew back to Delhi on the 18th morning, but astoundingly, continued to command the Corps from his sickbed at home in Delhi. Brig Palit writes, "*… With maps strewn over his bed and telephone handy, he continued to issue detailed orders for the movement of troops on the Namka Chu.*" From his sickbed, he issued a diktat for two more companies to be moved to Tsangle, with a threat to courtmartial anyone raising any objections thrown in for good measure.

Gen Kaul learnt of the massive Chinese attack on 20 October over a telephone call from his staff officer Brigadier KK Singh. He was now commanding a full-fledged shooting war from his sickbed thousands of kilometres away. Brig Palit describes in his book how he was sending instructions to Divisional and Brigade Commanders by signal, in the belief that they were in panic. He writes, "*as far as I recollect, it was a hotch-potch of instructions to move companies and platoons to Tsangle and other locations, and advice on how to fight a brigade battle in Namak Chu valley.*"

In addition, he was also advising the political leadership from his sickbed. As per his own account, Gen Kaul was visited by Prime Minister and the Defence Minister who sought his advice on evicting the Chinese incursions. Kaul writes, "*I made three concrete suggestions: firstly, to reorganise the command and control set up of the Indian Army in view of the prevailing situation along the Himalayas; secondly, to raise substantial forces within our own resources speedily and thirdly to seek military aid from some foreign power or powers.*" If all that he says is to be taken at face value – since he is prone to have a proclivity to exaggerate his own importance throughout his book – it would be pertinent to ask why was the political leadership seeking advice from a Corps commander instead of the Army Chief? As for the advice itself, the first had no meaning, especially since Kaul himself was commanding (by remote control) a formation that was recently created out of scratch to specifically deal with the situation. What other reorganisation he was talking about isn't fathomable. As for the other two suggestions, the second would take years – recruiting and training "substantial forces" was hardly a solution for an emergency like they were facing. The third suggestion amounted to admitting defeat and reversing our national policy of non-alignment – assuming that any foreign power would actually agree to bail us out at this stage beyond sending in some assistance in the form of weapons and equipment (Which did happen subsequently, but obviously did not arrive in time to be of use in the conflict).

Another absurdity, described in his own words by Kaul,

> *He* (Thapar) *said he needed me as CGS once again and that instead of reverting to my command, I should come back to him. My view was that for me to give up active command so soon after taking it over and specially after a reverse in battle and to accept an office job instead, whatever the reasons, would smack of either a punishment or evasive action on my part and hence, I said, was out of the question. I said I must go back to my men in the field, whatever the odds. Thapar agreed.*

So, we have a situation where, in the middle of an armed conflict, operational command of fighting troops was being decided, not by operational requirements or fitness of the commander, but on the basis of one General wanting to safeguard his reputation. And this General, a Corps Commander, was dictating terms to the COAS, who was meekly acquiescing instead of putting operational exigencies over personal requirements. In the normal course, the command of the corps should have been taken over by GOC 7 Div, Gen Niranjan Prasad. Since his was the only division Kaul was commanding, it would have been the most effective solution. But this was not resorted to, purely to allow Gen Kaul to save face and continue to be in command. Gen Thapar was quite helpless in the matter, as Kaul had Menon's blessings to continue in command "*because he did not want to add to the latter's embarrassments at a time when some newspaper reports had insinuated that the Corps Commander was feigning illness in order to avoid having to return to the front. … Kaul himself had reacted strongly against the suggestion of a replacement, even as a temporary measure, confident that he could continue to command 4 Corps from Delhi.*"

Gen Kaul was still on his sickbed when reports of the massive Chinese attacks along the border started being received at the Army HQ. As per Brig Palit, he received the information from the IB channels through BN Mullik as the Corps HQ was "*unable to give us a coherent account.*" As the news of the decimation of 7 Brigade trickled in, deliberations on the next course began.

Brig Palit was the most knowledgeable about the terrain amongst everyone in Delhi, having commanded 7 Brigade himself when it was first inducted into NEFA. He was of the view that 4 Div should consolidate its defences at Se La instead of trying to defend Towang, as the former had better defence potential. Having convinced the officiating CGS and COAS, he was asked to explain this at a meeting at Menon's office, attended by the Prime Minister and the foreign secretary. Palit explained the lay of the ground and the possible courses open to us and the Chinese troops. He writes,

> *After the Prime Minister had been briefed ... he unhesitatingly left the decision to his Army Chief. 'It is a matter now for the military to decide – where and how they should fight,' he said. ... I cannot lay down conditions about Towang or any other place on grounds other than military.*

On 23 October, the COAS along with Brig Palit and Mullik visited Tezpur where they held discussions with Gen Sen. Gen Kaul continued to be in his sickbed in Delhi. The argument about holding Se La vs Towang had become moot as the latter had been abandoned without a fight earlier that day, and 4 Div had fallen back to Dirang Dzong. As per Brig Palit's account, while Sen was briefing the COAS, he seemed hesitant and unfamiliar with the terrain and the operational plans of 4 Corps. The decisions taken at this meeting included strengthening of the Siliguri area, moving HQ 11 Brigade from Manipur to Walong to take command of the units deployed in Lohit frontier division from 5 Brigade, which was to focus on Subansiri and Siang divisions. A new division (which became 2 Infantry Div) was to be raised to command these two brigades and additional troops that would subsequently be allotted depending on the situation. The COAS also decided that Lt Gen Harbaksh Singh, a decorated and highly respected officer, was to take over command of 4 Corps. On Gen Sen's strong urging, he also agreed to remove Maj Gen Niranjan Prasad from the command of 4 Div and replace him with Maj Gen Anant Pathania. The COAS returned to Delhi that night while Brig Palit spent the next two days visiting the forward areas along with Gen Harbaksh and Gen Anant Pathania.

Meanwhile, the Chinese Premier Chou En-lai wrote another letter to Nehru on 24 October, repeating their earlier offer of pulling back troops 20 kilometres on either side. He summoned the Indian ambassador to personally convey his message to Nehru and the Indian government as well. In this meeting, Chou quoted Nehru's statements to the press about "instructing Indian Army to throw the Chinese out." He also referred to a press conference on 15 October in which Nehru had claimed that the Chinese had suffered heavier casualties than the Indians. He used all this to paint India as the aggressor, and justify the "defensive" actions taken by China. He emphasised that India could put a stop to this conflict now, by agreeing to the "fair and just" terms he had proposed in his letter to Nehru. This was, of course, a repetition of the stance that China had taken since 1961 about withdrawing 20 kilometres from the "line of control" in Ladakh and NEFA. He handed a copy of the letter to the ambassador, which had also been hand delivered by the Chinese ambassador in Delhi to the Indian government.

Acceptance of this proposal would leave China in possession of Aksai Chin and India would have to withdraw 20 kilometres south of McMahon Line. This hand not been acceptable to India in 1961 when the offer was first made, or in September when it was repeated. It was not acceptable even now, after the massive Chinese attacks of 20 October, and was summarily rejected once again. Throughout the period of the active hostilities, both countries continued to maintain diplomatic relations with each other. When questioned about it in the parliament by Mr HV Kamath of the opposition, Nehru replied, "*When we come to a conclusion on this matter, we will give effect to it.*" India never formally declared war with China. Nehru, in a letter to all Chief Ministers dated 21 October wrote, "*We have not declared war against China and we do not intend doing so at present or in the foreseeable future. ... But the fact is we are in military conflict with the Chinese, and all the consequences of this conflict will be borne by us.*" Notes were exchanged between the two countries on an almost daily basis while the conflict was on. A total of 81 notes, letters and memoranda were exchanged between 20 October 1962 and January 1963.

The series of reverses suffered by the Indian forces in Ladakh and NEFA had become common knowledge through news reports and radio broadcasts. The Prime Minister came under severe criticism, and though the people and the opposition rallied behind him, everyone including members of Congress party themselves demanded Defence Minister Menon's dismissal. Acceptance of the Chinese offer at a time like this would have been politically fatal for his own position – not something Nehru would have liked to risk.

But convinced about the seriousness of the Chinese to militarily enforce their territorial claims, Nehru was now willing to go back on his principles of non-alignment and seek foreign military assistance to meet the serious threat to national security posed by the Chinese incursion. It was now just a matter of time, it was thought, before the Chinese would be marching into the plains of

Assam. He sent out an appeal to all friendly powers for urgent supply of military equipment.

The two superpowers were, at this time, dealing with a confrontation of their own. A CIA aircraft had detected activity for construction of launch facilities for Russian medium-range ballistic missiles in Cuba on 15 October. What followed was a 13-day standoff between Russia and US, referred to as the "Cuban Missile Crisis." It is probably one of the times that the world came closest to a nuclear exchange between the two superpowers. The crisis peaked on 27 October when a CIA aircraft was shot down by Russia over Cuba. But it was diffused shortly thereafter, with Khrushchev agreeing to withdraw the missiles from Cuba if US promised not to invade Cuba. But normalcy was restored only by 20th November, by which time China had also declared a unilateral ceasefire. The small border conflict in far off Himalayas would have paled into insignificance in the eyes of US and Soviet leadership at a time like this.

The American ambassador in India Kenneth Galibarth offered political support to India, but not military aid initially. Accordingly, the US embassy in India issued a statement endorsing India's stance on the McMahon Line. On 28 October, President Kennedy wrote to Nehru promising "moral and tangible support" if India sought it. Russia, meanwhile, had informed India that it was holding in abeyance the supply of MiG 21 fighters that Menon had been instrumental in selecting for the Indian Air Force. Nehru's biggest fear in asking for arms was that India would be asked to join a military alliance, but fortunately this didn't happen.

Britain also agreed to provide military assistance in the form of weapons, equipment and clothing. Airlift of basic infantry weapons began almost immediately, and shipments of weapons started arriving. These included basic weapons like 7.62 mm Self-Loading Rifles, which could make a huge difference in the fighting capability of our soldiers. However, these needed to be carried forward and distributed, and more importantly, the troops had to be trained in using them before they could actually be put to use. And unfortunately, there just wasn't enough time for that. Apart from the flying in of weapons and clothing, US helped out India by putting pressure on Pakistan to ensure it doesn't exploit Indian preoccupation on the Tibet border to open another front in Kashmir or elsewhere on the Western front.

On 26 October, a national emergency was proclaimed across the country by the President under Article 352 of the Constitution. Simultaneously, a Defence of India Ordinance was promulgated, which was later passed by the Parliament as an act. Under the sweeping powers vested in the government through these provisions, prohibitions were placed on foreigners from visiting border areas. Government could now seize any moveable or immovable property, enforcing the continuation of production overriding labour laws. A National Defence Council (NDC) was also set up under the chairmanship of the Prime Minister, but it was a case of too little too late. The first meeting of this oversized body hastily constituted to include an assortment of members was held only after the war was over.

Gen Thapar visited Tezpur once again on 26 October, carrying the news that Gen Kaul would be back in command of 4 Corps again, as soon as he was declared medically fit. Apparently, Gen Kaul had sought and obtained the Prime Minister's blessings for this.

On return to Delhi, Brig Palit was asked to brief the Defence Minister the next day in his office. He writes that after updating the minister on the operational situation and the preparatory actions being taken, as he was about to leave, Menon asked him, "*Do you think we ought to bring back retired generals to take charge of the war?*" He was referring to Gen Thimayya and Gen Thorat, as per Brig Palit's reckoning, as such suggestions had also been made in the media. It seems that Menon was contemplating replacing Gen Thapar and Gen Sen, little knowing that it was he himself on whom the axe was about to fall shortly. On 1 November, under intense pressure from his own party, the opposition, press and public, Nehru had taken over the charge of Defence Ministry himself, while Menon had been made Minister for Defence Production. This did not satisfy those demanding Menon's head, who saw it as merely a cosmetic change of titles. Matters came to a head when, in a meeting of the Congress Parliamentary Party on 7 November, Nehru suggested that he might offer his resignation as well if the members insisted on Menon's. When even this did not cut ice with his own party men, Nehru had to finally let Menon go. As per Neville Maxwell, "*For the first time, Nehru had been openly defied by the Congress party, and his threat of resignation, formally an ultimate deterrent, had been exposed as a bluff. Menon's ouster had become a sacrifice necessary for his own survival.*"

The IB had received reports that the Chinese were working round the clock to build a motorable road from Bumla to Towang. Patrolling by the forward troops had also reported hearing continuous explosions, corroborating road building activities like blasting of rocks. The Chinese beat Indian intelligence estimate of the time it would take them to build the road, and in early November, a convoy of vehicle was reported by intelligence sources, indicating that the road was ready. The implications of this were ominous – it meant that China could now move, maintain and support large bodies of troops well within the Indian territory. There were also some indications that the Chinese were attempting to bypass Se La and isolate it by cutting off the road leading to it from Dirang Dzong. There were reports of about 2,000 Chinese troops in the Towang area. However, this number was actually much higher as the later attacks proved. The attacks on the Walong sector were seen by Army HQ as attempts to simultaneously bypass or outflank the brigade sector from the west.

On 29 October, Gen Kaul was back in command of 4 Corps terminating the short tenure of Gen Harbaksh Singh. He requested for an additional division to be allotted to 4 Corps to bring it up to full complement. What he refused to acknowledge was that the logistics set up wasn't adequate to sufficiently maintain even the troops he already had. Besides, all the reserves available with Army HQ had already been committed. However, foreign ministry had indicated that we had assurance from the US that "*they would hold the Pakistanis in check*" till the crisis on our northern and eastern border blew over. The move of two divisions deployed on the Pakistani border was therefore planned as a contingency. In his book, Kaul attributes the lack of the additional resources asked by him as one of the causes of failure, though the reality is that even the troops he had at Se La and Bomdila did not really give a pitched battle to the Chinese before withdrawing. Besides, even if additional troops had been made available, the wherewithal to sustain and supply them was simply not available.

The behaviour and conduct of Gen Kaul oscillated between unfounded bravado and abject panic during these critical days. One day he is reported to be "*surrounded by a crowd of admiring war correspondents from Britain and United States. Riding on a high, he had struck a 'Rommel like pose' for the cameramen and described with dramatic embellishments, how he was to deal with any Chinese who attempted to cross the Se La range.*" By his own admission, Kaul had flouted direct orders of the Defence Minister by allowing journalists in the forward areas. The party of reporters visited the forward areas including Se La and saw the jawans cheerfully going about their tasks of preparing defences – something that's a tribute to the resilience of Indian jawan's morale rather than an indication that situation was under control. Their reports made the people believe that the worse of the war was over.

Mullik, on a visit to Tezpur a couple of days later, found Kaul "*depressed, convinced that he had been given a hopeless task. He seemed to have resigned himself to defeat, to the extent he was taking no precaution to counter the Chinese threat...*"

After the attack on Walong, in a signal to the Army HQ Gen Kaul "*pushed all circumspection aside and starkly asked for foreign military intervention to save the situation.*" It read,

> *... you should ask the highest authorities to get such foreign armed forces to come to our aid as are willing, without which, as I have said before and which reiterate, it seems beyond the capacity of our armed forces to stem the tide of the superior Chinese forces....*

Gen Thapar's reaction to this was that Gen Kaul had "*finally lost his mind. He expects us to invite the Americans to fight our battles!*" The Prime Minister, after being shown the signal, dispatched Gen Thapar to handle the situation. On 17 November, he flew to Tezpur along with Brig Palit. At this time, the operational situation was as follows:

62 Brigade and one battalion of 65 Brigade were in Se La – Senge area. 4 Div HQ was at Dirang Dzong, along with a field battery of artillery and administrative elements. Although the GOC along with his tactical HQ were supposed to be with the forward brigades, Gen Anant Pathania had pulled out on grounds of ill health. He had also held back 65 Brigade HQ and two of its battalions for "protection of the Div HQ." Not only had this left Se La – Senge denuded of troops critical for its defence, it also left the Div HQ and almost a full brigade sitting in a valley susceptible to attack. 48 Brigade was in Bomdila along with a squadron of tanks and a battery of artillery. 67 Brigade and 181 Brigade were at Misamari and Daranga, respectively.

When Gen Thapar arrived at Tezpur once again on 17 November, he received reports of the raging battles in Se La and Bomdila, and reports of withdrawals from all around were trickling in. Gen Kaul was away to the Walong sector, and neither Gen Sen nor Gen Thapar was willing to take charge of the situation and control the tumultuous disintegration of 4 Div. Gen Kaul's arrival from Walong on the 17th morning did not make the situation any better. Despite the advice of Brig Palit, who knew the terrain well and was updated on the situation at the front, the orders for pulling back from Se La were issued, only to be withdrawn later. That night, GOC 4 Div called up once again asking for orders to withdraw, not only Se La but also from Bomdila, which had not come under attack at all. Gen Kaul's orders to him on telephone were ambiguous and vague. However, he justifies it in his book, claiming that the withdrawal was to take place only when the position became untenable.

What followed the next day, i.e. on 18 November onwards – the crumbling of 4 Division without a single pitched battle, described earlier – was summarised by Brig Palit as, "*Total silence reigned within the wireless and telecommunications network of 4 Infantry Division. There could be no doubt that everybody was on the run. 4 Infantry Division had ceased to exist...* (It had) *pulled out without orders and without offering a battle.*"

The confusion in the Corps HQ on these two days wherein the senior most officers in the army stood one of its finest formations disintegrate is recorded differently in different accounts by the protagonists. This wasn't an exception, but was symptomatic of the command failure that led to the overall debacle in 1962.

The talk at 4 Corps HQ now shifted to defending the Assam plains against a possible Chinese attack once they had consolidated their position. On the flight back to Delhi, Gen Thapar confided Brig Palit that he intended to hand over his resignation to the Prime Minister on return. By the time they reached Delhi, Bomdila had also fallen. On hearing about this, Gen Kaul decided to go forward himself "*in the hope that I might help in the restoration of the situation somehow.*" What he hoped to achieve, with none of the brigades or even the battalions left as intact fighting units, is not fathomable.

The next day confusion reigned supreme from Delhi to Tezpur. The news about Se La and Bomdila having fallen was all over the newspapers, and the civilian populace of Assam were suddenly faced with the prospect of the Chinese knocking on their doorstep. Speaking in the parliament, Nehru said, "*The enemy bypassed our main post (at Se La) by a wide flanking movement between Se La and Bomdila. They attacked in the early hours of Sunday and cut the road between Se La and Bomdila.... The situation is somewhat confused and fighting is going on, but our commander had to withdraw from Se La.*"

Unknown to the Army HQ or even the Ministry of Defence, the Home Ministry had passed orders to "*evacuate officials from Tezpur and other cities and to initiate a scorched earth policy, including the destruction of the Digboi oil fields and all the power plants in the valley. The Director General of Civil Defence was ordered to Gauhati and Tezpur to organise the evacuation of central government officials, leaving the Assamese and their government to fend for themselves.*" Gen Kaul also withdrew his HQ from Tezpur to Guwahati, a decision he claimed was taken with the assent of Gen Thapar.

The Prime Minister addressed a gathering of contingents of Territorial Army, Auxiliary Air Force and National Cadet Corps at the Red Fort on 18 November. Lashing out at China for its "*Naked, crude aggression*", he "*reaffirmed the nation's determination to drive out the Chinese aggressors and take back every inch of territory forcibly occupied by them*", as per a report in the next day's *Times of India.*

On 19 November, while NEFA and Assam were all but in a state of panic, Nehru wrote a second letter to President Kennedy. The content of this had been kept highly classified by the US Department of State, supposedly on the request of the Indian government and was only declassified in 2010. It has since been also published in *Selected Works of Jawaharlal Nehru Series 2 Volume 79* by the Jawaharlal Nehru Memorial Fund in 2018. The contents of this letter authoritatively answer a key question that every commentator has speculated about since – why wasn't the Indian Air Force used in an offensive role against the Chinese troops and logistic bases, usage of aircraft remaining restricted only to dropping supplies. India *did* restrain its Air Force in fear of Chinese retaliation by bombing its cities like Calcutta, as it lacked air defence resources to defend critical targets within Chinese aircraft range. Nehru wrote, "*We have repeatedly felt the need of using air arm in support of our land forces, but have been unable to do so as in the present state of our air and radar equipment, we have no defence against retaliatory action by the Chinese.*" Nehru requested for a minimum of 12 squadrons of supersonic fighters, two squadrons of B-47 bombers and radar coverage for air defence, along with USAF personnel to man both while Indian pilots and technicians were being trained. He assured Kennedy that air attacks inside Tibet would be undertaken by the Indian Air Force alone.

Bruce Reidler writes that Ambassador Galibarth had been informed about contents of this letter by Morarji Desai. In order to allow President Kennedy more time in coming to a decision about the huge commitment India was asking for, he cabled the contents in advance: "*Galibarth wrote that it reflects the new disasters and further large Chinese advances today and will ask for some form of back up support to the Indian Air Force by USAF amounting to join Air Defences to deter attacks on cities and lines of communications while the Indians commit IAF to tactical operations and attacks on Chinese communications which they believe is now the only chance of stopping Chinese and preventing cutoff of eastern India or more.*"

Nehru also wrote to the leaders of other countries including Britain and France for urgent military assistance. As someone who had considered himself a leading statesman of the Non-Aligned Movement, it must have been a bitter pill for Nehru to swallow indeed. Begging a superpower not just for supply of equipment, but also active participation of their troops to defend his country was nothing short of an ad hoc alliance. But he had only himself to blame, for not ensuring that our armed forces were strong enough to protect ourselves without having to ask for external help. However, credit is due to Nehru for ensuring that India continued to retain its non-aligned status, and that the help we received was without any strings of agreeing to alliances attached.

The leaders were willing to help India and the flow of small arms from the US and Britain started almost immediately. France announced a military aid package of 10 million US dollars in the form of helicopters and spares for French aircraft already in service with IAF.

On his return from Tezpur, Gen Thapar had decided to put in his resignation. However, he was given a face-saving exit by Nehru, being allowed to leave the army "on grounds of ill health." Lt Gen JN Chaudhuri, who was commanding the Southern Command, was to take over as "officiating COAS" in his current rank instead of being promoted and taking over as the permanent incumbent immediately. The DMO had prepared fresh orders for the defence of Assam plains, and this was approved by the new appointee after some discussion. But this was never promulgated, as the Chinese announced a unilateral ceasefire the next day.

Ceasefire

The news of the unilateral announcement of ceasefire by the Chinese was in the headlines of all Indian newspapers on 21 November. Surprisingly, the government and Army HQ also learnt of this through radio broadcasts rather than through diplomatic channels. In a statement in Lok Sabha, Prime Minister Nehru said, "*The Government of the People's Republic of China, it appears from Radio broadcasts, has announced that they will have ceasefire from midnight of 21/22 November, and will start withdrawing their forces from the positions they occupied from the 1st December. This is a unilateral announcement. We have thus far received no official confirmation of it.*" However, this news had been conveyed to the Indian embassy in Peking by the Chinese government on the night of 19th itself. The ambassador had been summoned by Premier Chou En-lai once again, and given a 45-minute-long monologue on "*the same old themes: his relationship with Mr Nehru, the glorious friendship with India, the fight against imperialism, the Bandung Conference, Asian-African solidarity....*" He also lamented that Nehru, who had championed the cause of non-alignment, was now seeking military aid from the United States. Chou was obviously aware of the appeal for help that Nehru had sent to President Kennedy, and possibly of the latter's acceptance. He concluded his long speech by telling the ambassador that "*Mr Nehru should realise when there was still time to stop the war and negotiate.*"

The details were also issued to all foreign correspondents by the Chinese next morning, from where Indian newspapers picked it up and published it before the encoded communication from the embassy could be decoded and disseminated through the government channels here. As per the ambassador, the timing and delays in transmission were deliberately planned by China to "*pre-empt Indian reaction ... and project before the world China's image as a peace loving, tolerant and forgiving country.*" Whatever, the reason, the fact is that while the ambassador was informed of the ceasefire on the night of 19th November, Prime Minister Nehru made a statement in the parliament admitting that his information was based on radio broadcasts.

As per the terms given in the ceasefire communication, the Chinese would withdraw up to the position as it existed in November 1959 in NEFA, while in Ladakh they would withdraw up to the position as it existed on the day the Chinese invasion began. In effect, they were vacating the area claimed by India in NEFA, and maintaining the territories occupied by them up to their own claim line in Ladakh. The Chinese premier Chou en-Lai had proposed this very arrangement in 1961, and the same had also been repeated in the Chinese offer on 13 September 1962, and 24 October 1962, after each major Chinese attack along the boundary.

So why did the Chinese stop and turn back when they could have easily advanced and cut off the entire North East India from the rest of the country? It could even have forced India to concede some territory in exchange of agreement to withdraw. Yet they chose not to press on the advantage they had gained. Speculating on the reasons for the ceasefire, the *New York Times* wrote in an editorial, "*The decision of the Chinese communists to call a halt to their border war with India is startling, inexplicable ... the Chinese communists, after all, do not believe in Santa Claus.... The military and political objectives of the campaign may have been achieved. The process of seeking to dominate south and south east Asia will certainly continue, but perhaps it is to be attempted in stages, with the second stage (Tibet was the first) now accomplished.*"

Bruce Riedel writes in his book *JFK's Forgotten Crisis: Tibet, the CIA, and the Sino-Indian War*,

> *Two reasons seem most important. First, Mao had accomplished his goal of humiliating Nehru: China had prevailed over its Asian rival. ... From Mao's perspective it was clear that the communist system was stronger in the contest for Asia between the People's Republic of China and democratic India. Nehru was forced to accept the border proposal Beijing had been advocating since at*

> *least 1959. By withdrawing from NEFA, Mao also demonstrated restraint. China would later point to its restraint in November 1962 as a sign that it was a responsible member of the international community and should be given its seat in the UN Security Council.... Undoubtedly other logistical issues motivated Mao's decision to withdraw from NEFA. Winter was approaching and the PLA's supply lines over Tibet and Himalayas would have been stretched, making very difficult the provision of food, ammunition, fuel and other supplies... The second reason for China's restraint was undoubtedly US support for India. JFK had made clear from the start of the crisis that the United States was on India's side. Regardless of the ill-advised Forward Policy, Kennedy blamed the war on China. The United States endorsed the McMahon Line as the rightful boundary; by crossing it China was the aggressor. The airlift of supplies by the USAF and the RAF were the visible manifestations that Washington and London were offering not only its moral support to India but also concrete and tangible military assistance.*

The second reason given by Riedel is borne out by Chou En-lai's remarks to the Indian ambassador on 19 November. The ambassador, in his book, lists several other factors that are likely to have gone into the Chinese decision to announce the ceasefire. Lack of political success despite having penetrated deeply into the borders was one. The Chinese expectation was that the Indian government would be pulled down by massive uprisings, led by the Communists in India, but this had not materialised. On the contrary, the opposition stood firmly behind the government, suspending its criticism for the time being. Under the overwhelming pressure of public opinion, even the Communist Party of India (CPI) was forced to take a clear stand against the Chinese invasion. In a meeting of its National Council, the party passed a resolution condemning the Chinese invasion on 1 November. It also agreed with the government's stance that negotiations could only happen after the Chinese vacated the Indian territory occupied by it. However, the hardliners in the CPI including Jyoti Basu and Pramod Dasgupta, resigned from the party in protest of the resolution. They went on to form the Communist Party of India (Marxist), CPIM, and thus the Chinese aggression was responsible for the split of the second largest political party in India at that time. The Communists never recovered from this blow and have remained a marginal political force at the centre in India ever since.

The people had also rallied against the national threat, a wave of patriotism having swept the country. People from all walks of life came forward to offer resources and services towards the national war effort. Akali leader Master Tara Singh called upon the people in general and Sikhs in particular to make sacrifices for the defence of the country. Legendary film producer V Shantaram even came out with an offer to produce a full-length documentary to highlight India's case against the Chinese aggression amongst the international audience. Newspapers offered free space to the government for carrying slogans relating to the war effort. A group of 35 MPs wrote a letter to the President offering their personal services to fight the Chinese aggression. "*We would be prepared to shoulder any responsibility offered to us, including that of going to the front if necessary*" read the letter. Even the leader of the Naga National Council AZ Phizo, which was fighting the government for an independent Nagaland, sent a telegram to Nehru proposing a ceasefire in the Naga dispute and offering the services of 40,000 trained guerrillas to fight for the country against the Chinese. "*Never before had India been so completely united, not even when the Congress Party under the leadership of Gandhi, had fought against the British for India's independence. Mao's dream of making India a client state thus crashed on the hard rock of Indian democracy,*" wrote Indian ambassador to China PK Bannerjee in his book *My Peking Years*.

Although the ceasefire ended the fighting on ground, the war of letters continued between China and India. On 28 November, the Chinese Foreign Office handed a letter to the Indian ambassador, addressed to Nehru, asking for a positive response to the Chinese offer of ceasefire and other provisions in the proposal of 20 November. On 1 December Nehru replied, rejecting the proposal of "line of actual control" and other provisions in the proposal. On 9 December, the Chinese government sought clarification whether Government of India agreed to the ceasefire, and to disengagement and withdrawal of 20 kilometres from the line of control as it existed on 7 November 1959. It also asked for Indian agreement to meeting of officials to discuss the mechanics of the withdrawal, forming of a demilitarised zone and return of captured personnel. It is pertinent to mention that while 3,968 Indians of all ranks were captured by the Chinese during the war, India did not have a single Chinese prisoner. The imbroglio continued and led to discussions in Colombo under an initiative by the Sri Lankan Prime Minister Mrs Sirimavo Bandaranaike, which included representatives of six non-aligned nations. After hectic parleys and active mediation by Mrs Bandaranaike, which included her travelling to Peking and Delhi as an intermediary, Indian parliament voted to accept the Colombo proposals by 349 votes against 59 on 25 January 1963. Nehru also offered to refer the matter to the International Court of Justice for arbitration. However, Chou rejected the suggestion citing "unreasonable haggling" by Indian government. Instead, China decided to unilaterally freeze the ceasefire line as the Line of Actual Control. He wrote, "*Now, thanks to the initiative and efforts of Chinese side* (attack on India), *there exists a de facto cease-fire line and de facto disengagement line along the border. Even if the officials meeting between the two sides is not held for the time being, the already eased border situation will not become tense again.*"

The civilian population started returning to NEFA in January 1963, once the Chinese had completely vacated the area. It was many months before the troops were re-ordered there though. The uneasy, informal ceasefire continued to hold, and though India ignored the Chinese condition of its forces remaining 20 kilometres behind the Line of Actual Control, there was no insistence from China to do so. They had already proven the point they wanted to – forcefully.

10

What Went Wrong

As would be obvious to the reader by now, the saga of 1962 is one of failure at multiple levels – starting from the failure of the Prime Minister and the government to formulate a coherent national security policy, to the failure of the diplomats to effectively engage and gauge the Chinese. It was a failure on the part of the senior military leadership to provide sound military advice to the political leadership. In fact, they are guilty of ignoring basic military percepts in order to meet political requirements. A total of 1,383 soldiers had lost their lives, 1,696 were missing and 3,968 had been captured, of which 36 died in captivity. Localising the blame for this disaster to any one quarter would be wrong, as there were lapses or shortcomings in each of these. While talking about the causes of the 1962 debacle, we need to look at the causes that led to the outbreak of the war itself, and then at the causes that led to the debacle during the war.

Causes of the War

The outbreak of war in October 1962 was a culmination of a slow buildup of mistrust, suspicion and acrimony between India and China that started sometime after the "Hindi Chini Bhai Bhai" phase of relationships. The downhill trend was accelerated after the grant of political asylum to Dalai Lama, which added fuel to the fire of Chinese suspicion about India's intent in Tibet. Then began a rush to show the flag in as much of the disputed territory as possible, leading to patrol clashes. India's aggressive forward policy, undertaken from the position of a false belief that a full-fledged war with China was not a possibility, resulted in China also aggressively flexing its muscles.

Boundary Issue

The border between India and China emerged from a frontier between two empires: China was essentially the Quing Empire up to 1911, and India was part of the British Empire till 1947. Frontiers under empires tend to wax and wane as empires grow and shrink, when territories are conquered or relinquished. That is exactly what had happened with the Sino-Indian frontier as described in the first chapter. Boundaries of independent nations, however, are fixed. Any infraction across them is tantamount to an assault on the sovereignty of the nation. When India attained independence, it began considering the existing "frontier" bequeathed to it by the erstwhile British Empire as its sacrosanct boundary. This would have been fine only if China did not have an issue with it. The moment China expressed a disagreement, the assumption that our definition of the border was binding and unquestionable became problematic. That there was some dispute about the acceptance of Shimla Convention 1914 by China was common knowledge with the MEA right from independence onwards. Knowing that our neighbour doesn't accept our understanding of the border, we had several options at that time.

First option was to initiate talks with them at the earliest, bring them to the table to discuss the opposing stances and come to a mutually acceptable solution. This may have involved some exchange of territory – possibly giving up Aksai Chin with China giving up its claim over NEFA. Given Nehru's unquestioning popularity with the people and lack of worthwhile opposition at that time, such a decision by him would not have met with much domestic protestations. Given how things played out subsequently, with China being in physical occupation of Aksai Chin to date, while continuing to press its claim over Arunachal (as NEFA is now known), such an early solution might not have been a bad deal. The second option was to openly declare our intention of adhering to our stance, and our willingness to use force to implement it if need arose. In the second case, it would become imperative for us to build our military strength to be able to fight against any encroachments. We would be required to have the capability to effectively exercise our control over the borders, and the wherewithal to fight off any attempts to violate them. It would have involved developing the road infrastructure connecting these areas immediately after independence, and once this was in place, creating permanent presence in these areas by deploying border police. Contingency plans to move in the army in case of any Chinese misadventure would also have to be formulated. Instead we chose the third, a non-option. Contrary to what is said by some philosophers, not taking a decision is NOT a decision in itself. We chose a path of inaction of neither raising the border issue with China nor preparing ourselves militarily. This reluctance to face the issue head-on either way led to the disastrous results in 1962.

We decided to ignore the problem in the mistaken belief that China would do so too indefinitely. We neither brought the land up to the borders we claimed under our effective control, nor did we make a concerted effort to strengthen our armed forces to fight to enforce our stance if – or rather when – the need arose. On the few occasions Nehru did broach the topic of settling any ambiguity in the alignment of the boundary between the two countries with his counterpart during the early days of "Hindi Chini Bhai Bhai," it was brushed off without any satisfactory response. This was not because China was as indifferent or naive about the issue as we were, but because it wanted to make sure it negotiates from a position of strength when it finally sits down across the table.

Amongst the entire disputed territory along the three sectors, Aksai Chin in Ladakh was the most critically important to China because it provided a short, direct route between Sinkiang and Tibet. So, taking advantage of India's negligence in keeping its borders under watch and ward, China enforced its own claim over it by physically occupying it and started constructing a road through it from Sinkiang to Tibet. Conscious that it would probably have to fight one day to uphold its claim, it made adequate preparations for this. It started work on improving the road networks all over Tibet to facilitate speedy buildup of troops right up to the border whenever the need arose. The Chinese had also probably carried out an analysis of the options available to them, and come to the conclusion that they could give up their claim over NEFA as a bargaining chip to retain its vital communication link in Aksai Chin.

When the Indian government learnt of the road-building activities in Aksai Chin – which, as per accounts, was at least as early as 1957 – it chose to ignore it altogether instead of confronting China with the news. We did not even consider it necessary to start planning on constructing roads to facilitate movement into far-flung areas on the border we claimed. In fact, the Border Roads Organisation was set up only in 1960, three years after learning of the completion of the Chinese highway through Aksai Chin. The government did not share the information about the Chinese occupation and road construction with the parliament and public. By 1959, when China publicly announced the inauguration of the road, the Indian government came under fire, both for keeping the information under wraps and for not doing anything to prevent or evict the encroachment. Now on the back foot, the government painted itself in a corner by aggressive posturing, although lacking the military might to back it up with concrete action. In doing a war dance for the domestic audience, the government made empty gestures like "handing over the borders to the army" or "ordering the army to throw out the Chinese." These, to use Brig Dalvi's words, were mere "political slogans," not military strategy, since we simply had not prepared ourselves for this while the crisis brewed. Having made these noises, the Indian government was now no longer in a position to make any territorial concessions whatsoever to reach a mutually acceptable solution. The unintended outcome of this hollow posturing was that it either provoked, or gave an excuse, to the Chinese to use force – something it had already prepared for and planned to do at the appropriate time.

While the boundary dispute lay at the root of the conflict per se, the mishandling of the entire issue on multiple fronts was what exacerbated the situation finally resulting in the war, and ultimately the debacle.

Institutions Ignored

In an effective democratic set up, the institutions are geared to allow the power of collective wisdom to prevail – especially when it comes to matters of grave national importance like dealing with a border dispute. The cabinet consists of senior politicians and statesmen, headed by the Prime Minister who is considered *primus inter pares*, or first among equals. Other members of the cabinet handle their respective portfolios and advise the Prime Minister to help in decision making. The ministers are supported and advised by professionals and experts in their ministries – bureaucrats, diplomats, generals, scientists, economists, depending on the ministry. However, this system was not really working as it was designed to during the years leading up to the war. A primary reason for this was the strong personality and political position of Prime Minister Nehru.

Neville Maxwell writes, "*... in the 1950s Nehru rarely bothered even to pretend the Cabinet was the centre of the system. Once in a long while there were complaints about the Prime Minister's 'cavalier and unconstitutional' methods ... generally his colleagues preferred to go along with him and adopt the same procedures themselves. There have been numerous cases of ministers who have ... announced publicly policy decisions without securing the prior approval of Cabinet.*"

Nehru, who was also the Foreign Minister, shaped the foreign policy of the country without bothering to seek inputs from the cabinet or its foreign affairs committee. The decisions taken by the ministry were not adequately debated as a result, and were strongly influenced by Nehru's personal opinions, sentiments and prejudices. This also had an impact on the quality of professional advice offered to him. There was "*too much eagerness to please the boss. ... This encouraged sycophancy, personal ad hoc approaches, and a mixture of amateurishness and subjectivity.*" He was trapped in an echo chamber, especially when it came to dealing with China. Since he desperately wanted to have friendly relations with China, and was lulled into the belief by Chinese leadership that war between the two countries was not possible, the people around him reflected the same in every input to him.

Nehru Vs Mao

While existing in such an echo chamber, Nehru's own world view shaped his beliefs and actions. The biggest influence in Nehru's life had been that of Mahatma Gandhi, and hence he had an idealistic belief in the non-violence philosophy. He continued to rely on non-violence being more expedient irrespective of the context. For example, he disassociated from the independence movement and condemned the mutiny in the Royal Indian Navy in 1946. He said, "*I deprecate the mass violence in Bombay during the past four days. I have not been convinced that there is a need to employ violence for winning freedom of India. If I am satisfied that violence is necessary to win freedom, I shall be the first to give the call, and I will come out openly with such a call.*"

This belief was manifest in his speeches and actions even after he took over as the first Prime Minister of Independent India. He is known to have been of the view that an independent, non-aligned and peaceful India had no need for an army at all, since it did not intend to go to war with anyone. Although the invasion in Kashmir by irregular militia backed and subsequently augmented by Pakistan army within months of independence had put to rest the belief on redundancy of an army, he continued to accord low priority to building up of the armed forces, choosing to ignore their role as instruments of national power. Instead, he focused on diplomacy, putting a great deal of faith in international bodies like the United Nations and the Non-Aligned Movement. Right up to the beginning of the war, he continued to labour under the belief that China would not risk international criticism by attacking India, despite ample indications to the contrary.

Unlike the non-violent nature of Indian independence movement, the communist government in China had been established through the power of the gun. The world view and philosophy of the Chinese leaders including Mao

Tse-tung and Chou En-lai were therefore diametrically opposite to Nehru's belief in peace and negotiations as means of dispute resolution. KM Pannikar, India's first ambassador to China, compares the personalities of Nehru and Mao in his memoirs: "*Both are men of action, but with dreamy, idealistic temperaments. While both may be considered humanists in the broadest sense of the terms, Nehru has his roots in Western liberalism which affects even his socialist thinking. Mao Tse-tung, being mostly self educated, with his economics and history learnt from Marx and Lenin, has perhaps no use for the liberal creed of individual liberty.*"

In his book *International Ambitions of Mao and Nehru*, Andrew Kennedy argues that the divergent personal backgrounds and experiences of Nehru and Mao gave rise to different beliefs about efficacy and morality of war. Both came to power in their respective countries shortly after the Second World War, at a time when the world was markedly bipolar, and the cold war was at an incipient stage. While both challenged the international system dominated by two super powers, Mao did it through military action like the Korean war, and Nehru diplomatically through calls for non-alignment and disarmament. (The irony of this is that when his diplomacy was put to extreme test, Nehru had to compromise on both and request US, UK and other countries for arms and other military aid.)

Kennedy differentiates their "beliefs about efficacy and morality of war" as "Martial efficacy" vs "Moral efficacy." These relate to a leader's conviction about the ability of his or her country to accomplish specific military and diplomatic goals vis-à-vis the material power it possesses. Martial efficacy means a leader has the confidence of overcoming material disadvantages on the battlefield, while Moral efficacy refers to a similar belief of being able to elicit cooperation from other countries through diplomacy. Simply put, Mao had a greater belief in war as a means to solve its problems, while Nehru believed in diplomacy to do the same. Kennedy writes, *These very different senses of national efficacy, in turn, played important roles in the courses that Mao and Nehru charted in foreign policy. Mao's great sense of martial efficacy was instrumental in the decisions he made to challenge the United States in Korea and Vietnam, whereas his weak sense of moral efficacy made him much more cautious in the diplomatic sphere. Nehru's … weaker sense of martial efficacy made him much less assertive in the military realm.*" On the flip side, his strong belief in diplomacy made him take personal charge of the MEA and micromanage the Indian diplomacy. He also ensured restraint in spending on weapons and equipment for the army and did not pay adequate attention to the development of domestic defence industries.

While Mao had worked closely with and had led the PLA during the revolution, Nehru did not have any positive interaction with the British Indian Army. On the contrary, because he had viewed it "*as an adversary most of his adult life, his relations with the officers of the Indian Army were far from easy after independence.*"This probably explains his distrust of officers like Gen Thimayya, who were in the old mould and spoke their mind freely, and his faith in Gen Kaul, who was a kinsman and personally known to Nehru.

The different outlook of the two leaders towards diplomacy and military were to result in much of the misunderstandings, friction and ultimate distrust between the two sides that led to the war. Nehru continued to believe that he could solve the problems with China diplomatically. Projecting his own thoughts and philosophy on the other side, he assumed that China would continue diplomatic parleys too, instead of resorting to a full-fledged war. It was under this false assumption that he undertook the Forward Policy, believing it to be an adjunct to his diplomatic moves. However, Mao's views differed, placing more credence on a military solution rather than a diplomatic one, viewing India's actions to set up more posts in the disputed areas as a military provocation.

A top secret CIA analysis of the Sino-Indian War, recently declassified, concluded that "*China played on Nehru's Asian, anti-imperialist mental attitude; his proclivity to temporise, and his sincere desire for an amicable Sino-Indian relationship. China's strategy was to avoid making explicit, in conversations and communications with Nehru, any Chinese border claims, while avoiding any retraction of those claims which would require changing Chinese maps. ... It was a masterpiece of guile executed by Chou En-lai.*"

As per PK Bannerjee, the Indian ambassador to China at the time of the war, one of the reasons China attacked India was to assert its supremacy as the Asian "superpower" and demolish India's position as a leader of the newly independent Asian and African countries – a position that Nehru was clearly working towards achieving himself. It was also, as per Bannerjee, part of China's attempt to spread the communist ideology in Asia, as it had in the case of its support to North Korea. He writes, "*Just before the attack Mao genuinely believed that the right time had come. With a sudden and surprise attack, the government of India would crash and a pro-Chinese Communist Party of India would take over power.*" It was true that in the initial stages of the boundary dispute and rising tensions between the two countries, the CPI had spoken out strongly in support of the Chinese. When CPI leader Amrit Dange had dubbed China as an aggressor in Ladakh in 1961, the party clamoured for disciplinary action against him for "lowering the prestige of the party." The National Executive of the party "*expressed faith that a socialist country like China could not have any expansionist desire, far less aggressive.*" It was customary for a delegation from China and also representatives from the Chinese embassy in India to attend the national congress of the Communist party.

Intelligence Lapse/Failures

The IB was the sole intelligence agency in the country at this time, dealing with internal and external intelligence gathering. The latter role is now carried out by the Research and Analysis Wing (RAW) that was raised subsequently. The constraints of limited resources and shortage of trained manpower that it was functioning under has been mentioned earlier. Despite these, it was doing a reasonable job of collecting intelligence, especially human intelligence from the far-flung borders. However, because of the proximity of its Director BN Mullik to the Prime Minister, he and consequently the Bureau itself, was playing a larger role than being merely an intelligence collecting agency. Military Intelligence (MI) on the other hand was rendered defunct by denuding it of any substantial role in gathering or analysing external intelligence. This had been carried out on the recommendations of the Himmat Singhji Committee in 1951. The Director MI therefore deployed no agents, inside or outside the country, and as per Brig Palit, "*Thereafter although the DMI retained a sizeable staff and had vast funds at his disposal, he had little to do other than act as sirdar of the military attachés or supervise field security tasks within the army.*" All the sources of information received by the armed forces were therefore second hand.

There was a Joint Intelligence Committee (JIC), which was meant to collate and analyse the intelligence collected by IB and available from other sources to draw coherent, actionable conclusions. Chaired by a Joint Secretary from the MEA, it included the Director IB, representatives from the Ministries of Defence and Home, and the service headquarters. However, the contribution of any of the members except the IB was limited. Brig Palit writes,

> *The IB had completely cornered the market in intelligence inputs that it had taken to presenting its reports as conclusions rather than items presented for the committees' assessment. No one challenged this unusual procedure where the provider of intelligence has also arrogated the responsibility for collation of information and assessment of threat. The chairman and other members appeared to play no role except that of a post office. Most astonishing of all, the representative from MEA seldom contributed information regarding diplomatic or international developments. I do not* recall *any mention of the incipient*

> *Sino-Russian rift, or of domestic convulsions in China caused by the severe economic crisis in 1961-2 after failure of the Great Leap Forward and withdrawal of Soviet economic assistance.*

Thus, while clear inputs about Chinese military buildup, road construction and logistic preparations in Tibet were available, the information was not correlated with other diplomatic or political indicators to correctly gauge Chinese intentions and motivations. As per defence analyst K Subrahmanyam, "*the 1962 debacle was more a failure of intelligence assessment than a failure in intelligence collection and reporting.*"

Foreign and Defence Policy Flaws

Lack of a coherent intelligence analysis, coupled with Nehru's own biases and the fact that he was taking virtually independent decisions on the foreign and defence policy (assisted by Menon, who mostly reflected Nehru's own thinking), led to policy formulation that was flawed. Brig Dalvi writes in his book *The Himalayan Blunder*, "*Mr Nehru's China and Defence policies were found wanting in 1962. His declared China policy was to confront China and not to surrender to force, and yet inwardly he hoped for a peaceful settlement. However his subsequent political actions were not designed to implement this policy. He did not prepare for a military decision. He ordered only limited preparations, misled the nation in various statements which he made from time to time and contributed more than his fair share to the euphoria and equivocation, prior to the Chinese invasion.*"

Forward Policy

Secure in the misplaced belief that war was not a possibility, Nehru treated the deployment of army posts on the border like a game of chess. The wide expanse along the Indo-Tibet border was Nehru's chessboard, on which he moved around forward posts like a player moves his pieces. The situation was such that the Prime Minister and Defence Minister were ordering the move and deployment of platoons – a task that is normally left to battalion commanders. Brig Palit recounts in his book that during a meeting to discuss the siege of Galwan post in July 1962, "*After I had finished explaining the situation on the map I added that the Chinese had deployed a whole battalion. ... Menon, usually word-bound in Nehru's presence, intervened for once, to suggest that we should also expand our forces by sending in a few more platoons.*" What Nehru and Menon probably didn't reckon with was an opponent who was more adept at this game of chess, and had better border infrastructure and greater strength to play it better. He adds, "*The Chinese moved vigorously to outsmart us in 'chessboard' manoeuvres, positioning their own posts in a manner designed to winkle out our ours. For instance, if one of our posts was located at some distance from the dropping zone, the Chinese would be sure to attempt to cut it off from the latter by interposing a series of pickets between them or even by physically occupying the dropping zone....*" With the advantage of better road connectivity and more strength, it was possible for the Chinese to outmanoeuvre us all the time. Besides, they also did not stick to what we assumed were the rules. When they had enough of the game, they demonstrated that they were capable of upsetting the entire board instead of obliging his weaker opponent by making one move at a time.

When the army was forced into pushing troops closer to the border in compliance with the "forward policy," the Chinese surmised India was being aggressive. As per Brig Dalvi, after he had been taken prisoner, in his interaction with a Chinese officer he learnt that when he, clearly a senior officer, arrived at Namka Chu on 19 September, it was viewed by the Chinese as an escalatory measure by the Indians. Shortly afterwards, Gen Kaul landed up at the border outpost. All these movements were clearly visible from the Chinese posts across the Namka Chu. They were convinced that the presence of a senior officer at the border implied Indians were preparing for a major operation. The Chinese officer blamed Brig Dalvi for "*escalating a small border incident into a major battle.*" While it is true that this was exactly what 7 Brigade had been ordered to do, the ones passing the orders had not anticipated the massive reaction by the Chinese in retaliation to what the Indian decision makers considered just another move in their game of chess.

It was the duty of the military leadership to render the correct advice to the political leadership. Even if the latter can be excused for not realising the consequences of rushing troops headlong to the borders without adequate preparations, the Generals cannot be absolved of the same. The military correspondent of the *Statesman* writing a special supplement in November 1967 has summed up the contributory responsibility of Generals Thapar and Kaul neatly and comprehensively. He writes,

> *The two Generals did not say that they could not assume responsibility for the Forward Policy and its consequences with the means at their disposal. They thus made themselves party to a dangerous decision. At various times they represented, implored and complained that they faced "logistical difficulties." But they did not say at any time that because of these difficulties the execution of the Forward Policy, at that time, was impossible or dangerous. They only*

questioned the means to implement the policy and not the policy itself. To wake up civilians, generals must protest against a policy which they know to be beyond India's military capacity, to the point of resignation. Instead Kaul and Thapar did not even make a written protest. It is the duty of soldiers to obey; it is equally the duty of senior soldiers on rare occasions, to say that certain orders cannot be obeyed. It is the duty of responsible military men not to take on an impossible assignment from their civilian masters without at least firm written protest and at best submitting their resignations.

The shift in the role of posts established under the forward policy from showing the flag to holding defences when the enemy reacted was not something that had been planned and catered for. The Dhola post is a case in point, which, in all probability, was the immediate spark that lit the fire of 1962 Chinese invasion. When it was initially sited by Capt Mahabir Prasad who led the Assam Rifles platoon there, there was ambiguity about the alignment of the boundary marked on his map, which showed the Thag La feature on the Tibetan side of McMahon Line. The MEA later admitted that this area was actually a "dispute within a dispute." While the McMahon Line itself was not accepted by the Chinese as a legal boundary, there was a disagreement about even the exact alignment of the line itself in this area. Hence, while in the rest of the areas we were on our own side of the McMahon Line as understood (though not necessarily accepted) by the Chinese, in Dhola we had actually attempted to cross it.

The post established by Capt Mahabir Prasad was in the river valley instead of on a commanding height on the far bank for two reasons. Firstly, in view of the doubt arising from the marking on his map, he had sought clarification of the exact alignment of the McMahon Line. The fate of that query has been described in the previous chapter. Secondly, locating a small post on the other side of the river would increase the maintenance problems and likelihood of being cut off by the Chinese. Ideally, the post should have been located on our side of the river on a tactically sound position. But since this was considered as a "flag-showing" post that was not expected to fight to defend itself, it remained in the river valley. Dhola became a name that was known to everyone in Delhi, and without realising the geographical limitations, control over it suddenly became a prestige issue. The expectations and role changed from merely a show of presence to tactical defence, and ultimately to "throw the Chinese out." The Chinese in question, the ones required to be "thrown out," were deployed in strength in a tactically sound position across the river with better arms and ammunition in greater quantity. When, despite the protestations of military commanders in field about the unviability of this task given the terrain, strength and logistic constraints, the area was hurriedly strengthened, the Chinese took it as an extreme provocation and decided to move in first to exploit their advantage.

Political/Media Outcry

China was a virtual dictatorship, and Mao could exercise absolute powers without worrying about having to justify himself to any opposition (there was none), the media (it was all state controlled) or the people (he didn't have to ask them for votes). In a democratic India, even though Nehru had very little opposition in parliament to contend with, and could rarely do wrong in the eyes of the media and the people, he was ultimately accountable for his actions to all of them. Not having to worry about public opinion one way or the other gave the Chinese leadership a much greater leeway to act as compared to Nehru. Similar was the case with international opinion – China was not concerned about playing to the international gallery, while Nehru, with his firm belief in his stature as an international statesman, felt compelled to take world opinion into consideration while taking decisions. A lot of the Indian Prime Minister's actions and omissions were therefore swayed by the burden of having to take into account such pressures. Thus, when the parliament and press created a noise about Nehru not taking the country into confidence about the Chinese occupation of Aksai Chin for almost two years, he initially tried to explain it away by assertion that the area was of practically no significance being uninhabited and completely barren. Subsequently, he painted himself into a tight corner by jingoistic assertions about not allowing "even an inch" of Indian territory to be lost.

Brig Dalvi writes,

> *By letting matters drift, the border poser became a convenient stick to beat Nehru's Congress government. Mr Nehru, in defending his policies was compelled to make bombastic and reassuring statements, knowing fully well that he could not back his words with guns. Once the Chinese began nibbling at our territory, any concessions made would have been looked upon as appeasement and surrender. Government thus lost the initiative and had no alternative but to proclaim a tough and uncompromising posture. The border problem became the test of government's will and determination, and was heatedly debated at every session of the Lok Sabha.*

It is interesting that it was simple for Nehru to satisfy the outcry by media and opposition by grand assurances about the state of readiness of the army and taking them into confidence about the orders he passed to the army – like handing over the NEFA border to army in 1959, or the order on 12 October 1962 "to throw the Chinese out". None amongst his critics were knowledgeable enough about military matters to be able to raise informed questions about the lack of capabilities by the army to carry out the impossible tasks assigned to it. It was, thus, solving problems by passing orders. As Dalvi writes,

> *There were no probing questions, and no one asked where the additional forces were to come from. Surely, the army did not have surplus troops standing by for just such a contingency? The army had always been restricted both in its manpower and its budget to ceilings fixed by the cabinet. Were troops to be withdrawn from the Pakistan borders? If so what diplomatic action was proposed to ensure that we did not get involved with Pakistan while we were undertaking this additional commitment? … Would the government need more money to meet this extra commitment? If so what were the government's supplementary budget proposals? Was there to be an increase in the strength of the Army? Had the army the necessary mountain warfare equipment?*

Initially, Nehru had an absolute say and his word was rarely questioned. Later when questioned and under attack, he used bluster and unrealistic tasking. Dalvi further says,

> *Mr Nehru had never permitted foreign affairs to be decided by anyone but himself, advised by Mr Menon and a few External Affairs Ministry officials. Without meaningful debates, with a compliant Parliament and an adoring public, Mr Nehru was left to his own judgement and he continued to drift along, living in fond hopes of a peaceful settlement of the Sino-Indian border dispute. Later, in 1961-62 he succumbed to taunts from Right opposition parties and tried to simulate a posture of resolute determination to guard India's frontiers. He may have quietened his critics but he did not dissuade the Chinese from overrunning our pitiful military outposts.*

And indeed, they were pitiful, without the wherewithal or geographical advantage to put up a credible defence.

Another blunder was that government decisions and orders passed to the army were released to the press by the government. This was possibly an attempt to fend off criticism from opposition and media, and assure the people that adequate steps were being taken to counter the threat to the nation. However, these also gave a heightened impression of Indian belligerence to the Chinese government, resulting in escalatory actions from their side in return. The announcement to the press immediately after passing orders to "throw the Chinese out of Thag La" in September, and Nehru's statement to the press on 12 October before his departure for Sri Lanka were both immediately followed up with swift offensive actions by the Chinese. The raising of 4 Corps with Kaul having been given the task to throw the Chinese out was another such instance. This news was not part of the official release by the government, but probably leaked to the press by Gen Kaul himself. As per Brig Palit, when he went to meet Gen Kaul at his house on the day he was appointed, he found Prem Bhatia, the editor of *Times of India*, there. His newspaper next day reported that a "Special Task Force" had been created with Gen Kaul in command to throw the Chinese out. The story did not, of course, go into details – that the "Special Task Force" was nothing but a handful of officers under a more compliant commander taking over the command over troops existing on the front. The Chinese would be justified in not knowing the story behind the faux corps, and assuming that a full-fledged formation was on its way to reinforce the Indian borders in NEFA, possibly expediting their plans to push Indian troops back.

China's Internal Crisis

With the failure of the "Great Leap Forward", the domestic situation in China was alarming. As per a declassified CIA report, "*After delivering a decade of solid economic growth and prosperity between 1949 and 1959, Mao had embarked on a radical socio-economic policy called the 'Great Leap Forward' to modernise China rapidly. Three years of poor weather, combined with that policy's detrimental effects on agriculture and the withdrawal of almost all Soviet economic and military advisers in 1960, resulted in 'economic chaos' across the country. Malnutrition is widespread, foreign trade is down and industrial production and development have dropped sharply.*" The possibility of internal unrest as a consequence of the economic crisis, and the need to find a diversion, could have been a factor that contributed to the decision of attacking India over the boundary dispute.

CAUSES OF THE DEBACLE

Lack of Preparedness

The army had received low budgetary allocations right since independence, with the government prioritising expenditure on development over armaments. They cannot be faulted for doing so, given that India was a poor country struggling to set up an industrial base, build infrastructure while also trying to feed millions of hungry mouths. Yet, having taken a conscious decision about this priority, the government should also have given a serious thought to alternatives for safeguarding national security after carrying out a realistic assessment of possible threats in the near and middle term. As is evident from the narratives of all concerned – whether it was the chief of the IB, the diplomats or the generals of the time – no such exercise was even contemplated. It appears that the government just believed (or hoped) that we would not go in for a war. As a consequence, the army was not geared up for one. Brig Palit in his book *War in the High Himalayas* writes,

> *There were material shortages in all spheres – arms, ammunitions, equipment and General Staff reserve holdings. In addition, I found the army's order of battle was not balanced and there were dangerous gaps in the supporting arms and technical services; even field formations were under strength. Reasons for this deplorable state of affairs were many. Politically, the armed forces had, since independence, been accorded low priority in allotment of resources. PM Nehru displayed marked indifference to the Defence Ministry (as was made evident by his choice of ineffective nonentities as defence minister before Krishna Menon came on the scene) and was grudging in his allotment of funds to the armed forces. Thus, military procurement programs were best by a number of drawbacks, such as shortfalls in production by the ordnance factories, restriction on imports due to lack of foreign exchange, expansion programs outstripping procurement and heavy drain on both manpower and equipment stocks caused by formations and units serving overseas under UN.*

Besides the shortages of essential equipment, the training of the army was also not geared for war – let alone a war in high altitude. Complacency of a peacetime army had set in, so much so that troops were being used as labour to construct accommodation instead of spending time in training. Whatever little training happened was also pro forma. As per Brig Dalvi, "*In those days the Indian Army had developed a flair for stage managing training exercises. There would have been many well-got-up files passed around. The area would have been swarming with umpires, 'observers' and VIPs. The main aim would have been buried in the spate of opening and closing addresses, comments from the Chief Guest and so on. A note would be made in the dossier of the General 'conducting' the exercise and everybody would go back happy that the Army was being trained and gingered up.*"

The formations were moved directly from their peacetime locations in the plains to the operational area in high mountains, with no time to train for the changed role or acclimatise to the terrain and climate. Once they arrived there, they were deployed in penny packets and were too occupied with preparing their defences, patrolling or carting up their own supplies to carry out any worthwhile training. Brig Palit writes, "*From the days of 7 Brigade's move to*

Kameng three years previously, our troops had been unable to carry out any collective training; even individual training was spasmodic, owing to the numerous calls on the men. Furthermore, all the new brigades that now formed part of 4 Infantry Division had been sent up from the plains, unacclimatised and untrained in high altitude operations."

Aside from lack of equipment and training, the troops and even officers were clueless about the enemy they were up against. There had been no efforts to study the Chinese tactics in previous wars and draw lessons out of them, again, as we believed we won't really have to fight them.

Weak Military Leadership

The effect of change in military leadership at the helm with the exit of Gen Thimayya and appointment of Gen Thapar and Gen Kaul as COAS and CGS has been commented on earlier. Their amenability, or inability to object to, militarily imprudent decision by the political leadership led to a steady rise in hostilities till it resulted in a full-fledged attack by the Chinese.

After the initial clash at Thag La on 8 September 1962, the decision to launch offensive action against an obviously superior enemy located in a tactically better position, by an unprepared, ill-equipped force, was taken on 22 September by a minister whose charter was looking after defence production rather than operations. It was taken after overruling the military advice of the Army Chief, favouring over it the foreign secretary's advice using his own assessments and assumptions. If ever there was a time for a military leader in India to take a stand, it was this. Gen Thapar could have stuck to his guns at this critical juncture. He had the option to resign on the grounds that the order being passed was not implementable in his view. Neville Maxwell quotes Napoleon in his book about Gen Thapar's situation:

> *A commander in chief is not exonerated for his mistakes in war, committed by virtue of an order of his sovereign or of a minister, when he that gives it is far from the field of operations and knows little or nothing of the latest developments. Hence it follows that any commander in chief who undertakes to execute a plan which he considers bad is guilty. He should give his reasons, insist that the plan be changed, and finally resign rather than become an instrument of the ruin of the army.*

Instead, Gen Thapar merely insisted for the order to be given to him in writing – possibly an attempt at absolving himself of all responsibility. To make matters worse, while passing the orders down to the Eastern Command and lower formations, strict deadlines were laid down for implementation by the Army HQ on its own – this, despite the government not having fixed any specific deadline for the eviction of Chinese, leaving it for the COAS to decide when he was ready to do so. This was clearly indicated in the written orders given to him.

If Gen Thapar was weak in opposing the government orders, Gen Kaul was strong in pushing them down the chain of command despite serious objections by the field commanders.

In insisting on the deadline of 10 October for launching attack to "throw the Chinese out" of Thag La, Kaul was probably motivated by reasons other than sound tactical reasoning. He had been handpicked and sent to deal with a situation that his predecessor Gen Umrao Singh had refused to accede to carry out under political pressure. Kaul's lack of combat experience to date was one of the biggest gaps in his supposedly brilliant career. He saw this as an opportunity to plug that gap by carrying out this task successfully. When it was objected to by the lower commanders, he assumed they were merely stalling or being timid. When he arrived on the site and saw for himself that the task was actually impossible, the sound course would have been firstly to re-deploy the troops of 7 Brigade in a more tactically defensible position. This would ensure they could prevent being ousted by a sudden Chinese attack (as actually happened). Once in a position to hold on firmly against the Chinese, he could have built up the logistics and strength of troops in a phased manner to be actually strong enough to launch an offensive if required. But in doing so, he would have to agree to an initial withdrawal of troops from the river line to the heights to its south. To begin his combat command with a withdrawal would be an anticlimax to his audience back in Delhi, something that would hurt his carefully cultivated image as a dashing commander of a "special task force." Besides, the pause in the buildup would be necessary during the winter, which was just about one month away. The offensive would therefore only be able to go in during the next year, and he was impatient for immediate results. Thus in the quest for personal glory, he seemed to have lost sight of practical considerations.

Another aspect that stands out about Gen Kaul's style of leadership is aptly captured in the following lines by Brig Palit: "*It was typical of Kaul to want to escape from his HQ and its implied command accountability, and dash off towards the front to undertake some imagined feat of derring-do.*" His primary role as a Corps Commander should have been ensuring the fighting troops are provided the wherewithal to undertake the allotted task, and coordinating the battle in the different sectors under his command. Instead, he was found at Thag La or Walong, trying to fight the brigade commander's battles for them. Thus, he neither did his own job, nor allowed the brigade commanders to do theirs.

Micromanagement by Senior Officers

While we suffered a defeat in both NEFA and Ladakh sectors, there was a substantial difference between the ways we fought our battles in the two. In both theatres, we fought against overwhelming odds – posed by a superior enemy and underdeveloped communications. The effect of political leadership was also the same in both. However, the basic difference lay in the effect of military leadership. For whatever reasons, the leadership at Army Headquarters focused all its attention on NEFA once the attacks commenced, leaving the Army Commander Western Command to fight the battle in Ladakh on his own.

While the deployment and strength of posts in NEFA was dictated by Army HQ, it was left to the Brigade Commander in Ladakh. The only place where the deployment was dictated to the field commander in Ladakh was at Galwan, and this post faced the toughest time, remaining under siege by the Chinese for more than two months. In NEFA, every commander from the Chief downwards was commanding the one brigade that was in the forefront initially, i.e. 7 Infantry Brigade. The Corps Commander and the GOC 4 Div were, in fact, camping there for days before beating a hasty retreat when the Chinese threatened to attack. This micromanagement by senior officers denied the brigade commander and commanding officers, who knew the ground better, from exercising their initiative and judgement. They were left to follow orders, which were more often than not impractical, and driven by anything but tactical considerations.

In Ladakh, the brigade commanders – Brig Garewal and later Brig Raina – had more leeway to exercise command and control over their troops. The morale of the troops and commanders therefore remained high throughout, and whenever posts were ordered to withdraw, the movement was orderly and with exercise of command and control. There was no post that was abandoned without a fight, unlike the withdrawal from Towang, Sela and Bomdila in NEFA.

The quality of junior leadership and the fighting spirit of the soldiers were equally formidable in both the sectors, as is evident by the fiercely fought battles by units like 2 Rajput, 4 Garhwal and 1 Sikh in NEFA. It was the excessive interference and micromanagement from the very top that led to the ignominy faced there.

Faulty Deployment

Right from the initial stages of the deployment of the Army in Ladakh and NEFA, the location of posts was being dictated by the government on political considerations, usually based on the advice of the Director IB. The tactical unviability of holding them against an enemy attack was not a factor in their decision, and this was not resisted by Army HQ as well. To quote one instance from Mullik's book, "*To prevent the occupation of the area between Chang Chenmo and Spanggur we suggested that we should send our troops into this area immediately and set up posts at Nyingri and Dambu Guru.*" Similar was the insistence by Menon on the occupation of Dhola. These decisions were taken under the false conviction that Chinese would never really attack to evict our troops from them and thus such posts were merely place markers to assert our presence and claim over territory. But when the Chinese onslaught started, it was impossible to hold on to these posts, as they were deployed in penny packets over unfavourable ground. Almost complete lack of artillery support and limited availability of ammunition on these posts made matters worse. It was through sheer grit and courage that the soldiers manning these posts fought back till they could, before they were wiped out or forced to withdraw.

Another example of faulty deployment was the decision to hold Se La instead of Bomdila after the fall of Towang. It meant loss of less territory to the Chinese that was a political requirement but of no military importance. Se La, at a majestic height of 4,450 meters, would have been a tough nut for any enemy to crack. On both of its flanks stood even higher peaks, and suitably deployed troops could dominate the road from Towang, making any enemy movement impossible. But the altitude also meant that it would be tougher for our own troops who had been rushed from the plains and were not acclimatised to fight there effectively. Stocking and maintenance of troops with supplies and ammunition was relatively difficult because of the road condition, and the difficulties in air dropping due to the terrain. Also, since the Chinese were not necessarily road bound, and there were many foot tracks that bypassed Se La, the troops holding Se La could easily be bypassed and isolated from the rear. And this is exactly what they did, necessitating the Se La garrison to withdraw when the Chinese cut off their rear.

The decision to withdraw from Se La was another hasty one, taken against the Brigade Commander's advice. As per Brig Hoshiar Singh, even if cut off, Se La was strong enough to hold and fight back for at least a week. But the GOC did not heed his advice and ordered the withdrawal.

Logistic Difficulties

All the posts in the forward areas were several days walk from the nearest road head. Buildup of troops, heavy weapons, ammunition, defence stores and supplies was therefore extremely difficult. In the mountainous terrain, flat areas of a requisite size for dropping zones for air dropping supplies were difficult to find. When supplies were air dropped in these makeshift dropping zones, a large portion of it drifted and ended up in irretrievable places. Thus, only a fraction of the stores dropped were actually recovered. Even these had to be physically carted to the forward localities, some of which were a full day's walk. To make matters worse, there was an acute shortage of air dropping equipment and parachutes. So the orders were to recover these and return them to the rear locations for reuse. Doing this needed extra effort. Since civilian porters were not readily available in the sparsely inhabited far-flung frontiers, troops had to do this task themselves. This was in addition to manning defences and patrolling. Hence, there was very little rest for the men.

Although the troops were operating at high altitudes under extremely cold weather, they did not have the appropriate clothing. Some units were inducted in their cotton uniforms, and even those who had winter uniforms were suited only for the milder winters of the plains. There were no sleeping bags, no shelters, and often men huddled together in shared blankets whenever they got some time off to sleep. Exposure to cold and hard conditions led to sickness in large numbers, further depleting the fighting strength of the units.

Because of all these factors, the quantity of ammunition that could be stocked at forward posts was extremely limited. When the hostilities broke out, this ammunition was quickly used up. The exhausted soldiers, with their fighting capabilities severely restricted due to lack of proper winter clothing, still fought on till their ammunition ran out. Thereafter, there was very little they could do to stop the oncoming Chinese waves. The enemy, on the other hand, had motorable roads running almost right up to the border on their side. They could thus easily bring forward their heavy weapons, logistics and reinforcements.

The causes are aptly summed up in these lines by Brig Palit:

> *India had been unnecessarily provocative in both Ladakh and Thag La regions, but its military initiatives had been no more than hollow posturing; the troops sent up to the high frontiers to execute them had been despairingly under strength, under armed, under provisioned and, in many cases, under inept military leadership. The result was that, when the time was ripe, the Chinese found no difficulty in rudely slapping them back from the border.*

It would be going amiss not to mention the two factors that formed the saving grace amidst the disastrous causes spoken of earlier. These were the robust junior leadership and steadfastness of the Indian Jawan. The leadership at battalion, company, platoon and section commanders levels was inspirational and without blemish. Everywhere small bodies of men fought isolated battles under desperate conditions and extreme shortages. In every instance, the junior leaders on the spot led from the forefront, often to their last breath. And the jawans followed their leaders unquestioningly, unhesitatingly and uncomplainingly. Never once were the "Naam, Namak aur Nishaan" let down. This was a testimony to the strong esprit de corps forged by the regimental system of the army, which continues to stand the test of time even to date.

11

Lessons Learnt

It is always easier to find faults and point fingers in hindsight after a disastrous defeat like the one faced by India in 1962. It *was* India's defeat, not just the defeat of Indian Army in the field, as it was a failure of the national security policy. As pointed out in the previous chapter, there were amalgamation of factors and actions or omissions by multiple people and agencies that led to the ultimate fiasco. It is important to talk about the shortcomings rather than sweeping them under the carpet, so that substantial lessons can be drawn, to avoid recurrence of past mistakes again. The lessons have been drawn and commented about, discussed and debated in books, articles, seminars and lectures endlessly over almost six decades that have passed since the war. The government had even ordered a formal inquiry under a serving Lt Gen, which resulted in the famous Henderson Brooks Report – one that remains classified to date, although parts of the Top-Secret document are purportedly available on the internet. There were considerable changes brought about as a result of the lessons learnt. The Indian Army emerged from the depths of this ignominious defeat to give a commendable account of itself in the subsequent wars it fought. In 1965, it emerged in a commanding position against Pakistan although the war was stopped by a ceasefire before a decisive victory could be obtained. We did get an indisputably decisive victory in 1971, which resulted in the surrender of Pakistan Army and the creation of Bangladesh. Some of the shortcomings persist though, as systemic reforms required to remove them haven't been implemented in full, despite numerous committees and experts recommending them year after year.

A significant diplomatic lesson learnt was that while adherence to principles is important, the country needs a pragmatic foreign policy keeping our own national interest supreme. While we espoused the principles of non-violence and peaceful settlement of disputes, we were wrong to assume that the adversary would also play by the same rules. Even when we went the extra mile to appease the Chinese by playing down the invasion of Tibet and atrocities thereafter, China continued to harbour suspicions about our motives. It appeared that either we were sending mixed signals about our attitude towards Tibet, or our diplomats and politicians were unable to convince China about any lack of ulterior motives by us. A pragmatic approach could have been to actually use the unrest in Tibet to our advantage, by covert or overt support to the Tibetans in their fight against Chinese occupation.

Another big takeaway from the war was the need for the nation to have a well-defined national security policy with clearly stated national aims, a realistic threat assessment and the security wherewithal to be able to meet these. Brig Dalvi writes,

> There is no gainsaying the fact that there was something amiss in the manner and methods we had adopted to arrive at the national aims and implement them in peace and war. On paper we had a sound enough system which was largely copied from the British. Unfortunately the system was not allowed to function in the recognised way. Even during the years preceding the Chinese aggression, the enunciation of national policy had become the prerogative of a few people, whose views prevailed even when there was unmistakable evidence that the policy was faulty. There was no harmonious fusion of civil and military thinking. The politician, soldier and civil servant had not evolved a smooth working arrangement whereby each could have his say, and each could get a respectful hearing.

At the height of the 1962 crisis, the government set up a National Defence Council with the charter to take stock of situation and arrangements for national defence from time to time and assist in defence buildup. It was a large, unwieldy body that had the expected ex officio and invited members including prominent retired Generals, Chief Ministers of several states including Maharashtra and Tamil Nadu, industrialists like Naval Tata and Ashok Mehta, and Nehru's daughter Mrs Indira Gandhi. The council was a classic example of too little, too late, and it never met during the course of the war. It remained a defunct body during the 1965 and 1971 wars, though the higher defence planning, and the interface between the government and the armed forces was decidedly better. Yet there was still no effective formal institutional mechanism for this.

After India became a nuclear power in 1998, some of the national security apparatus at the apex level was formalised. We now have a Nuclear Command Authority that controls the nuclear assets with a tri-services Strategic Forces Command as its executing arm. We also have a National Security Council with a permanent National Security Advisor (NSA) at its head. The Joint Intelligence Committee has been energised and placed under the supervision of the NSA. Our technological means of gathering intelligence have seen a radical improvement thanks to the highly developed indigenous satellite program. Systems for tasking these assets, receiving inputs and expertise for analysis have undergone tremendous improvement.

The armed forces now have a written doctrine that presumably derives from a pragmatic assessment of the threat perceptions, visualisation of likely scenarios we could be faced with, and suitable contingency plans to deal with each of these. One longstanding reform that has recently been addressed is the creation of the post of a Chief of Defence Staff with a seat at the high table. With the appointment of the first CDS and the creation of a separate Department of Military Affairs in the Ministry of Defence that he would head, the process of integration of the Ministry with the Service Headquarters has begun.

The need for expanding the army to cater for a two-front war has been talked about ever since 1962. With the emergence of terrorism as an additional threat to national security, the talk now is of two and a half fronts. Large-scale raising took place after the war, and force accretions have been happening at regular intervals ever since, based on studies and threat perceptions. The latest was the recent raising of a mountain strike corps, although as per reports there are some delays in raising all the complements of this.

Our weakness due to lack of self-reliance in defence production became apparent when we had to plead for weapons, ammunition and equipment from foreign powers when the Chinese were well inside our territory. While their response was positive and prompt, the newly arrived weapons were of no immediate use as it would have taken time for troops to get trained in using them. Sadly, we remain amongst the largest importer of weaponry even after six decades and lakhs of crores of rupees in research, development and setting up Ordnance Factories.

The disastrous effect of political interference in promotions in the senior ranks in the army was apparent in the inept handling of the situation by Gen Kaul. Despite his lack of requisite experience as an infantry company or battalion commander, he was allowed to command an infantry brigade and division, and later promoted to the rank of Lt Gen overruling the objections of the COAS, because he was close to the Prime Minister and the Defence Minister. Throughout the operations, he used his proximity to the ministers to override the chain of command. It is therefore necessary for the government to ensure that the selection of officers for promotion to senior ranks is completely free from political interference and any other factor except seniority and merit. Strict adherence to the chain of command by political leadership while exercising their control over the armed forces is also an inviolable principle, especially during war. It is their charter to lay down the aims and objectives they want the armed forces to achieve, and allow them to work out options available for achieving them based on the resources available and other military factors. The political leadership can exercise their choice amongst the options available. If none of these are acceptable, then there may be a need to either augment the resources available to the forces, or to look for alternative means of achieving those objectives. However, micromanaging the armed forces, or tasking them without providing the wherewithal to accomplish the task would lead to disastrous consequences.

The same is also true about senior commanders passing direct orders downwards, bypassing the chain of command. Gen Kaul's presence at Namka Chu and Walong during the early phases of the battle created more confusion rather than serving any meaningful purpose. Although visits by higher commanders to forward areas before outbreak of active hostilities serve to raise the morale of troops, their presence is more fruitful in their headquarters while the actual fighting is on. If they do visit forward localities during a lull in the battle, adequate communication arrangements should be available for them to be in constant touch with their own headquarters, other parts of their command as well as higher headquarters. Also, having issued their operational orders to lower formations, they must allow the formation commanders to exercise their own judgement in how these are to be executed instead of micro-managing them. The commanders on ground are better informed of the developing situation, their own dispositions and most importantly, the terrain, to be able to take decisions.

While on the issue of command and control, there must be a clear chain of succession laid down and adhered to in case a commander is incapacitated for any reason. The highly questionable decision of allowing Gen Kaul to continue commanding the Corps from his sick bed in Delhi also led to an immense amount of confusion in the lower formations during critical stages of the war. Allowing such arrangements merely to cater for the aspirations of an individual was an indulgence allowed by the political leadership to whom Kaul was close, and this proved a costly mistake. To make matters worse, the large-scale changing of commanders in the midst of war was another step that should have been avoided. Reversing the decision to replace Gen Kaul with Gen Harbaksh within a few days of the latter having taken over command was another mistake.

The hesitation in using our Air Force in an offensive role against Chinese troops and logistic bases was an example of excessive caution. The fighters and bombers of the Air Force were kept in check for fear of Chinese counter-bombardment on Indian cities like Calcutta. The basis of such a fear is not clear, but the outcome of the battle could have been very different if we had used our offensive air power to its full effect.

The disruption in training activities of units in peace locations by involving troops in non-professional tasks such as projects to construct accommodation (Project Amar) had affected the operational preparedness of the units. The hurried induction of unacclimatised troops into high-altitude terrain, without time for either acclimatisation of specialised training for high-altitude warfare had an adverse impact on the fighting efficiency of the units. Allowing units in peace locations time for continuous training, and also having sufficient reserves of acclimatised and trained troops to meet contingencies in high-altitude areas was another lesson that emerged.

It became clear that rushing in troops into forward areas without adequate arrangements for logistics in place was counterproductive. The fighting troops should not be tied down by the burden of having to involve themselves in catering for their own lines of communication, stocking and replenishment. Sufficient arrangements for these should be in place before any offensive operation is contemplated, as was lacking in the ill-fated Operation Leghorn. For defensive operations, establishment of forward maintenance bases with adequate stocking located within acceptable turnaround time is essential. Selection of suitable dropping zones to avoid losses during air drops is also vital.

It is necessary for officers and men to have adequate knowledge about the enemy's tactics and weapon systems. Such information must be constantly updated by the intelligence setup and fed down to the unit levels. Had the commanders at the lower level been aware of the tactics that the Chinese had adopted during the Korean war, they would have been better prepared to guard against being cut off by infiltrating Chinese columns. The irrationality and impossibility of holding every inch of the ground during defensive operations was also driven home forcefully. Careful use of ground must be made to deploy troops in a manner that enemy is forced to follow our own design of battle, especially in the mountains where the approaches are limited. It may be necessary to initially trade space for time. This means allowing the enemy to come in into our own territory instead of fighting him strongly at the border itself, where the terrain may not be suitable for positional defence. The three-tiered system of defences proposed by Gen Thorat would have probably served us better, as Menon himself had later acknowledged. It would force the enemy to fight on ground of our choosing, where we have an advantage as a defender. It would also ensure we would have adequate artillery fire support and reserves including ammunition and that our own maintenance lines were shorter while those of the enemy were extended.

Withdrawal as an operation of war is important to be planned for and practiced. While it is vital to imbibe an offensive spirit in the troops even while on the defensive, the circumstances under which they would be required to withdraw must be laid down clearly, along with the authority empowered to order it. The headquarters controlling the withdrawal must remain in control of the withdrawing troops at all times, and for this it is essential that adequate communication links are ensured. Responsibilities of various units and subunits, the order in which they would vacate their defences, arrangements for carriage or destroying of heavy equipment and stores such as ammunition must be made. Plans must also be in place for measures to deny routes of advance to the enemy while withdrawing. At no stage must a withdrawal be allowed to turn into a panicked flight, as it happened at Se La, Bomdila and Dirang Dzong. In contrast, the withdrawals that were executed in Ladakh, during October and November 1962, took place without such confusion, panic or disorder because the commanders at all levels retained control throughout.

The Last Word

It is now almost 60 years since the Chinese crossed over the mountainous frontiers to forcefully make a point about their stance on the border issue. Yet there is still no resolution in sight. Aksai Chin continues to be under Chinese control, along with the areas occupied by it as per its 1960 claim line. China still does not recognise NEFA (now Arunachal Pradesh) as a part of India. However, both the countries have learnt to isolate the border disagreements and segregate it from other bilateral issues like diplomacy, trade, travel, tourism etc. Occasional irritants and flare-ups occur – like the most recent standoff between Indian Army and PLA at Doklam in 2017, or the periodic insistence by China to "staple" the visa on the Indian passport of residents of Arunachal Pradesh. It suits both the regimes to put the contentious issues on the back burner, just as it suits China to occasionally remind us that the border issue remains open by incidents like Doklam and stapled visas.

The geopolitical situation has changed beyond recognition since 1962. Sino-Pak relations, which were at an incipient stage before the war, have now transformed into a strong partnership of mutual benefit and a common adversary in the form of India. China has made substantial investments in Pakistan, especially in the China–Pak Economic Corridor (CPEC) that is part of the Belt and Road Initiative (BRI) and gives China an access to the Gwadar port. China has also secured a foothold all around India in its "string of pearls" strategy. Most importantly, China, India and Pakistan are all nuclear powers now. Economically, China and India are neck to neck in the race for the largest growing economy. They are both also vying to emerge as regional and global superpowers in a future multipolar world order.

The million-dollar question is, What does the future hold for Sino-Indian relations? Is the boundary issue still a potential cause of conflict between the two countries? Is there a possibility for a mutually acceptable resolution to the problem? If so, is it the very same that Chou En-lai proposed to Nehru several times in the run-up to and during the 1962 war, which is also the present status quo? That India give up her claim on the territory under Chinese occupation in the north including Aksai Chin, in exchange for Chinese reciprocity in Arunachal Pradesh? Would any Indian government accept such a solution and survive politically? Would it be acceptable to the people of India, or would they see it as a surrender of Indian sovereignty? There are precedents of such tradeoffs with Bangladesh, but these involved much smaller pieces of land and were not as prominent in public consciousness as Aksai Chin.

The examination of these questions is well beyond the scope of this book, but merely mentioned as food for thought for the reader, and for possible deliberation by crystal gazers and strategic experts. Whatever be the conclusion of such thoughts and deliberations, one thing should be clear, eternal vigilance is the price of liberty.

Bibliography

1. China Invades India, VB Karnik (Editor), Allied Publishes, 1963.
2. Chinese Invasion of Ladakh, Maj Sitaram Johri, Himalaya Publications, 1969.
3. Chinese Invasion of NEFA, Maj Sitaram Johri, Himalaya Publications, 1968.
4. India's Defence Problem, SS Khera, Orient Longman, 1968.
5. The India China Border: A Reappraisal, GN Rao, Motilal Banarsidas Publishers, 2009.
6. More on Nehru's Philosophy in Light of the Sino-Indian Boundary Question, Renmin Riabo (Editors), 1962.
7. My Peking Memoirs of the Chinese Invasion of India, PK Bannerjee, Clarion Books, 1990.
8. The Red Eagles, a History of Fourth Division of India, KC Praval, Vision Books, 1982.
9. From Reveille to Retreat, Lt Gen SPP Thorat, Allied Publishers, 1986.
10. Lest We Forget, Capt Amarinder Singh, Variety Books, 2005.
11. Aksaichin and Sino-Indian Conflict, John Lall, Allied Publishers, 1988.
12. Understanding the Sino-Indian War 1962, Gautam Das, Har Anand Publications, 2013.
13. The Saga of Ladakh, Maj Gen Jasjit Singh, Vanity Book, 1983.
14. Recollections of the Se La Bomdila Debacle 1962, Maj Gen JS Datta, KW Publishers, 2013.
15. The Battle of NEFA, GS Bhargava, Allied Publishers, 1964.
16. The Unfought War of 1962, Lt Col JR Saigal, Allied Publishers, 1979.
17. Unsung Battles of 1962, Lt Col GS Kler, Lancer Publishers, 1995.
18. 1962: A View From the Other Side of the Hill, Maj Gen PJS Sandhu, Vij Books, 2015.

19. A History of Sino-Indian Relations, John Rowland, D. Van Nostrand Company, 1967.
20. All the Prime Minister's Men, Janardhan Thakur, Vikas Publishing House, 1977.
21. Ambassador's Journal, John Kenneth Galbraith, Houghton Mifflin Company, 1969.
22. Ballot Box China, Kerry Brown, Zed Books, 2011.
23. Asian Rivalries – Conflict Escalation, and Limitation of Two Level Games, Sumit Ganguly & William R Thompson (Editors), Stanford University Press, 2011.
24. Between the Lines, Kuldip Nayyar, Allied Publishers, 1969.
25. China's India War: Collision Course on the Roof of the World, Bertil Lintner Oxford University Press, 2018.
26. Defending Kashmir, Publication Division Government of India, 1949.
27. Fall of Towang 1962, Niranjan Prasad, Palit & Palit, 1981.
28. Great Game East: India, China and the Struggle for Asia's Most Volatile Frontier, Bertil Lintner, Harper Collins, 2012.
29. The Guilty Men of 1962, D.R. Mankekar, Tulshi Shah Enterprises, 1968.
30. Himalayan Blunder, Brig JP Dalvi, Thacker & Company, 1969.
31. India From Curzon to Nehru & After, Durga Das, The John Day Company, 1970.
32. India's China War, Neville Maxwell, Jaico Publishing House, 1970.
33. Jawaharlal Nehru and Foreign Policy, Yuri Nasenko, Sterling Publishers, 1977.
34. Krishna Menon, a Biography, TJS George, 1964.
35. After Nehru, Who?, Welles Hangen, Rupert Hart-Davis, 1963.
36. War in High Himalayas, Brig DK Palit, C. Hurst & Co. Publishers, 1991
37. 1962: The War that Wasn't, Shiv Kunal Verma, Aleph Book Company, 2016.
38. The Untold Story, Lt Gen BM Kaul, Jaico Publishing House, 1973.
39. My Years With Nehru: The Chinese Betrayal, BN Mullik, Allied Publishers, 1971.
40. With Nehru in Foreign Office, Subimal Dutt, Minerva Associates, 1977.
41. In Two Chinas: Memoirs of a Diplomat, KM Panikkar, George Allen & Unwin Ltd, 1955.
42. JFK's Forgotten Crisis: Tibet, the CIA, and the Sino-Indian War, Brude Riedel, Harper Collins, 2015.

Index